The Digital Phoenix Effect

The Digital Phoenix Effect

How Legacy Companies Can Lead the Platform Revolution
Without Burning Everything Down

Daniel Trabucchi & Tommaso Buganza

Inspiring **Stories**. Real world **Examples**.
Concrete **Tools**. GenAI **Co-Thinker**

THINKERS 50
RADAR THINKERS

The Digital Phoenix Effect

How Legacy Companies Can Lead the Platform Revolution Without Burning Everything Down

Find out more at https://platformthinking.eu
For any information write at
daniel.trabucchi@polimi.it & tommaso.buganza@polimi.ikt

Cover design by Georgia Medin

First published in 2025 by Platform Thinking Publishing.

ISBN-13: 979-12-210-9347-6 (paperback)
ISBN-13: 979-12-210-9349-0 (hard cover)

To Calliope & Ludovica
Daniel

To Clara & Aline
Tommaso

Praise for
The Digital Phoenix Effect

"Platform thinking made practical—this is a great playbook for turning legacy complexity into innovation ecosystems that scale."
— MARSHALL W. VAN ALSTYNE, Professor at Boston University and co-author of 'Platform Revolution'

"This book is for managers who confront the challenge of innovating within complex existing systems. The Digital Phoenix Effect provides practical examples to help firms understand how they can make progress on their platform journey."
— GEOFFREY G. PARKER, Professor at Dartmouth College and co-author of 'Platform Revolution'

"Trabucchi and Buganza's engaging book offers highly applicable business insights with a sharp focus on how legacy firms can build platforms. Weaving in lots of stories and examples and research-backed yet accessible step-by-step frameworks, it is a must read for those who want to learn concretely how to benefit from digital opportunities!"
— ANNABELLE GAWER, Professor at University of Surrey and co-author of 'The Business of Platforms'

"In a world dominated by platform business models, no company can afford to get left behind. But platform strategies aren't just for tech-natives. In *The Digital Phoenix Effect*, Daniel Trabucchi and Tommaso Buganza show that Platform Thinking is a state of mind as much as a state of technology, and lay out the platform playbook for established firms to turn their legacy into competitive advantage."
— DES DEARLOVE, Co-founder, Thinkers50

"*The Digital Phoenix Effect* is a must-read. The book serves as a practical guide for leaders in established companies who want to navigate the challenges of digital transformation. The authors provide valuable insights on how to leverage legacy assets as a foundation for innovation, rather than seeing them as obstacles. Filled with real-life examples from companies like AXA and Siemens, this book offers clear, actionable strategies that readers can implement immediately. The practical tools and frameworks make it easy to understand and apply the concepts to your own organization. If you're looking for guidance on how to drive meaningful change and build a successful digital platform, this is an essential resource."

— PIERRE DU ROSTU, CEO at AXA Digital Commercial Platform

"In today's world, not change but disruption has become the norm around the globe. As an incumbent with a significant business volume, you should always be ready to transform yourself when market conditions change to stay in the game. Our own transformation and those you will find in this book are testimonies that incumbents can disrupt their traditional set-ups into new business models and find new avenues for exponential growth through platforms. This book is an inspiration for all who need to prepare their companies to transform!"

— BETTINA ROTERMUND, Head of Strategy & Analyst Relations Siemens Xcelerator at Siemens

"The book explores how Platform Thinking can transform businesses by addressing complex challenges and fostering innovation through the creation of platform-based models. With a practical approach, it provides concrete tools to enhance collaboration among stakeholders and leverage the value of data, overcoming interoperability issues and promoting transparency across supply chains. Our contribution illustrates their practical application in real-world scenarios, showcasing their tangible impact on the growth and competitiveness of businesses engaged in the twin transition challenges."

— STEFANO FASANI, Open-es Program Manager & Head of Supplier Sustainability, Coordination & Development at Eni

"*The Digital Phoenix Effect* is an essential guide for any company seeking to navigating the next era of competition. Trabucchi and Buganza outline in actionable terms how legacy assets, often seen as burdens, can be transformed into strategic advantages through the power of Platform Thinking. In today's interconnected world, success hinges no longer on solitary effort but on working through collaborative ecosystems. This book provides a roadmap for leaders to reimagine their organizations, transforming existing strengths into platforms that foster innovation, resilience, and shared growth."
— KAIHAN KRIPPENDORFF, Founder of Outthinker Networks

"An insightful guide for leaders navigating complexity. Trabucchi and Buganza show how dormant assets and legacy systems—often seen as burdens—can become unexpected catalysts for transformation. A timely reminder that value often hides in plain sight, waiting to be activated with the right lens."
— CHRISTIAN BUSCH, Professor, USC Marshall School of Business and author of "The Serendipity Mindset"

"*The Digital Phoenix Effect* delivers critical insights for today's leaders: platform transformation isn't just about technology—it's about reimagining how people come together in new organizational forms to drive strategic outcomes. Trabucchi and Buganza provide a clear, actionable framework for legacy organizations to design platforms that are adaptive, inclusive, and innovation-ready. This book is a must-read for executives looking to align their talent, data, and collaboration models to thrive in the platform era."
— ELIZABETH J. ALTMAN, Professor, University of Massachusetts Lowell, Research Affiliate, MIT Initiative on the Digital Economy, co-author of "Workforce Ecosystems"

"Most books on digital platforms focus on the power of new firms, unencumbered by old business models and technologies. But established companies have unique assets and capabilities that can provide powerful advantages – if only they knew how to deploy them. That time has come. *The Digital Phoenix Effect* delivers a structured and field-tested methodology to turn legacy systems into platform-based engines of innovation. With real-world case studies and practical tools, Trabucchi and Buganza make platform transformation not only accessible, but actionable for any organization."

— ALAN MACCORMACK, Professor, Harvard Business School

"*The Digital Phoenix Effect* offers a structured and realistic guide for executives in traditional firms aiming to compete in a platform-dominated landscape. Rather than urging firms to mimic startups, the authors present "Platform Thinking" as a method to unlock the hidden potential of legacy assets—turning inertia into leverage.

What sets this book apart is its practical ambition: it shows how executives can bridge the gap between traditional companies and Big Tech—not by copying Silicon Valley, but by building scalable, ecosystem-guiding models rooted in their existing strengths. The inclusion of a GenAI "co-thinker" tool reinforces the book's hands-on approach.

The Digital Phoenix Effect is not about disruption for its own sake. It is about reinvention through creative thinking and vision at a time of accelerating innovation. It is a strategic manual for firms that in these turbulent times want to remain relevant, competitive, and influential in shaping their industry's future."

— FRANCESCO CAIO, Multiple times Chairman and CEO of multinational companies

"*The Digital Phoenix Effect* has the great merit of reminding us that even within the most mature and structured organizations lie valuable yet often untapped resources, which can serve as the foundation for innovative and transformative business models."

— CAMILLA FOLLADORI, Chief Strategy Officer at Sisal

"Trabucchi and Buganza masterfully reveal how AI chatbots transform from mere digital assistants into strategic innovation partners that resurrect aging enterprises. Their 'Digital Phoenix' framework doesn't just explain technological adoption—it charts a

flight path for legacy organizations to emerge stronger and more agile in the face of relentless market evolution."
— FAISAL HOQUE, Founder, Shadoka & NextChapter, #1 Wall Street Journal, Los Angeles Times, and USA Today bestselling author of 'Transcend'

"As an advisor to legacy companies navigating digital transformation, I've found *The Digital Phoenix Effect* to be an essential resource. Trabucchi and Buganza offer a research-backed, practical framework that redefines the legacy-liability equation. Their book provides actionable strategies to leverage existing assets and evolve into platform-based ecosystems. I look forward to integrating this approach into my future workshops."
— GIUSEPPE STIGLIANO, 3xCEO, Keynote Speaker and Executive Advisor, Author of 'Redefining Retail'

"This book finally brings Platform Thinking to established companies in a very practical way. The hands-on approach is further augmented by the application of GenAI. It was great to partner with Daniel and Tommaso in applying GenAI as a co-thinker to real platform case building. The GenAI co-thinker helps practitioners discuss key questions and trade-offs with a GPT companion to design a winning platform. This is the first-of-its-kind experiment in human-AI collaboration for strategy formulation in platforms"
— ELISA FARRI and GABRIELE ROSANI, Authors of the HBR Guide to Generative AI for Managers, Capgemini Invent's Management Lab

"Having spent years studying how technology shapes human experiences, I'm genuinely excited about this book. Trabucchi and Buganza masterfully show established companies how to transform their core strengths into dynamic platforms. Through compelling examples and practical frameworks, they demonstrate that platform strategies aren't just for tech startups — they're essential for any business ready to grow sustainably. Most importantly, they reveal how companies can innovate while staying authentic to their values.

This is the guide business leaders need to create lasting value in our rapidly evolving digital world."

— KATE O'NEILL, Tech Humanist and author of 'What Matters Next'

"Trabucchi and Buganza transform traditional business models into fuel for digital reinvention. *The Digital Phoenix Effect* delivers a compelling and necessary playbook to unlock your organization's hidden strengths through Platform Thinking."

— DAN PONTEFRACT, award-winning author of 'Work-Life Bloom' and 'Open To Think'.

"Platforms are disrupting economies and industries at high speed, redesigning the rules of business for incumbents and leaders. In a very cohesive and comprehensive way, The Digital Phoenix Effect provides deep conceptual frameworks, insightful examples, and rich practical advices to traditional companies and markets for their successful platform transformation from thinking to building. The authors offer an exceptional synthesis of cutting-edge research findings and organizational cases that makes it must-reading for any business trying to become a platform or a "platfirm" as I renamed it"

— COSIMO ACCOTO, Tech Philosopher, MIT Research Affiliate, UNIMORE Adjunct Professor

"*The Digital Phoenix Effect* tackles one of the most pressing questions for the survival and competitiveness of established companies with clarity and depth: how to innovate without denying your history and identity. Trabucchi and Buganza show that the answer does not lie in copying the models and approaches typical of start-ups, but in strategically rethinking existing assets, adopting Platform Thinking as a new paradigm for innovation.

The book masterfully integrates theory and practice, offering academically sound yet accessible models, enriched with real-life cases and ready-to-use tools.

Particularly interesting is the proposal to leverage GenAI tools as "co-thinkers" to support strategic planning: an experiment that

opens up new perspectives not only for business innovation but also for management training."
— FEDERICO FRATTINI, Professor & Dean at POLIMI Graduate School of Management

"Multi-sided platform marketplaces dominate many industries and are rapidly invading the remainders. Yet most existing 'non-platform' companies cannot shift their entire business model to address this threat. However, as Professors Trabuchi and Buganza explain in clear and practical terms, they can - and perhaps must - create ancillary platforms with the resources that are necessary but not sufficient to give them a market edge. This strategy deserves immediate attention from all business managers."
— TED LADD, Harvard University, Hult International Business School, and 7-time platform entrepreneur

"In recent years, Trabucchi and Buganza have demonstrated an exceptional ability to analyse change in the business models of large technology companies, showing how the platform model has often been a decisive competitive advantage.
But it is with *The Digital Phoenix Effect* that the big insight comes: this advantage is not exclusive to Silicon Valley start-ups but can also be adopted by more traditional and less 'tech driven' companies. In this case, the platform model becomes essential to ensure survival in an ever-changing market."
— RICCARDO BASSETTO, Head of Operations at Chora & Will Media and co-host of *Actually*

"*The Digital Phoenix Effect* focuses on the major untapped potential by legacy companies by demonstrating the power of Platform Thinking. While platforms have conquered the consumer space a long while ago, established organizations are yet to fully embrace their potential. This book provides a wealth of pragmatic evidence on the numerous opportunities already out there, and practical guidance how to get started with platformization."
— PAAVO RITALA, Professor of Strategy & Innovation, LUT University & Co-Editor in Chief of R&D Management

"*The Digital Phoenix Effect*" offers a compelling roadmap for leaders navigating disruption in a digital world. Drawing on deep insights and real-world cases, it shows how companies can rise stronger from crisis. The book balances strategic thinking with practical frameworks. It is a timely and thought-provoking read. I highly recommend it to executives and scholars alike."

— WIM VANHAVERBEKE, Professor, University of Antwerp, Co-Editor in Chief of Technovation

Table of Contents

Introduction

A decade in the world of platforms: from startup to legacy firms

Around a decade ago, the two of us started talking about platforms, inspired by the brilliant work of colleagues around the world. Back then, it was a conversation among tech enthusiasts, something you'd expect at geek meetups, with discussions revolving around freemium apps and the sustainability of their business models. The world was only beginning to realize the potential of data and its value, with many referring to data as the "new oil." We could see that platforms would power this new reality, but how it would unfold wasn't clear. There was excitement but also confusion. Data-driven business models were emerging, yet the challenge was understanding how these models could be sustainable and scalable, and how they could impact traditional industries.

We published numerous articles exploring platforms from every angle—how they work, how they differ from linear businesses, and the hidden potential they offer. We were particularly intrigued by their scalability at quasi-zero marginal cost. The cost that Airbnb would have to double the number of rooms offered to the market is not zero, but really negligible if compared with the cost that a traditional company like Hilton would have to achieve the same result. Back then, we started talking about multi-sided platforms, which facilitate transactions between two distinct user groups. These platforms, such as Airbnb and Uber, were becoming the new business norm by solving market friction through network effects. The idea that network externalities could reshape industries became a central focus in our early discussions.

However, as we immersed ourselves in platform research, something crucial became clear. This wasn't just about startups or

Silicon Valley companies like Google, Facebook, and Uber. We began to engage with professionals and managers from large, legacy firms, all grappling with a common issue: how to stay relevant in an increasingly digital and fast-changing world. These firms had a significant legacy—decades of market dominance, loyal customer bases, knowledge and know-how, and an immense workforce. But they also had something else: inertia. The question was, how could they evolve in a digital age dominated by platforms?

This realization shifted the conversation. We saw a widening gap between the tech-driven startups disrupting industries and the traditional firms that had long defined them. While tech startups thrived on platform-based business models, incumbents were left questioning if platforms could be relevant for them as well. Could Platform Thinking—a mindset that focuses on unlocking value through platform-based mechanisms—help them in maintaining (or in some cases regaining) their market relevance?

The answer was a resounding yes[1]. Over time, we began introducing Platform Thinking to these managers and executives. We started exploring how legacy firms could leverage their existing assets, partners, data, and customers to create their own platforms in their own field. In short, we helped them understand how to build an ecosystem that could transform their traditional value chains into something more dynamic, resilient, and future-proof.

Our early conversations were hypothetical, but today, the phenomenon is visible in the market. Over the last few years, 92% of the S&P 500 have approached the idea of platformization, but only a few of these companies have actually developed a platform and integrated Platform Thinking into their business models. Those that succeeded proved that even the most traditional, legacy firms

---

[1] See Hagiu and Altman, 2017, Dell'Era et al., 2021; Zhu and Cao, 2024; Springer et al., 2025.

can reinvent themselves[2], not only in B2C but even in industrial and B2B settings[3].

We studied them, we worked with them, and we developed tools and processes to support their transformation. And now, it's time to share what we've learned. While only a few companies have fully made this leap, those that have succeeded are now reaping the benefits. Their stories, and the lessons they offer, are ready to be shared with you.

As you dive into *The Digital Phoenix Effect*, you'll see how Platform Thinking can transform not just startups or tech giants, but any business that's willing to embrace a new way of thinking. Whether you're managing a small family business or leading a global corporation, this book is your guide to building platforms that can drive innovation, growth, and long-term success.

20 years...that changed the world

In the last two decades, the business landscape has undergone a radical transformation, and nowhere is this more evident than in the S&P 500. If we take a look at the top 10 companies listed in 2004 and compare them to the leading firms in 2024, the difference is striking. In 2004, the list was dominated by companies in industries like energy, finance, and manufacturing—titans like ExxonMobil, General Electric, and Citigroup were among the top names. Their business models were linear, built on supply chains, large workforces, and physical assets. Fast forward to 2024, the picture couldn't be more different. Today, platform-based companies such as Meta (formerly Facebook), Alphabet (Google), Amazon, Apple, and Microsoft dominate the S&P 500 list.

This shift reflects the broader platform revolution that has taken place in the last 20 years. Companies that have embraced platform-based mechanisms have redefined their industries and transformed millions of people's daily lives. Consider how Uber has changed the

[2] These numbers were first presented in the 'Platform Thinking Magazine Vol. 1' (2023), released at the end of the first edition of the Observatory Platform Thinking HUB.

[3] See Jovanovic et al., 2022; Meier et al., 2024; Patrucco et al., 2024.

way we think about transportation, Airbnb, how we book travel accommodations, and Spotify or YouTube, how we consume music and video content. These platforms thrive on a simple but powerful idea: they connect two or more interdependent groups—drivers and passengers, hosts and travelers, or content creators and consumers—triggering network effects. As more users join one side, the value for users on the other side increases exponentially.

The impact of platforms has been profound, extending far beyond just the digital and tech sectors. Platforms have penetrated nearly every primary industry, including healthcare, manufacturing, finance, and energy. Martin Kenney and colleagues'[4] extensive research showed how platforms have evolved from niche digital marketplaces to central actors in reorganizing traditional industries. Their analysis reveals that 70% of service industries in the U.S. are now either directly or indirectly affected by platforms.

However, this platform revolution has not been evenly distributed across the globe, at least in terms of where the platforms are created. A significant portion of the platform economy is concentrated in a few key regions. If we consider the top 100 platform companies worldwide, 85% of their total market capitalization is based in the United States, with companies like Amazon, Apple, and Google leading the charge. The Asia-Pacific region, particularly China, accounts for another 11%, driven by giants like Alibaba, ByteDance and Tencent. Europe and Africa combined to contribute a mere 3%, highlighting the platform divide across regions[5]. This disparity raises critical questions about the future of traditional firms in regions like the American and Asian-Pacific markets, but even more in Europe, where established industries based on linear economics models continue to dominate and serve as the backbone of the economy.

---

[4] See Kenney et al., 2022.

[5] See Hamidreza Hosseini from Ecodynamics.io https://www.linkedin.com/posts/hosseinihamidreza_chatgpt-activity 7287387946591092736-wCJ2/

Traditional firms cannot afford to ignore this reality. They are at a crossroads: either embrace Platform Thinking and reinvent themselves or risk being left behind. The harsh truth is that the companies that once formed the backbone of the global economy now face unprecedented disruption from platform businesses, many of which didn't even exist two decades ago. Yet, the path forward is not necessarily bleak for legacy firms.

Traditional companies can learn from the platform game; some of them already have, and the results were astonishing. They are now enhancing and even surpassing these models. By effectively deploying platform strategies, these legacy firms are tackling global challenges such as sustainability and digital transformation, often exceeding the impacts made by their digital-native counterparts. This shift suggests a pivotal lesson for other industrial companies: the path blazed by these pioneers might offer more relevant insights and actionable strategies than those traditionally highlighted by Silicon Valley.

The first step is relatively simple: the platform revolution is not just about technology. It's about rethinking business models, relationships, and the very nature of value creation. As we move forward, the question for every company—large or small, established or new—is this: How can we leverage Platform Thinking to unlock new opportunities, foster innovation, and ensure long-term success? The answer lies not in holding on to the past but in embracing the future through platforms.

Structure of the Book

This book is your guide to understanding how platforms can transform legacy companies and how to design your new platform-based value creation model effectively. Over the past decade, we've dedicated ourselves to researching and working with over 20 companies that were once like yours, wondering how to stay competitive in a world increasingly dominated by platform-based business models. We've also analyzed over 800 initiatives from S&P 500 companies, selecting 140 actual platforms to extract a well-researched foundation for understanding platforms and their potential. Now, we want to share this journey with you and give you the tools to apply Platform Thinking to your organization.

The book is divided into three parts, each designed to guide you step by step through the process of embracing platforms. Whether you're a newcomer to Platform Thinking or an experienced manager looking for deeper insights, this structure will make your transformation journey clear and actionable.

Part 1: Rethinking Platforms in Established Firms

We start with examples that might resonate with your own company's situation. You'll read about AXA, Eni, and Siemens—three industry leaders who faced major challenges but managed to use Platform Thinking to turn things around. AXA created its Digital Commercial Platform to keep up with new challenges due to climate change. Eni developed Open-es, a platform focused on sustainability in the energy sector, and Siemens launched Siemens Xcelerator, a platform that helped them stay competitive in the manufacturing world seeking digital services. Each case study shows that platforms are not just for tech startups. They are a powerful tool for solving industry-specific problems, even in traditional companies.

By reading these stories, you'll see how platforms can be the spark that ignites transformation in even traditional businesses. You'll understand that this isn't just about tech companies but about how any organization can use Platform Thinking to adapt, innovate, and thrive.

Next, we'll explore how you can use platforms in different areas of your business. We've identified three key strategies that companies like yours can use to drive transformation. In addition to developing new services, we propose using platforms to reshape the core of your business by transforming core business activities and revamping support functions.

Part 2: 5 Business Problems to be solved through Platform Thinking

We continue with an in-depth dive into the business problems that can be solved through platforms, and the relative Platform Thinking hacks to solve them.

Here, we don't just give you high-level ideas; we go through five concrete business problems that can be solved through concrete tactics that we call Platform Thinking Hacks. They emerge from real-world examples from the hundreds of cases we studied in the S&P 500. These examples will inspire you and show you practical ways to apply Platform Thinking to your unique challenges. We want you to walk away from this section not just understanding the theory but knowing exactly how to put it into practice in your business.

Part 3: Building Your Platform

Finally, when you're ready to start building your platform, this part of the book will be your hands-on guide.

The core of this section is the Platform Thinking Journey, a four-step process that will take you from identifying a problem in your business to designing and evolving a platform that solves it. We've also created a set of cards to help you work through each step systematically. You'll have the tools you need to frame your problem, design your ecosystem, and develop a business model that works in a platform-based world.

The whole methodology has been developed with the support of roughly 20 legacy companies that believed in Platform Thinking and experimented with us in the Observatory Platform Thinking HUB at Politecnico di Milano.

Plus, to ensure you have support at every step, we've developed a dedicated GPT model designed specifically to guide you through the platform-building process.

We introduce GenAI as a powerful tool that will act as your co-thinker[6] throughout your platform journey. GenAI will ask you the

[6] As explained by Elisa Farri and Gabriele Rosani in the usage of GenAI in the management world, who inspired us in the development of the PlatformThinkingJouneryGPT, acting as our sparring partner.

right questions, support you in identifying options, and guide you through a complex process, one step at a time.

This tool will help you move from theory to action, ensuring that your platform journey is both thoughtful and efficient.

By the time you finish *The Digital Phoenix Effect*, you'll be equipped not only with the knowledge of how platforms work but also with practical tools and strategies to start building your own. Whether you lead a small team or a global corporation, this book will empower you to embrace platforms and stay ahead in today's competitive world.

PART 1
Rethinking Platforms in Legacy Companies

1

Three Faces of the Digital Phoenix

Uncovering the Platform Within Legacy Firms

"Every block of stone has a statue inside it, and it is the sculptor's task to discover it."

These words, pronounced initially by Michelangelo, echoed powerfully on October 16th, 2023, in Milan, the business heart of Italy. That day marked the first public convention of the Platform Thinking HUB, an initiative born at the Politecnico di Milano to bring Platform Thinking into the spotlight for businesses across industries. Standing on stage was Francesco Caio, a visionary CEO who had guided some of Italy's and Europe's most influential companies through transformative journeys. His career reads like a roadmap of Europe's industrial evolution. CEO of Omnitel (now Vodafone Italy), pioneering mobile operators in Italy, leading the restructuring of Cable & Wireless in the UK as Group Chief Executive, and guiding Lehman Brothers Europe as president of the board of directors. His work also spanned to Avio S.p.A., a General Electric aerospace company, Poste Italiane, where he spearheaded a major digital transformation, Saipem, a key player in energy infrastructures, and consulted for the governments of Italy and the UK on digital strategies. His ability to navigate such diverse industries, transforming each through digitalization, made him the perfect figure to help launch this initiative.

That day, we talked about companies from all walks of life—John Deere, the American agricultural machinery giant; Walmart, the largest U.S. retailer; Telepass, the Italian company managing highway toll systems. We also touched on global leaders like AT&T,

NVIDIA, Ford, and PepsiCo, among others. Despite operating in very different sectors, all these businesses were the focus of our attention because they share a common trait: they embraced Platform Thinking, transforming aspects of their long-established operations through platform mechanisms and network effects.

But ask anyone in the business world to name a "*platform*," and they'll probably not mention any of the abovementioned companies. Most likely, the answer would be Uber, Airbnb, Spotify, YouTube, Amazon, or Meta. These are the names that dominate headlines and conversations. However, that day wasn't about these tech giants. The room was filled with managers from well-established, non-digital-native companies, all eager to discover how to maintain or regain their business leadership and competitive advantage in an increasingly digital and fast-changing world. The energy was palpable. We spent the entire morning in deep conversations about platforms, exploring their potential with these managers, each representing companies that have been pillars of their industries for decades. Their challenges were clear, as was their ambition to drive change.

As Caio continued, he drew upon Michelangelo's words again: "*As Michelangelo said, the statue is in the block of marble, you just need to know how to find it. The platform is within the company, and you just need to know how to find it. Those who do... develop and create an impressive amount of value.*" That's what this was all about—finding the platform within each business, with the singular mission of solving the most pressing problems.

"*The truth is,*" Caio continued, "*there has been exponential growth for those who embraced platforms, while others have remained stuck in linear progress.*" His statement was a wake-up call to everyone in the room. In the past decade, companies like Meta, Uber, and Airbnb have seen explosive growth, riding the wave of network effects and data-driven scalability that platforms provide. These companies have grown at a pace that traditional businesses can only dream of, thanks to their ability to leverage platforms to scale rapidly while maintaining near-zero marginal costs.

But the room grew more reflective when Caio pointed out another harsh reality: "*North America and Asia have led this revolution, while Europe has lagged. There is a huge gap between those who have adopted this way of thinking and those who have not.*" It was a sobering thought for many European executives in the room. The stark contrast between regions that have embraced platforms and those that haven't was evident. Companies like Google, Amazon, and Tencent dominate the platform landscape, and none of them is European.

This gap, however, also presented an opportunity. *"We are talking about new business paradigms,"* Caio emphasized. *"It's time to rethink what we have defined as a company until now."* The message was clear: traditional businesses must evolve or risk falling behind in a world where platforms are redefining how value is created and captured. The words are strong: platforms are not only for the digital tech elite. They are far more than just technology; they are a new business paradigm, and as such, can be embraced by every company in every possible industry. This is a call to action to all the managers in legacy firms; traditional businesses must evolve. But this evolution can be seen more as an opportunity to stay relevant than as a risk of falling behind in a world where platforms are redefining how value is created and captured.

Since that day, we have met visionary leaders who introduced us to platform-based initiatives created by large, established organizations. Bettina Rotermund brought us into Siemens Xcelerator, Pierre du Rostu introduced us to AXA's Digital Commercial Platform, and Lorenzo de Filippi and Stefano Fasani shared with us the story of Open-es powered by Eni.

What became strikingly clear in those conversations was that all three companies (legacy companies very far from being start-ups) were heading in the same direction: they were building platforms to solve urgent problems within their organizations. They had recognized that their core issues couldn't be addressed by traditional linear methods. Instead, they needed platforms that could reconfigure their ecosystems, accelerate innovation, and create new forms of value. It wasn't about starting from scratch; it was about leveraging the assets they already had and using Platform Thinking to bring them together in powerful new ways.

These projects are real and concrete examples of how legacy organizations can not only learn the platform game from tech giants but master it to an even higher level, targeting relevant social problems like sustainability, digital transformation, and climate change. Using Francesco Caio's words: *"The platform is already within your company, and it can help you maintain your leadership as you embark on the digital transformation journey."*

These projects contained *The Digital Phoenix Effect* that this book is all about. They represent the future of business—a future in which platforms are at the core of solving problems, creating value, and driving long-term success. These three case studies will open this book and serve as real-world examples of how Platform Thinking can ignite change, even in the most established organizations.

Siemens' Digital Dilemma: A Legacy at Risk

"Today, we want to talk about speed, how we can accelerate digital transformation, and how we can do this for you and with you, our customers and partners."

In June 2022, at the global launch event of Siemens Xcelerator, CEO Roland Busch opened his speech with this powerful statement. He set the stage for the urgency and vision behind Siemens's next big move: its transformation from a legacy industrial giant into a tech company, capable of solving customer challenges in new, innovative ways. For Siemens, the stakes were high—remain relevant or face the risk of obsolescence in a rapidly changing world where digitalization was not just an advantage but a necessity.

Founded in 1847 by Werner von Siemens and Johann Georg Halske, Siemens has a storied history as one of Europe's most iconic companies. Initially established as a telegraph manufacturing company in Berlin, Siemens quickly grew into a global leader in electrical engineering and electronics. Over the decades, the company expanded into sectors ranging from healthcare and energy to manufacturing and transportation. Today, Siemens operates in more than 200 countries, with 2024 revenues exceeding €75,9 billion. The company is a dominant player in industries such as automation, electrification, and digitalization.

However, even with its vast portfolio and global reach, Siemens was increasingly facing a familiar challenge for legacy firms: the digital disruption posed by software-centric companies. Competitors from Silicon Valley and elsewhere were offering cutting-edge digital solutions that connected physical products with the cloud, enabling real-time data analysis, predictive maintenance, and unprecedented operational flexibility. The question facing the company was simple but existential:

Could Siemens remain competitive in an increasingly digital world?

To clearly understand the problem Siemens wanted to target, we can still rely on the words of Busch: "*During the pandemic, many organizations turned to technology to keep their operations running. When supply chains broke down and assembly lines ground to a halt, digital technologies saved us. I'll give you an example—when we didn't have the parts in Amberg to make a specific version of our SIMATIC controllers, we used our digital systems to shift production to Chengdu, China, in real time. That flexibility allowed us to deliver when others couldn't. This is the kind of transformation we want to make easier for you*".

Siemens acknowledged that customers needed more than hardware—they needed agility and digital solutions that could adapt quickly to market changes and operational disruptions. Despite the undisputed quality of Siemens' products, customers were struggling with problems that traditional hardware alone could not solve. What they needed were integrated solutions that combined both physical and digital elements to unlock their digital transformation.

But, enabling digital transformation in industrial companies that relied for decades on hardware products to sustain their competitive advantage is not an easy task. Busch is absolutely aware of it: "*…for all its promises, digital transformation is hard and that moving beyond proof of concept and integrating legacy systems and fusing data silos can be costly, slow and difficult to scale up*".

All these elements lay at the bottom of the vision behind Siemens Xcelerator, the company's ambitious new digital platform.

A Hardware Giant in a Software World

Siemens' challenge was not just external but also deeply rooted within its organizational DNA. As a company built on over a century of producing high-quality physical goods, Siemens was seen as the epitome of industrial excellence. Its core competencies lie in manufacturing and engineering, not software development. This became a significant barrier to digital transformation, both internally and in terms of market expectations. Its greatest asset and biggest obstacle was Siemens' brand, long synonymous with precision and reliability.

This legacy of excellence in hardware created several challenges. First, the market expected Siemens to continue delivering world-class products that had defined its reputation. Second, even if Siemens, for the last 30 years, has led many vertical software areas with integrated software, for example in the AI field, it remained mainly known for hardware. This sustained resistance to change, especially in a company whose history and perception were so intertwined with the production of physical goods.

Finally, Siemens had to contend with the fact that hardware alone was no longer enough to meet the demands of modern industry. Customers needed integrated solutions that combined sensors, data, and real-time analytics capabilities that were traditionally outside of Siemens' core expertise. In this environment, the company faced the risk of being left behind by faster, more agile competitors who were born digital. As Bettina Rotermund, Siemens Head of Strategy & Analyst Relations, Siemens Xcelerator, reflected, "*We needed to understand that our core strength wasn't just in making great products—it was in helping our customers succeed through those products, and that now included digital solutions*".

The rise of startups and digital-native companies only intensified the pressure. Giants like Amazon, Google, and NVIDIA were setting the pace for digital innovation, leaving traditional companies like Siemens at risk of becoming irrelevant in key sectors. In fact, the future of the industry was increasingly being shaped by digital platforms—interconnected ecosystems of hardware, software, and data that could scale quickly and provide value far beyond the physical product itself.

For Siemens, the need to evolve was clear. But the path forward wasn't. How could a company with over a century of history transform itself without losing the qualities that made it successful in the first place? How could it maintain its leadership in industrial hardware while also becoming a leader in digital solutions?

In response to these challenges, Siemens recognized that it couldn't go it alone. The company's core strength lies in its relationships—with its customers, its technology partners, and its vast ecosystem of suppliers and service providers. By leveraging these relationships and combining them with cutting-edge digital technologies, Siemens saw an opportunity to reinvent itself. This vision would soon take shape in the form of Siemens Xcelerator, a platform designed not only to drive Siemens' digital transformation but to empower its customers to achieve their own.

Siemens Xcelerator—A Digital Revolution Takes Shape

The solution to this dilemma? Siemens Xcelerator. Launched in June 2022, Siemens Xcelerator is not just a product or a service; it is an open digital business platform designed to accelerate digital transformation across industries, from manufacturing and infrastructure to mobility and energy grids. More than a suite of tools, Xcelerator represents a fundamental shift in how Siemens interacts with its customers and partners, combining hardware, software, and digital services in one integrated ecosystem.

As Roland Busch, Siemens CEO, remarked at the launch event: "*Siemens Xcelerator will make it easier than ever before for companies to navigate digital transformation—faster and at scale. By combining the real and digital worlds across operational and information technology, we empower customers and partners to boost productivity, competitiveness, and scale-up innovations*".

At its core, Siemens Xcelerator is built on three pillars: a curated portfolio of IoT-enabled hardware, software, and digital services, a growing ecosystem of partners, and an evolving marketplace. This combination makes digital transformation more accessible for companies of all sizes, allowing them to connect physical assets with digital solutions to optimize performance, reduce costs, and increase efficiency. The portfolio is modular, cloud-connected, and built on open standards, making it easier for businesses to integrate it into their existing infrastructure.

But Siemens Xcelerator isn't just about Siemens' own products. It brings together an ecosystem of partners, from industry giants like Microsoft, NVIDIA, and SAP to smaller, innovative developers, all working to create solutions that complement and enhance each other. Through this growing network, companies can access a wide range of digital services, customize them to their needs, and scale solutions as their businesses grow.

The Xcelerator marketplace allows customers to discover, customize, and purchase solutions from both Siemens and certified third-party providers. This marketplace acts as a hub for innovation, bringing together different players to solve problems collaboratively. Whether a company is looking to optimize its factory operations, build smart buildings, or manage energy grids more efficiently, Xcelerator offers a one-stop solution that brings together the best-in-class tools available on the market.

As Bettina Rotermund explained: "*The beauty of Xcelerator is that it doesn't force Siemens to do everything alone. Our strength lies in collaboration, in bringing together the best ideas from different partners and integrating them into solutions that work for our customers*".

One of the standout collaborations within Siemens Xcelerator is with NVIDIA, a leader in graphics processing and artificial intelligence. Together, Siemens and NVIDIA have partnered to create a powerful industrial metaverse, using digital twin technology of Siemens paired with the Omniverse of NVIDIA to enable companies to simulate their operations in a virtual environment before implementing changes in the real world.

Mike Geyer, working in NVIDIA, said in a LinkedIn video: "*Looking forward, we see opportunities to further expand the ecosystem by connecting more of Siemens digital industry software, Siemens hardware and PLCS's edge devices into the NVIDIA ecosystem through Omniverse and other technologies, so that we can ultimately bring more AI automation to solve the problems of our customers.*".

Consider the case of a manufacturing company facing challenges in optimizing its production lines. Traditionally, these companies would have to physically test and adjust their machinery, a process that could be time-consuming and costly. With Siemens Xcelerator digital twin technologies paired with the Omniverse technology of NVIDIA, companies can now create an exact digital replica of their factory, test different configurations, and simulate outcomes—all without touching the actual production line. This not only reduces downtime but also allows companies to experiment with innovative solutions without the risk of failure.

The impact of this collaboration is profound. Customers can achieve higher operational efficiency, faster time-to-market, and a more sustainable production process. Siemens Xcelerator, through partnerships like the one with NVIDIA, is enabling companies to solve some of their most pressing digitalization challenges with confidence and ease.

A Seamless, Scalable Solution

At its heart, Siemens Xcelerator is designed to be flexible and scalable, offering solutions that can grow with a company's needs. This is particularly important for smaller companies that may not have the resources to develop their own digital infrastructure from scratch. Xcelerator provides them with the tools, support, and ecosystem to build and expand their digital capabilities.

By focusing on openness, interoperability, and collaboration, Siemens Xcelerator makes it easier for companies to connect their physical products to the digital world, unlocking new value in previously unimaginable ways.

The launch of Siemens Xcelerator wasn't just a technological advancement; it was a strategic move designed to solve some of the most fundamental barriers to Siemens' digital transformation. For a company with a rich legacy in hardware and manufacturing, the platform approach allowed Siemens to embrace the future without compromising its strengths. The core of Siemens Xcelerator lies in how it leverages the company's core competencies while introducing external innovation. Siemens did not have to reinvent itself completely or abandon its expertise in hardware; instead, it integrated that expertise with digital services and solutions provided by partners. The Xcelerator platform is built around Siemens' historical strength in industrial products. Still, now those products are enhanced by cutting-edge software and IoT capabilities from a growing ecosystem of partners.

By creating an open platform, Siemens avoided the pitfall of trying to do everything on its own. As Bettina Rotermund emphasized, "*We are not challenging what Siemens does best—rather, we're changing how we do it and, importantly, why we do it. The platform allows us to focus on solving customer problems, not just delivering products*". This shift in mindset is critical: Xcelerator transforms Siemens from a product manufacturer into a solution provider, where the value is created together with a network of contributors rather than by Siemens alone.

Siemens Xcelerator allowed the company to modernize its brand without losing sight of what has always made it successful. Siemens' name remains synonymous with reliability, precision, and quality—qualities that still underpin the Xcelerator ecosystem. However, the digital platform repositions Siemens for the future, aligning it with modern trends like interoperability, cloud computing, and AI.

This was critical for overcoming internal resistance. Employees and customers alike needed reassurance that Siemens wasn't abandoning its roots but enhancing them. As Bettina Rotermund pointed out, "*For many inside Siemens, there was a fear that digital transformation would mean giving up the products we are known for. Xcelerator proved that wasn't the case. It's not a threat to our legacy but a way to make it even more valuable in the digital age*". The platform preserved Siemens' reputation while also expanding the offerings it could provide to its customers.

One of the most significant advantages of adopting a platform-based approach is speed. Xcelerator allows Siemens to move faster by integrating digital solutions from its partners rather than developing everything in-house. This reduces the time-to-market for new solutions, allowing Siemens to respond more quickly to customer needs.

Additionally, the platform model is inherently scalable. Whether a customer is a small business looking for a basic digital tool or a large enterprise needing an advanced industrial metaverse, Xcelerator can grow with them. It offers a flexible, modular approach that allows companies to start small and scale up as needed, paying only for what they use through subscription-based models. This not only lowers the initial investment but also makes digital transformation more accessible to companies of all sizes.

Finally, Xcelerator's reliance on external partnerships reduces Siemens' need to build all capabilities internally, lowering costs. By co-creating solutions with partners like NVIDIA and SAP, Siemens can offer more innovative services without the expense and risk of developing everything in-house. This strategy also makes it easier to attract new partners, further enriching the platform's offerings and increasing its value to customers.

A Shift in Mindset: Integrating with External Innovation

At the heart of Siemens Xcelerator is a fundamental shift in mindset. Rather than seeing external players as competitors, Siemens embraced them as partners. This is the essence of Platform Thinking: value is created not by hoarding resources but by opening up to collaboration. As Bettina Rotermund noted, "*The platform is an acknowledgment that Siemens cannot do it alone. By building partnerships, we can deliver more value, faster, and at a lower cost*".

Through the platform, Siemens could combine its expertise in industrial hardware and software with the digital innovations of its partners. This opened up new possibilities that Siemens alone could not have achieved. For example, the partnership with NVIDIA to develop the most comprehensive digital twins not only revolutionized Siemens's ability to serve its customers but also accelerated the company's digital transformation.

Siemens Xcelerator was the right move at a critical moment for the company. Faced with growing competition from digital-native companies, Siemens had to find a way to remain relevant without losing the strengths that had made it an industrial leader for over a century. By adopting a platform strategy, Siemens unlocked the full potential of its traditional offerings while integrating new digital capabilities from an ecosystem of partners.

The platform model allowed Siemens to move faster, scale more effectively, and lower costs, all while staying true to its brand. As a result, Siemens is not just keeping up with the digital revolution; it is driving it, showing that even the most established companies can lead the way in a platform-driven world. Through Siemens Xcelerator, the company has proven that the future of industry is not about going it alone—it's about collaborating, innovating, and building a stronger ecosystem for everyone involved.

Weathering the Storm: AXA's Dilemma in the Age of Climate Change

"The risks we're facing today—whether it's climate change, cyber threats, or geopolitical instability—require us to rethink the way we approach insurance. It's no longer just about looking backward at historical data; we need to innovate and build new capabilities for the future."

These are the words of Pierre du Rostu, CEO of AXA Digital Commercial Platform, talking about the need for his platform. The world is facing unprecedented challenges as climate change alters the landscape of risk management. The increasing frequency of natural disasters, rising sea levels, and unpredictable weather patterns have not only impacted individuals and communities but also fundamentally changed the nature of risks that businesses and insurers must handle. For insurance companies, climate change has presented a particularly daunting challenge, undermining traditional business models that have long been based on predictable patterns of risk and stable premiums. As extreme weather events become more common, the ability of insurers to assess, price, and underwrite risks is stretched to its limits, threatening their financial sustainability.

The essence of the insurance business lies in predicting risk and pooling it across a broad base of customers. But climate change has shifted the goalposts, making risk harder to predict and control. Insurance firms are now grappling with how to protect their clients against more frequent, more severe events, while ensuring their survival. AXA, one of the world's leading insurance companies, has felt the full brunt of these changes. The company, known for its historical strength in offering personal, life, and commercial insurance, faces a new reality where the very nature of risk is evolving faster than ever before.

Founded in 1817 as Mutuelle de l'Assurance contre l'Incendie in France, AXA has grown into a global leader in insurance and asset management. With operations in 54 countries, over 120,000 employees, and a presence that spans Europe, Asia, North America, and beyond, AXA provides a range of services, including health, life, and property insurance, as well as financial planning and investment services. In 2022, AXA's revenues exceeded €100 billion, making it one of the top players in the insurance world.

Historically, AXA's strengths include its expertise in traditional insurance products, strong customer base, and conservative approach to risk. The company has built a reliable reputation, consistently delivering solid returns to investors. Its core competence lies in developing and deploying insurance products tailored to customer needs, focusing on underwriting and risk assessment.

But as the climate crisis worsened, AXA's strengths began to feel more like burdens. The company's traditional risk assessment methods—relying on historical data and actuarial models—struggled to keep pace with climate change's unpredictability. The question facing the company was simple but existential:

Could AXA remain competitive in an unpredictable climate change world?

In this shifting environment, AXA faced two parallel challenges that impacted its B2B customers. First, there was the immediate issue of climate risk: how to gather, analyze, and act on new kinds of data to better understand and price the emerging risks associated with climate change for its business clients. Traditional data sources were no longer sufficient; AXA needed access to more sophisticated, real-time data streams—from satellite imagery to geospatial data and climate models—to assess risk for companies operating in an increasingly volatile world.

For example, a large agricultural enterprise might rely on AXA's B2B insurance products to protect its operations from crop loss due to severe weather conditions. To offer more accurate insurance coverage, AXA would need to utilize satellite data and climate models to assess the business's specific risk and tailor their insurance solutions accordingly.

Second, AXA faced a more existential challenge from the rise of new digital players targeting business insurance markets. Insurtech startups, which adopted agile, tech-driven models, could quickly respond to the evolving risks faced by businesses. Unburdened by legacy systems and traditional ways of doing business, these startups posed a serious threat to AXA's B2B market share. They leveraged big data, artificial intelligence, and machine learning to provide real-time, personalized risk solutions to companies, outpacing traditional insurers like AXA.

For instance, an insurtech competitor might offer a manufacturing company a dynamic insurance policy that adjusts based on real-time data from production systems, potentially lowering premiums during periods of reduced activity. Such innovations challenged AXA to reinvent its own B2B offerings to remain competitive in this rapidly evolving landscape.

As Pierre du Rostu shared with us during an interview, "*Startups today are able to move quickly, leveraging new data and technologies in ways that we, as a larger organization, need to catch up with. The challenge for AXA lies in integrating vast amounts of new, real-time data into our systems fast enough to compete.*"

In many ways, AXA's legacy was becoming its biggest obstacle to change. As a historical brand, AXA had built its reputation on expertise in product development and risk management. This deep-rooted competence had earned it the trust of customers and markets alike, but it also created expectations that were difficult to break free from. Customers expected excellence in traditional insurance products, and internal teams were trained to perfect these offerings over decades. But this created inertia—a resistance to the unexplored digital and technological transformation that the future required.

As Thierry Fabing, Chief Product Officer at AXA Digital Commercial Platform, explained in an event, "*Established companies like AXA are not born platforms. We have a legacy system, a historical business model, and a mindset that was developed in a world of more predictable risks*". The challenge was clear: AXA had to overcome internal resistance, market expectations, and a legacy of doing things the "old way" in order to evolve into a company that could thrive in a rapidly changing world.

In response, AXA embarked on an ambitious journey to reinvent its approach to risk management. The solution? A digital platform that could not only modernize its risk models but also position AXA as a leader in the new age of insurance. The result was the AXA Digital Commercial Platform—a bold step into the platform economy, designed to help businesses manage emerging risks in a way that was faster, more agile, and more scalable than ever before.

This transition, however, would not be without its challenges. AXA's history of excellence in product development and risk assessment, while a source of strength, also risked becoming a barrier to the kind of innovation required to compete with the new wave of digital-first players. But with the creation of the AXA Digital Commercial Platform, AXA took a bold step into the future—one that would help it navigate the turbulent waters of climate risk and digital disruption.

Redefining Risk: The Power of the AXA Digital Commercial Platform

AXA Digital Commercial Platform (ADCP) serves as a comprehensive digital solution for AXA's commercial clients, offering new tools and services that extend far beyond traditional insurance products. The ADCP not only helps businesses manage and mitigate emerging risks but also provides AXA with a modern approach to data-driven risk analysis.

At its core, the ADCP is designed to support businesses by providing real-time insights and predictive analytics, helping them to understand better and manage risks associated with environmental changes, cyber threats, and supply chain disruptions. The platform embodies AXA's commitment to digital transformation and is an essential part of the company's strategy to stay relevant in a world where risks are increasingly volatile and unpredictable.

The AXA Digital Commercial Platform thrives on collaboration between multiple stakeholders. These key players form an interconnected ecosystem that enables the platform to deliver value.

AXA's Commercial Clients are the first players of the platform. Businesses across a range of industries—such as retail, logistics, and manufacturing—rely on the ADCP to better navigate the unpredictable risks they face. These clients are at the center of the platform's design, using its tools to assess and mitigate threats like extreme weather, cyberattacks, and operational disruptions. The ADCP allows them to make informed decisions based on real-time data, ultimately reducing their exposure to unforeseen risks.

External Service Providers and Data Partners play the role of partners and support. The platform integrates data from various third-party providers, including cybersecurity firms, geospatial analysts, and environmental data organizations. These partnerships provide AXA's Commercial Clients with a broader view of their risk landscape. For example, real-time weather data can help a logistics company monitor potential disruptions to its supply chain, while cybersecurity alerts allow a financial institution to stay ahead of emerging digital threats.

Finally, and perhaps more importantly, internal AXA Stakeholders like underwriters, claims teams and product developers also benefit from the ADCP. The platform feeds them valuable data that improves decision-making processes, from pricing new insurance policies to handling claims more efficiently. This internal integration strengthens AXA's ability to adapt its offerings to the needs of the modern business world.

Imagine a large retail chain operating hundreds of stores, each exposed to risks like severe weather or cyberattacks. Before adopting AXA's Digital Commercial Platform (ADCP), the company often found itself reacting to problems rather than anticipating them, leading to costly disruptions. Without a centralized system, the retailer struggled to track how different threats—like regional storms or cyber vulnerabilities—could affect specific locations.

With the ADCP, this situation changes dramatically. By integrating its own operational data (such as store locations, inventory, and supply chains) with external data sources, including climate models and cybersecurity feeds from partners like IBM Security and Microsoft Azure, the retailer gains real-time risk monitoring for all its locations. Now, when a storm is forecasted, the platform sends early warnings, enabling the company to relocate stock or reinforce vulnerable stores in advance, minimizing potential damage.

But ADCP's value goes beyond managing immediate threats. With predictive analytics, the platform helps the retailer foresee long-term risks, like an expected increase in hurricanes next season for coastal stores. This allows them to plan proactive measures, such as pre-arranging alternative supply routes or enhancing physical protections, improving long-term resilience. The retailer can also integrate its supply chain data into the platform, allowing for quick responses to disruptions in supplier regions, such as rerouting deliveries when a supplier is affected by extreme weather.

Additionally, the ADCP offers collaboration tools that enable the retailer to easily share risk insights with key partners and suppliers. For instance, if a critical supplier's warehouse is at risk of flooding, the retailer can quickly coordinate backup plans and minimize disruption to their operations.

For AXA's internal stakeholders, the ADCP creates significant value as well. The platform allows AXA to better assess and price risks, using more accurate and up-to-date information, which reduces the likelihood of unexpected large claims. By providing more tailored, data-driven insurance solutions, AXA can strengthen its relationships with B2B clients like this retailer, enhancing client satisfaction and loyalty. Internally, AXA benefits from improved operational efficiency, as underwriters and claims teams can make more informed decisions, reducing the need for reactive adjustments to policies or coverage. This also helps AXA stay ahead of insurtech competitors, maintaining its market leadership by offering cutting-edge, tech-enabled insurance products.

In essence, AXA's ADCP transforms risk management for both the retailer and AXA itself. By helping businesses anticipate and mitigate risks, while also providing AXA with better tools for assessing and managing their own risk exposure, the platform is a win-win, improving resilience for clients and operational efficiency for AXA.

Breaking Barriers: Why the AXA Digital Commercial Platform Was the Key to Innovation

For AXA, creating the ADCP wasn't just a technological upgrade—it was a strategic move designed to overcome fundamental challenges inherent to being an established company in a rapidly changing world. The platform has allowed AXA to maintain its competitive edge while addressing the evolving needs of its customers in a way that a traditional business model could no longer support. In doing so, AXA has reaffirmed its role as a leader in the insurance industry, positioning itself as a modern, data-driven risk management provider.

The ADCP has proven to be a multi-faceted solution that works both externally for AXA's commercial customers and internally for its operational teams. Externally, it provides businesses with the tools to navigate modern risks, from climate change to cyber threats. Internally, the platform serves AXA's own functions by streamlining risk assessment processes, improving underwriting accuracy, and facilitating more efficient claims management. This dual-purpose approach ensures that AXA remains relevant in a landscape where both customer expectations and the nature of risk are shifting rapidly

.

As Pierre du Rostu emphasized, "*The ADCP keeps our product at the center while adapting to the contextual changes we see today. We aren't changing what we do—we're enhancing how we do it*". This perspective reflects the careful balance AXA has struck: staying true to its roots in insurance while embracing new, platform-driven business models.

One of AXA's greatest strengths in launching the platform was its established brand. Over the years, the company has built a foundation of trust with its customers, and the ADCP leverages that trust to introduce new services without alienating its core market. Unlike tech startups that must build credibility from scratch, AXA's longstanding relationships with its clients gave the platform a strong launchpad. Businesses were already turning to AXA for risk management, and the ADCP expanded that relationship by offering more innovative, real-time tools for understanding and mitigating risks.

The platform's brand continuity is also a key element. It is not just a departure from traditional methods—it's a seamless extension of what AXA has always done best: helping customers manage uncertainty. In this sense, AXA's deep industry expertise forms the core of the ADCP, ensuring that the platform delivers value while maintaining the company's reputation for reliability and excellence.

However, building the ADCP wasn't without its challenges. As with many established companies, AXA faced internal resistance to change. The shift from product-centric to platform-centric thinking necessitated a significant cultural transformation within the organization. Historically, AXA's core competency has been developing and deploying insurance products—a process steeped in traditional methods and legacy systems. The move to a platform model, which emphasized collaboration, open ecosystems, and data sharing, required teams to think beyond the product and embrace new ways of working.

This resistance, however, was overcome by emphasizing that the ADCP wasn't replacing AXA's core business—it was enhancing it. "*We are not trying to change what AXA is known for*," said Pierre du Rostu. "*We're simply leveraging new technology to get better at what we've always done—manage risk*". By positioning the platform as an evolution, rather than a revolution, AXA was able to foster internal buy-in and align the platform with its longstanding mission.

Building the ADCP as a platform, rather than developing a series of standalone products, has provided AXA with significant advantages. Platforms, by design, are faster, more scalable, and require less internal investment than traditional product development. The ADCP benefits from external data providers, artificial intelligence, and real-time analytics, reducing the need for AXA to build every capability in-house. This also enables faster adaptation to market needs, as new services can be easily integrated into the platform with relative ease.

Additionally, the platform's scalability enables it to grow in tandem with AXA's business. As more data is integrated and more customers join, the platform's value increases through network effects, making it a more powerful tool for both AXA and its clients. This scalability, combined with the cost efficiencies of leveraging external data and partners, positions the ADCP as a long-term growth driver for AXA.

In the end, the AXA Digital Commercial Platform is more than a technological solution; it's a strategic transformation that positions AXA for the future. By addressing the twin challenges of climate change and digital disruption, the ADCP helps AXA not just survive but thrive in a new era of risk.

Open-es and the challenge of sustainability in the energy sector

> "*Sustainability requires planning, pragmatism, constant monitoring of results, and medium- to long-term strategies. It is a challenge that must be addressed not only by large companies, but by the entire economic system, with a collective and inclusive vision, involving all actors along production chains and economic sectors.*"

These are the words of Stefano Fasani, Open-es Program Manager. The world has recently witnessed a growing focus on green transformation, sustainability, and environmental, social, and governance (ESG) standards. These themes are no longer just trends; they have become critical imperatives for businesses, particularly those in traditionally resource-intensive and environmentally impactful industries, such as energy production. However, the shift to sustainable practices is a significant challenge for legacy companies rooted in conventional energy sources. They must embrace new energy sources and transform their entire supply chain to be more sustainable. This complex transformation requires innovation, collaboration, and a reassessment of core business models.

Eni, one of the world's largest energy companies, is a prime example of this challenge. Founded in 1953 by Enrico Mattei, Eni (Ente Nazionale Idrocarburi) has grown into a multinational corporation operating in the energy sector. Eni is a global energy company operating in 61 Countries, with over 30.000 employees. Originally an oil & gas company, it has evolved into an integrated energy company, playing a key role in ensuring energy security and leading the energy transition. Eni's goal is to achieve carbon neutrality by 2050 through the decarbonization of its processes and of the products it sells to its customers.

The purchasing function within Eni has become a critical focal point for this transformation.

Procurement has always been crucial for managing relationships with thousands of suppliers worldwide. These suppliers, spanning various industries and geographies, present significant variability in their sustainability practices. Ensuring that all players in Eni's supply chain adhere to strict sustainability standards is a daunting task, particularly because many of these suppliers are small and medium-sized enterprises (SMEs) with limited resources to invest in ESG compliance. The question facing the company was simple but existential:

Could Eni remain competitive in a world asking for sustainability?

The challenge of Eni is at the root of Open-es, as Stefano Fasani effectively described: "*Sustainability is increasingly becoming a key driver of competitiveness. Companies today, to be able to deal with the financial world or participate in calls for proposals, must be able to measure sustainability and declare improvement plans, and so the goal of the Open-es alliance is to make sure that no one is left behind on this path.*" As the world moves towards stricter environmental and social standards, companies grapple with a network of suppliers that often lack the resources, expertise, and awareness to adopt sustainable practices. Lorenzo De Filippi – Eni's former Head of Procurement & Contract Management System – further highlights the urgency of the issue: "*Sustainability has become a relevant, important issue for all companies. This path has also been stimulated by Eni's strategy and the Procurement Director's vision, which has driven a strong focus on these issues. [...] The regulatory revolution is making the obligations for companies to prepare sustainability reports more and more stringent, and it is crucial to address this challenge now.*" Large industrial companies are aware that if they lag in their sustainability transformation, they risk falling behind competitors that are quicker to adapt to the changing market and regulatory landscape. Companies like Eni must rapidly drive sustainability throughout their entire value chain, but this task is monumental when so many suppliers are unprepared, underfunded, and unaware of the stakes.

Eni was in the perfect position to solve the problem through the Open-es platform that soon became a solution for other partner companies facing similar problems.

Eni supports a socially just energy transition to preserve the environment and ensure affordable energy for all. Eni believes in a common commitment and participation of all stakeholders, including the supply chain. Eni recognizes the key role of the supply chain in the transformation process and promotes its sustainable development. Stefano Fasani's words clearly describe Eni's challenge: *"Sustainability is increasingly a competitive factor and key to a company's market positioning, and therefore there is a risk that each large organization will want to launch its own ESG initiative to its stakeholders, resulting in a multiplication of demands on the same companies creating bureaucracy and confusion.".*

This is where Open-es, a digital platform designed to support the sustainability journey of businesses across Eni's supply chain, emerged as a solution.

Open-es: the open platform for ecosystem sustainability

To address the challenge of embedding sustainability across its vast supply chain, Eni supported the launch of Open-es (soon open to other partners), a platform designed to bring together different players who are invested in the journey towards sustainability. On one side are industrial firms acting as suppliers (many of which are small and medium-sized enterprises (SMEs) for the leading company (Eni at the beginning and others like Snam or Saipem later). On the other side are external companies specializing in measuring, certifying, and improving sustainability practices. These external partners include ESG (Environmental, Social, and Governance) metrics experts, offering services that help companies align their operations with the United Nations' Sustainable Development Goals (SDGs) and with the international and European reporting standards, such as ESRS, GRI, IFRS, and VSME.

For companies navigating the complex requirements of the abovementioned standards, Open-es provides a straightforward, user-friendly process to track, assess, and improve sustainability practices. For example, a company might want to measure its carbon footprint or improve labor conditions within its supply chain. Through Open-es, they can access services provided by specialized partners, such as certifications for environmental performance or benchmarking tools for governance practices. A small supplier could, for instance, use Open-es to get certified in sustainable practices with support from external auditors and ESG certification bodies, ensuring they meet global standards while also aligning with sustainability goals.

The Open-es platform creates a connection between these different players, allowing suppliers to work towards achieving ESG compliance while giving the main companies visibility into the sustainability practices of their entire supply chain. As Manuela Lunetta, Eni's Head of Supplier Sustainability & Management Services put it: *"In 2021, we decided to implement the Open-es initiative, a project that was the brainchild of Eni, but designed to involve other entities as well. Today we are an alliance of 30 partners and a community of more than 29000 companies, mostly small and medium-sized ones, using tools made available free of charge by all partners. These tools enable companies to measure their ESG profile, improve it and grow through guides, solutions and, most importantly, training and development resources available within a digital platform."* Through this collaborative approach, Open-es not only ensures that individual companies improve their ESG performance but also creates a broader network of businesses working towards common sustainability goals.

The development of Open-es began in 2021, rooted in a collaborative effort between Eni, Google Cloud, and Boston Consulting Group (BCG). This partnership was key to laying the technological and strategic foundations of the platform. The early vision for Open-es was clear: to simplify the way companies within a main company supply chain measure and report their ESG performance, with a focus on collaboration with the right technological and strategic partners from the outset to build an ecosystem capable of supporting thousands of businesses.

Initially, Open-es focused on onboarding Eni's suppliers into a digital ecosystem that allowed them to track key ESG metrics. Many of these suppliers lacked advanced digital systems, so the platform was designed to be accessible and straightforward, helping them start their sustainability journey. Over time, Open-es was opened to many key industrial players. Snam and Saipem were among the first companies to join Eni in creating and utilizing the platform, thereby opening it to their suppliers. Soon, they were These companies not only joined Open-es bringing their own s followed by other large organizations, including Baker Hughes, Unicredit, TIM, Autostrade per l'Italia, and many others. The primary objective remains the same: utilizing the platform to evaluate their own supply chains and promote sustainable practices. By involving such key players, Open-es created a multi-firm ecosystem that went beyond Eni's own needs and supported broader industrial transformation.

These companies not only joined Open-es, bringing their own suppliers into the fold, but also creating a ripple effect that expanded the platform's reach and impact.

As Open-es grew, it evolved from a simple data-tracking tool into a comprehensive solution for businesses of all sizes. To support businesses on their sustainability journey, Open-es now offers a range of services beyond basic ESG measurement. One notable extension is the Open-es Camp, a 60-hour training program designed for SMEs. This initiative provides specialized sustainability training, focusing on environmental and social impact, helping small companies improve their ESG practices. Through these programs, Open-es has become not only a platform for data-sharing but also an active force in improving sustainability standards across industries.

Additionally, the platform has partnered with various research institutions to create research opportunities on the data gathered through the platform and integrate certification processes, offering businesses the opportunity to obtain verifiable ESG certifications. This not only helps companies meet regulatory requirements but also enhances their competitiveness in a market increasingly driven by sustainability.

In just a few years, Open-es has grown into a vital resource for companies across various sectors. By fostering collaboration and providing tools for ESG compliance, companies like Eni, Saipem, or Snam have transformed a daunting challenge into a shared opportunity for growth.

Advancing an Ecosystem: why Open-es was the best move in the platform world

Eni's decision to address its sustainability challenges through a platform like Open-es was not only innovative but also strategically sound. By embracing Platform Thinking, with Open-es, Eni solved the immediate problem of aligning its supply chain with ESG standards. Still, it also demonstrated how platforms could support a wider ecosystem, benefiting other businesses and promoting sustainable transformation across industries.

Open-es directly supports Eni's original challenge: ensuring that all its suppliers meet sustainability standards without overwhelming them with administrative burdens. The platform provides suppliers with a simple, accessible tool to assess and improve their ESG performance, while allowing Eni to monitor and manage compliance efficiently. As Stefano Fasani emphasized: "*Only by joining forces between all industrial, financial and institutional players can global goals such as reconciling environmental protection, social care and economic growth be achieved quickly and effectively. Hence the idea of creating an open, cross-sectoral, non-profit system alliance to collaborate between the large realities of the economic system and to support, with simple and free tools, the most representative realities that most need help in this journey, the micro-small and medium-sized enterprises.*".

But Open-es does more than improve internal operations. It has evolved with its own brand, board, and governance structure, which includes multiple companies from different industries. Firms like Unicredit, Saipem, and TIM, previously mentioned, have joined the platform not just as participants but as active contributors, bringing their own suppliers into the ecosystem. This collaborative approach has turned Open-es into a multi-company initiative that transcends Eni's original scope, generating network effects and creating value for the entire industrial sector.

The platform's evolution highlights a key benefit of Platform Thinking: scalability. By building a platform, Eni was able to scale its sustainability efforts far more rapidly than it could have through traditional means. With over 29,000 businesses now using Open-es, the platform has become a self-sustaining ecosystem, continuously growing as more companies and their suppliers join, creating a virtuous cycle of improvement and collaboration.

Internally, platforms like Open-es have the advantage of reducing resistance by aligning with existing business models while introducing new opportunities for growth. By focusing on procurement and supply chain transparency—an area where Eni already had deep expertise—the platform made it easier for internal stakeholders to accept and integrate into the company's broader operations.

Eni's strong brand and decades of experience managing complex industrial relationships were key assets in the platform's successful kickoff. The company's reputation allowed it to build trust with suppliers and partners, encouraging them to adopt Open-es and participate in the broader sustainability mission. Eni's leadership in promoting ESG standards also resonated with Italy's broader industrial transformation, reinforcing the company's role as a pioneer in sustainable business practices.

One of the significant advantages of using a platform to solve Eni's sustainability challenges was speed. Traditional approaches to transforming a supply chain could take years, requiring significant internal resources and investments. With Open-es, Eni was able to leverage external expertise to deploy a scalable solution rapidly.

Platforms also enable scalability at a relatively low cost. Instead of building every capability in the sustainability field in-house, Eni could rely on external partners and ecosystem participants to co-create value. This reduced the need for heavy upfront investments in technology and training, as the platform could grow organically with the help of its users. As more companies joined, the platform became more valuable for everyone involved, reinforcing its network effects.

Three Digital Phoenixes, three different impacts on the original value chain

In this chapter, we explored the stories of three companies—Siemens, AXA, and Eni. Each company represents a successful response to a set of modern business challenges through platform development. Siemens, a leading industrial giant, launched a platform to offer value-added services to its customers beyond their core product offerings. AXA, a global insurance leader, responded to the changing environment by building a platform that revolutionized its R&D function, creating new ways to assess and mitigate risks for its business customers. Eni, a global energy company, focused on solving a sustainability issue within its supply chain by engaging partners through a platform model.

These cases demonstrate the vast potential of Platform Thinking. While the specifics differ, there's an underlying pattern that connects them all. Siemens, AXA, and Eni are all established firms with a rich history and market dominance. They each faced a critical challenge that required a strategic shift, and in all three cases, they turned to Platform Thinking to solve their problems.

The Shared Challenge: Platform as a Strategic Response

Though Siemens, AXA, and Eni operate in entirely different industries, they share several commonalities. Each of them is a long-standing, established company that initially built its success on traditional, linear business models. Over time, they encountered new external pressures—customer demands, sustainability concerns, and technological disruptions—that threatened the sustainability of their core business models. To address these challenges, each firm implemented a platform strategy. This strategic shift allowed them to go beyond the confines of their traditional value chains, moving into new territory that would future-proof their businesses.

In essence, Platform Thinking was their common answer. Siemens developed a platform to enhance customer services; AXA deployed a platform to improve risk assessment in its R&D process. And Eni leveraged a platform to tackle sustainability challenges. Each of these companies identified that their traditional, product-centric approach was insufficient in today's fast-paced business environment. By shifting to platforms, they embraced an ecosystem-driven model that extended their reach and adaptability.

Being an established company brings unique challenges when adopting a platform approach. Siemens, AXA, and Eni all faced similar hurdles in terms of legacy systems, organizational inertia, and complex value chains. These companies had built their success on traditional models, which meant that moving toward a platform approach required a shift not only in technology but in mindset as well. The cultural shift—convincing teams to look beyond established processes and embrace a more open, collaborative approach—was significant. In addition, established firms often need to navigate more complex stakeholder landscapes, balancing existing customer expectations with the need for innovation.

Yet, the benefits of Platform Thinking for these established players were immense. For Siemens, the platform allowed them to unlock new revenue streams by offering services that complemented their products. AXA's platform, on the other hand, gave them a tool to stay ahead in the ever-evolving insurance industry by allowing them to innovate faster and more efficiently in risk assessment. For Eni, the platform enhanced the transparency and sustainability of their supply chain, which directly aligned with broader global concerns about sustainability and corporate responsibility.

These firms not only succeeded in solving the immediate challenges but also unlocked future potential. The platforms they built enabled them to become more agile, engage with new ecosystems, and tap into new markets. This agility is crucial for legacy firms, as it offers a way to stay relevant in a fast-changing environment[7]. They didn't just build platforms; they built resilience.

Three Different Paths to Platform Success: 3 Platform Thinking strategies

While the similarities between Siemens, AXA ed Eni are notable, there are significant differences in how each company approaches Platform Thinking.

AXA applied Platform Thinking to complement its core business by changing and evolving its services to commercial clients. The platform allows the collection of data and information that support the company in revising its approach to insurance and pushing towards prevention activities for its customers.

Eni's platform, on the other hand, focuses on injecting sustainability into the supply chain processes. By engaging partners and suppliers through the platform, Eni tackled a critical challenge, acting on the heart of its business operations.

Finally, Siemens developed a platform that complements its core business by offering additional services. Their platform sits next to their business, providing a new layer of value for customers without disrupting the core product-based model.

The stories of AXA, Eni, and Siemens remind us that Platform Thinking is versatile. It can apply to various parts of an organization, whether it's a primary function like production and supply chain or a support function like R&D. This flexibility makes platforms a

[7] See Magistretti and Trabucchi, 2024

powerful tool not only for new business models but also for enhancing existing ones.

This chapter has shown how platforms are not a one-size-fits-all solution but rather a strategic tool that can be adapted to fit the specific needs of established companies. These stories illustrate that platforms can strengthen every aspect of value creation, ultimately enabling firms to respond to new challenges while staying true to their roots. Platform Thinking is a mindset, not just a business model—it's about continuously evolving, embracing change, and looking beyond the traditional value chain to drive sustained success.

2

What is a platform? And, how Platform Thinking can support innovation?

Platform: is a broken word

Words are powerful. They align minds, enabling people to share a common understanding instantly. But sometimes, words lose their superpower—they become so broad and overused that they no longer mean the same thing to everyone. The word "platform" has reached that point. Once, it was clear what a platform meant, but today, the term is fragmented, stretching to mean anything from physical structures to software, business models, and digital ecosystems[8].

Depending on your industry, the word "platform" might bring up vastly different images. You might think of an oil platform in the ocean, a subway platform where passengers await the next train (minding the gap between the train and the platform), or even a type of shoe. In the business world, platforms often refer to businesses like Uber, Facebook, or Airbnb, and for some – in the tech world -, platforms are simply the operating systems that support apps. The diversity in meanings creates confusion, which is why it's crucial to bring clarity back to the word, especially in business discussions.

The journey to understanding platforms in the business context starts by defining what they are and what they are not. The roots of most modern platform discussions can be traced to the academic

[8] See Jacobides et al. 2015, 2018.

literature on two-sided markets[9], which outlines two key conditions for something to be considered a platform. First, it must have two sets of interdependent users. Second, it must generate cross-side network effects (or indirect network externalities) between them, meaning that as more users join one side of the platform, the value to users on the other side increases[10].

Let's use Uber as an example. Uber connects two sets of users: drivers and riders. The more drivers on the platform, the faster a rider can find a ride. Similarly, the more riders there are, the more drivers have business. This makes both groups of customers willing to join the platform. This dynamic demonstrates the cross-side network effects that are critical for a business model to be called a platform.

Finally, it is important to highlight that both riders and drivers are customers of the platform provider. In other words, drivers are suppliers in the eyes of riders, but from the platform's perspective, they are customers as well. This last point is easy to prove, as drivers pay the platform for its services through a fee on each transaction. If they were suppliers, the dynamic would be opposite, and they would be paid by the platform instead.

However, not all platform-based business models are the same. Other companies like Facebook, Google, or Microsoft offer variations of the model. While Uber allows single drivers to meet single riders, Facebook allows single advertisers to be seen by as many users as possible, as well as Google, and Microsoft allows app developers to use part of their technologies to satisfy the final users. Despite functioning in slightly different ways, all these cases bring together two or more distinct groups of users and make them perceive more value depending on the number of actors on the other side. Advertisers on Facebook will be happier if more users see them, and app developers if they can reach a higher number of people using Windows.

---

[9] See Rochet and Tirole, 2003; Evans and Schmalansee, 2016; Parker and Van Alstyne, 2005; Parker et al., 2016.

[10] See (and Shapiro, 1985, Karhu et al., 2024.

Despite sharing these characteristics (two or more customers and network externalities), these cases also have many differences that are crucial to fully understanding the platform-based value creation mechanisms. But before we dive deeper into the different types of platforms, let's first take a step back and consider what platforms are not.

Misunderstanding platforms can lead to missed opportunities or poor strategic decisions[11]. This is why, in this book, we take great care to define platforms precisely and explore their true potential for value creation. The first step is to clear the confusion and agree on a shared understanding of what platforms mean in today's economy. Platforms are not just digital businesses; they are dynamic systems designed to foster exchanges and create value across different sets of users. Before we can build a proper definition of platforms, we need to remove the broken meanings and misinterpretations that cloud our understanding. Only then we can explore the power that platforms hold as engines for innovation in the digital age.

NOT all Digital Businesses are Platforms

We can start by analyzing the difference between platforms and traditional, linear businesses. Linear businesses operate through a straightforward value chain, where goods or services flow in a single direction—from suppliers to the business and then from the business to customers. A useful example here is Nike's direct-to-consumer (D2C) e-commerce site. When you buy sneakers directly from Nike.com, you're interacting with a traditional business model, even though it's digitally enabled. Nike designs and produces the shoes, manages its own online store, and sells those products directly to individual customers. The flow of value remains direct and unidirectional—typically represented from left to right. Nike controls its supply chain, handles operations and logistics, and delivers a finished product to the consumer. This is a classic linear value chain, simply implemented through a digital channel.

---

[11] See Trabucchi and Buganza, 2022.

To better understand this point, let's look at the value chain model popularized by Michael Porter[12].

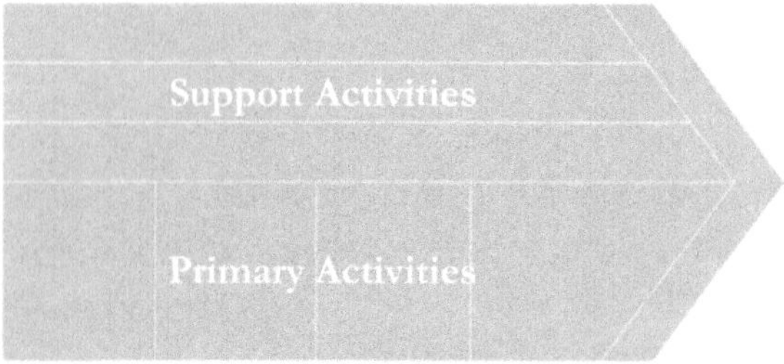

Figure 2.1 – Linear Value Chain

Porter's value chain is divided into two broad categories (Figure 2.1): primary activities, which are directly involved in creating and delivering a product, and support activities, which facilitate and enhance those primary operations. Primary activities include inbound logistics, operations, outbound logistics, marketing and sales, and after-sales service. Support activities include infrastructure, human resource management, technology development, procurement, and so on. These support functions do not directly create value but are essential in enabling and sustaining the core business activities.

Porter's framework can help us describe more precisely the linear value creation mechanism of Nike's e-commerce business. First, Nike sources raw materials—rubber, leather, fabric, plastic, and other components—from a global network of suppliers. This is the inbound logistics phase: gathering and transporting inputs to Nike's factories, where they are stored and prepared for manufacturing. Then comes operations: Nike's manufacturing process, which transforms those raw materials into finished sneakers and apparel through standardized production systems across its facilities.

[12] See Porter, 1985

Once manufactured, the products are moved to Nike's distribution centers and ultimately shipped to individual customers who place orders online. This is outbound logistics—getting the product from factory to consumer. Next, Nike invests heavily in marketing and sales: from brand storytelling and social media to influencer campaigns and digital ads, all designed to drive traffic to Nike.com and convert that attention into purchases. Finally, there's after-sales service: handling returns and refunds, responding to customer service inquiries, and providing digital support through chatbots or helplines.

Behind these primary activities, several support functions operate to sustain Nike's linear business model. The firm's infrastructure includes strategic planning, financial operations, and legal compliance, ensuring global alignment across regions and channels. Human resource management supports recruiting and training talent, from designers to logistics specialists. Technology development enables the maintenance and evolution of Nike's digital platform—its e-commerce website, mobile apps, and backend systems. Procurement plays a vital role in selecting and negotiating with suppliers for raw materials, components, and even digital tools that support operations.

This is a textbook example of a linear value chain. Nike controls the entire journey—from material sourcing to product design, manufacturing, distribution, and customer engagement—and value is added at each sequential step. Although the customer interface is digital, there's no interaction between multiple sides of a market. Buyers don't create value for one another. They don't interact with Nike's suppliers. And they don't participate in a peer-to-peer network.

At this point, someone might argue: isn't Nike.com a platform, since it allows users to customize their sneakers? You can choose colors, materials, and somctimes even add your initials. It's called "Nike By You"—that sounds like a platform, doesn't it? Well, no. Designing your own product doesn't make you a participant in a multi-sided system. You are still a customer, personalizing a product built entirely within Nike's controlled value chain. No interaction occurs between users, and no external group of providers is facilitated by Nike to create that value. You are a consumer, not a contributor.

This distinction becomes crucial when we contrast it with platform business models, which are built on multi-sided interactions. In platforms, value is not generated by a single firm managing the entire process but by enabling exchanges between two or more interdependent user groups—like hosts and travelers on Airbnb, developers and users in the Apple App Store, or content seekers and advertisers on Google. These are all platforms, but with fundamentally different dynamics, which we'll explore in detail later.

Some might argue that Nike.com is a platform because it allows customers to customize their shoes. That's fair—but misleading. Letting users design their own product is not the same as letting users co-create value for one another. Customization is a feature, not a business model. A true platform doesn't just let customers interact with the brand; it lets multiple groups interact with each other, often without the company being at the center of every step.

Nike.com looks modern, behaves like a tech product, and offers customization. But it remains a linear, industrial model at heart. That's the trap: many digital services look like platforms, but act like pipelines. And that confusion is not only semantic—it's strategic.

Three types of Platforms (and related examples)

Now that we have cleared the field of common misunderstandings and mistakes, it's time to focus on different typologies of platforms, diving into the technical differences between their value creation mechanisms. Over the years, three main archetypes of platforms have emerged from the innovation literature: transactional platforms, innovation platforms, and orthogonal platforms. Each has a unique way of connecting users and generating network effects, but they all share the fundamental trait of fostering interactions between two or more groups and triggering some kind of network externalities. Let's explore these three platform types, along with real-world examples that illustrate how they work.

Transactional Platforms: Matchmakers

The most well-known type of platform is the transactional platform[13]. These platforms facilitate direct exchanges between two or more groups of users, typically buyers and sellers, or service providers and consumers. They act as intermediaries that reduce friction in the marketplace, allowing users to connect and transact easily (Figure 2.2[14]).

Airbnb is a prime example of a transactional platform. On one side, it has travelers looking for a place to stay; on the other side, it has hosts offering accommodations. The platform's job is to connect these two groups and facilitate their exchange, whether it's a booking for a night in Paris or a weekend getaway in a countryside cottage.

Figure 2.2 – Transactional Platform

The power of Airbnb, like all transactional platforms, lies in the (bidirectional) cross-side network externalities it generates. As more hosts join the platform, travelers have more choices, which increases the value of Airbnb to the traveler. Conversely, as more travelers use Airbnb, hosts find it easier to rent their properties, increasing the value of the platform to them. This creates a virtuous cycle: the more

[13] See Parker and Van Alstyne, 2005; Gawer and Cusumano, 2014; Tauscher and Laudien, 2018; Cusumano et al., 2019; Trabucchi and Buganza, 2022.

[14] In all our representations, we always put the demand side (traveler for Airbnb) on the left and the supply side (host for Airbnb) on the right. This is a deliberate choice to stress the difference with the typical Porter's value chain that flows from left (suppliers) to right (customers).

users on one side, the more valuable the platform becomes to users on the other side.

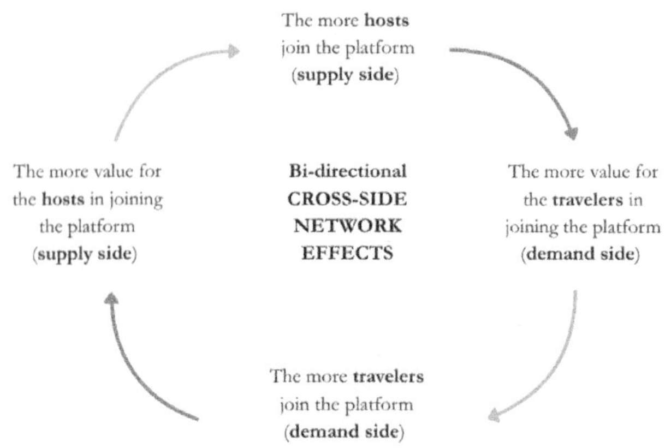

Figure 2.3 – Bi-direction Cross-Side Network Effects (or Exertnalities)

However, transactional platforms face a fundamental challenge known as the "chicken and egg" paradox[15]. Which comes first: the supply (hosts) or the demand (travelers)? In the case of Airbnb, the platform had to solve this paradox by simultaneously attracting enough hosts to make the service appealing to travelers while also ensuring there were enough travelers to make the platform worthwhile for hosts.

Because transactional platforms are typically marketplaces, they often do not have intrinsic value without users. The value comes entirely from facilitating interactions between the two groups. This makes these platforms highly dependent on user growth and engagement. Without users on both sides, the platform has little value to offer.

[15] See Caillaud and Julien, 2003; Trabucchi, 2020.

Innovation Platforms: Creating New Opportunities for Complementors

Innovation platforms[16] are different. These platforms provide a foundation upon which other businesses, often called *complementors*, can build additional products or services. Unlike transactional platforms, innovation platforms typically have intrinsic value that exists even without a vast number of complementors because they offer something fundamental, like infrastructure, tools, or software, which customers can directly use.

Apple's iOS operating system is a classic example of an innovation platform. On one side, you have iPhone and iPad users, and on the other side, you have app developers—the complementors—who build software for the platform. With its basic functionalities (calls, text messages, camera, and so on), the phone itself already has an intrinsic value for the final customers. Still, a huge added value comes from the apps that complementors can build upon the basic infrastructure. The iOS platform enables this additional value creation, providing the complementors with the tools, frameworks, and APIs (application programming interfaces) they need to create apps. These apps, in turn, add value to the platform by giving iPhone and iPad users more reasons to stay within the Apple ecosystem. The power of iOS, like all innovation platforms, lies in the (bidirectional) cross-side network externalities it generates (also in this case, have a look to Figure 2.3). As more developers join the platform and publish apps, users have more functionalities and experiences to choose from, which increases the value of iOS to the user. Conversely, as more users adopt iOS devices, developers find it more rewarding to build and monetize their apps, increasing the value of the platform to them (Figure 2.4).

One of the key differences between innovation platforms and transactional platforms is that innovation platforms may not face the same "chicken and egg" problem. The iPhone has intrinsic value for users (with an operating system that powers their devices), and sales

[16] See Gawer and Cusumano, 2014; Cusumano et al., 2019; Trabucchi and Buganza, 2022

can easily start even without the App Store and the apps. When a critical mass is reached, opening this potential customer base to developers is easier and triggers a reinforcing platform effect. The more apps that are developed, the more valuable iPhones and iPads become for users. Meanwhile, the larger the user base, the more attractive iOS becomes to developers. This creates a reinforcing cycle, but it's not dependent on reaching a critical mass of users right away to be valuable.

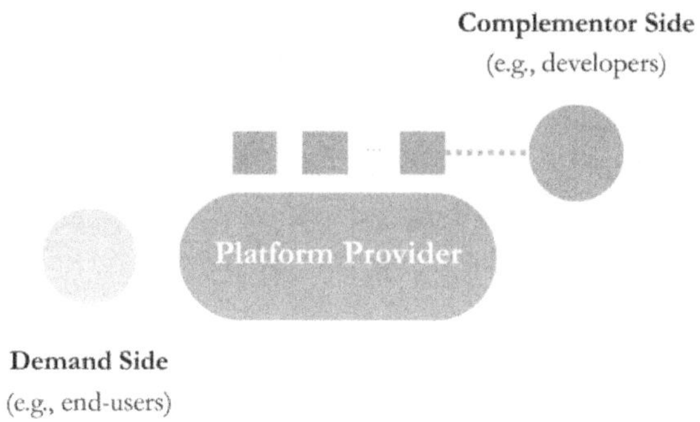

Figure 2.4 – Innovation Platform

Orthogonal Platforms: When the second customer is not always obvious

The third type of platform is the orthogonal platform[17], which operates in a slightly different way. Orthogonal platforms have two distinct sides, like transactional and innovation platforms, but the network effects between the sides are often *unidirectional*, meaning that only one side benefits from the presence of the other side.

[17] Fllistrucchi et al., 2014; Trabucchi et al., 2017; Trabucchi and Buganza, 2022

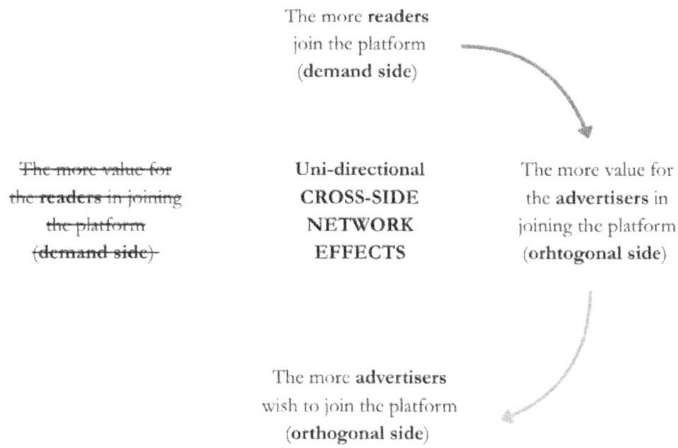

Figure 2.5 – Uni-direction Cross-Side Network Effects (or Externalities)

Consider a traditional newspaper with both readers and advertisers. In this orthogonal platform, readers consume the newspaper's content (the service), while advertisers pay to reach the newspaper's audience. There is no direct interaction between readers and advertisers. They do not exchange goods or services like hosts and travelers on Airbnb or users and app developers on iOS. The network externalities are unidirectional: advertisers benefit from a larger audience while the reverse is not true (Figure 2.5). Platforms that serve two distinct customer groups without enabling direct interaction between them, where the platform engages with each side independently, are referred to as Orthogonal platforms [18], and they can be of two types: CaaT (Client-as-a-Target) or CaaS (Client-as-a-Source). Newspapers are an example of CaaT orthogonal platforms, as the orthogonal players (advertisers) are interested in "targeting" the users with their messages. These platforms are quite popular in the digital space; other examples are the Google search engine, Facebook, and TikTok (Figure 2.6).

Strava, a popular fitness app, provides an example of a *Client-as-a-Source* orthogonal platform (Figure 2.7). In these platforms, the final user is not seen as a target to hit but as a valuable source of

[18] This name is meant to stress the lack of a horizontal transaction between sides.

information. Strava gathers GPS data from its users (who use the app to track their runs or rides) and aggregates it to serve an orthogonal actor. Having data about hundreds of thousands of rides, for example, allows Strava to map where riders cycle in a city, and this information turns out to be incredibly valuable for municipalities, always struggling about where to spend their limited budgets to add bike lanes. Many other companies we interact with daily, apply a similar strategy. During the 2012 US election campaign, Twitter (now X) created Twindex. This index measured public sentiment toward the presidential candidates Barack Obama and Mitt Romney by analyzing millions of tweets to assess real-time public opinion. Similarly, many social media, like Facebook, Instagram or TikTok, leverage both the CaaT and the CaaS strategies to personalize the advertising messages.

In orthogonal platforms, the cross-side network effects are unidirectional. In both the newspaper and Strava examples, more users mean more value for the orthogonal player (advertisers or municipalities), while increasing the number of advertisers or municipalities served does not directly benefit readers or bikers.

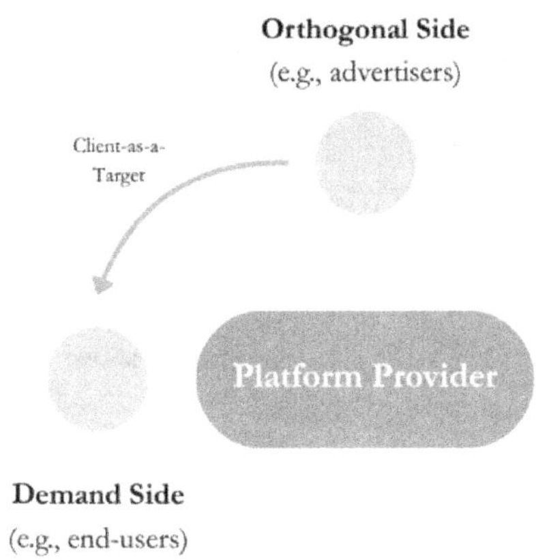

Figure 2.6 – Orthogonal Platform: Client-as-a-Target

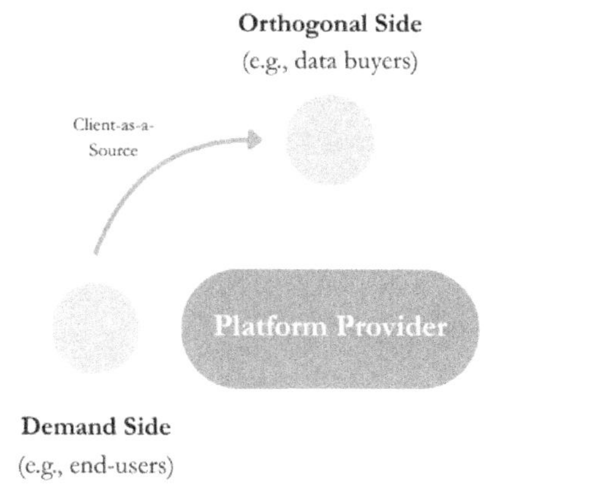

Figure 2.7 – Orthogonal Platform: Client-as-a-Source

Hybrid Platforms: When Models Combine

While these three archetypes—transactional, innovation, and orthogonal—are distinct, platforms can often combine elements of each. Multi-sided platforms, like Uber, can operate across multiple lines of value creation (Figure 2.8).

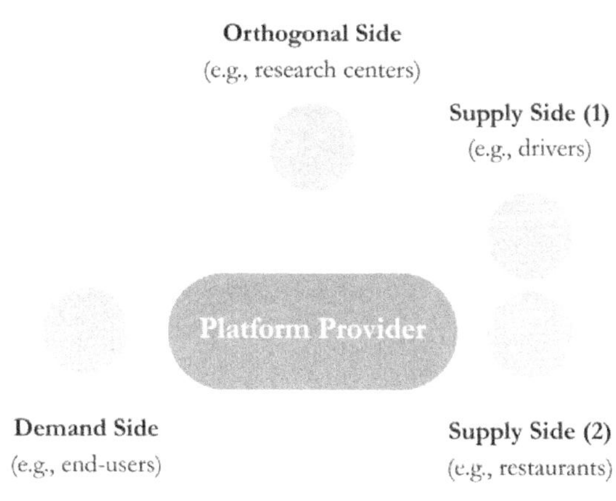

Figure 2.8 – Hybrid Platform

Uber started as a purely transactional platform, connecting drivers and riders. But over time, it expanded its offerings to include

Uber Eats, a food delivery service that adds another transactional layer. Uber also introduced *Uber Movement*, a service that leverages aggregated platform data to deliver insights into urban mobility trends. This is an example of an orthogonal extension[19], where Uber uses data generated by its users to offer a service that doesn't involve direct interaction between users. Here, Uber demonstrates how a platform can evolve to encompass multiple types of value creation within a single ecosystem.

These three archetypes—transactional, innovation, and orthogonal—provide a comprehensive framework for understanding how platforms create value. Each type addresses a unique way of facilitating interactions and leveraging network effects. These network effects are the most relevant element of the platform-based value-creation mechanisms, as they are responsible for fast growth, scalability, and quasi-zero marginal cost. Their relevance is easily explained by comparing the traditional linear business model with platforms when scaling. If a traditional hotel company like Hilton wanted to double the number of rooms offered to the market, they would have to go through a huge upfront investment (to buy and furnish buildings) and almost double its operating costs (cleaning, concierge, and so on). On the other hand, a platform-based business like Airbnb would probably have a lower investment (maybe advertising) and a very marginal increment in operational costs.

However, as seen in the case of Uber, platforms are not bound to just one archetype. Many of the most successful platforms combine elements from all three models, adapting to different opportunities for value creation.

To explore the peculiarities of each platform type and how they can transform businesses, we'll refer to our earlier work in *Platform Thinking - Read the Past, Write the Future* as well as the Platform Thinking MOOCs on Coursera, where we dive deeper into platform strategies for innovation.

---

[19] See Trabucchi and Buganza, 2023

Figure 2.9 – QR Code for the Platform Thinking specialization on Coursera - https://bit.ly/PTCourseraSpecialization

Siemens Xcelerator, AXA Digital Commercial Platform, and Open-es as Platforms

In this section, we revisit the three cases we introduced earlier—Siemens Xcelerator, AXA's Digital Commercial Platform and Open-es—and examine them through the lens of the platform models we've just discussed. Each of these companies has embraced Platform Thinking to solve specific business challenges, but they've done so in different ways, aligning with the three platform archetypes we explored: transactional, innovation, and orthogonal platforms.

By mapping these real-world examples to platform typologies, we can see how established businesses can leverage platform strategies not only to remain competitive but also to lead innovation in their industries.

Siemens Xcelerator as a platform

Launched by Siemens to drive digital transformation in industrial sectors, Siemens Xcelerator exemplifies a hybrid platform that serves as both an innovation hub and a transactional platform.

At its core, Siemens Xcelerator functions as an innovation platform. It allows developers (complementors) to build advanced solutions upon Siemens hardware and software through APIs (Application Program Interfaces). For instance, a fire safety monitoring service can use Building X APIs to track alarm systems in real-time, automatically logging events across multiple locations for enhanced safety and compliance. Similarly, an emission management tool can consolidate emissions data across a supply chain, giving companies a comprehensive view of their carbon impact to support sustainability goals. Both solutions utilize Siemens APIs to deliver powerful insights for operational safety and environmental performance.

However, Siemens Xcelerator also operates as a transactional platform by creating a marketplace for industrial customers and service providers. Business customers can purchase software solutions or services directly through the platform, regardless of whether they are built on Siemens hardware. For instance, businesses can use Xcelerator's low-code platform to quickly develop custom applications, automating workflows and integrating seamlessly with various business systems through open interfaces, all without Siemens-specific devices. Another option for companies focusing on sustainability is the Building X environmental suite, enabling carbon tracking across operations with tools to analyze and reduce emissions, which integrates directly with existing non-Siemens infrastructure (Figure 2.10).

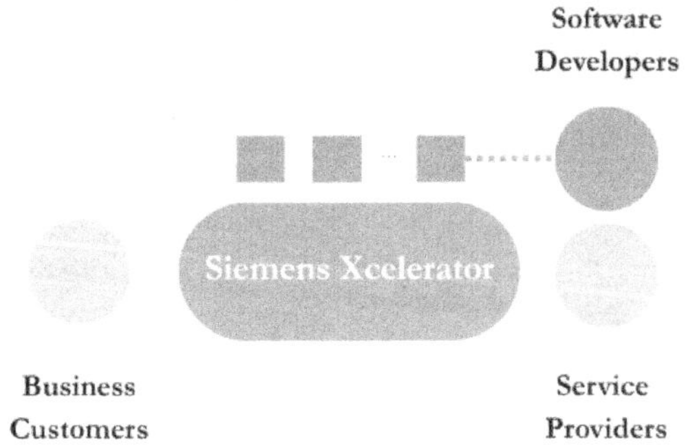

Figure 2.10 – Siemens Xcelerator as a Platform

One of the key innovations of Siemens Xcelerator is its ability to integrate both platform types seamlessly. On one side, it drives technological innovation by providing tools for developers to build new solutions and proactively invites customers and partners to co-create and co-innovate. On the other side, it facilitates direct transactions between industrial customers and service providers, creating a marketplace that adds further value to the ecosystem. This hybrid approach ensures that Siemens can support both long-term innovation and immediate customer needs through a single platform.

Siemens Xcelerator's Idle Assets

Siemens was uniquely positioned to develop the Siemens Xcelerator platform by harnessing several idle assets. In Platform Thinking, idle assets are resources already in use within the company, but only partially exploited—their full potential remains untapped and can be unlocked by applying platform-based mechanisms. The high-tech products Siemens already sells to the market, such as industrial hardware and automation software, became the backbone of the Xcelerator platform. These products provided a strong technological base for developers (complementors) to build upon, creating new software solutions that enhanced the functionality of Siemens' equipment.

In addition to its product portfolio, Siemens' global brand—an idle asset built through decades of leadership in industrial innovation and automation—added significant credibility and trust to the Xcelerator platform. This trusted brand helped attract both developers and industrial customers, reassuring them that they were engaging with a platform built by a well-established player in the B2B space. Finally, Siemens' deep know-how in managing B2B relationships—along with its existing customer base on the demand side—represented another idle asset. Already central to its traditional business, this expertise played a crucial role in establishing immediate critical mass for the Xcelerator platform when activated through platform mechanisms.

These assets were essential in facilitating the emergence of strong network effects on Siemens Xcelerator. Siemens' product portfolio—and, with it, a broad base of existing customers already positioned on the demand side—provided a tangible and credible foundation for developers and service providers, who saw the platform as an opportunity to extend the capabilities of industry-leading offerings. As more developers and service providers joined and created new solutions, Siemens' business customers gained access to an ever-expanding array of tools and services. This, in turn, made the platform increasingly attractive to additional developers, who recognized the growing demand from a well-established industrial client base.

Crucially, these assets—ranging from a trusted brand to deep domain knowledge and long-standing customer relationships—would be extremely difficult, if not impossible, for a startup to replicate. In the language of innovation strategy, they constitute an unfair advantage: deeply embedded capabilities that give Siemens, as a legacy company, a privileged position to launch and scale a platform. Rather than being held back by its history, Siemens was able to reframe its legacy as leverage—turning dormant potential into active value through Platform Thinking. The resulting cross-side network effects created a self-reinforcing loop: more developers brought more value to customers, and more customers attracted more developers, fueling the platform's growth.

Siemens Xcelerator not only supports innovation by enhancing its product ecosystem, but it also adds a completely new activity to Siemens' traditional value chain: servitization. By offering the Siemens Xcelerator platform as a service, Siemens extends its core business model beyond selling technologically advanced hardware and software. The platform creates an ecosystem where Siemens products are integrated with complementary software services, enabling customers to optimize and personalize their equipment through third-party innovations. Moreover, the platform has the ability to support with financial services as well as consulting through community and experts, as well as the Learning Hub, where Siemens helps customers to educate themselves in order to drive more informed decisions about the future of their organization.

This shift represents a significant transformation in Siemens' business model. Historically focused on selling industrial products, Siemens is now offering a platform-based service that elevates the value of those products. The Siemens Xcelerator platform allows customers to continually enhance and improve their systems, turning Siemens from a product provider into a solutions provider. This new layer of services fosters continuous innovation within Siemens' ecosystem, creating a dynamic and evolving relationship with customers, who can now derive greater long-term value from their investments in Siemens products.

"*Siemens is about connecting the real and the digital world unlike any other company. Making hardware smart involves equipping machines with sensors, connecting them to the Internet of Things, and utilizing artificial intelligence to enhance their intelligence. This is the foundation for industrial digitalization. Yet the best solution becomes a bad solution if it does not work well together with other technologies,*" says Peter Koerte, Member of the Managing Board and Chief Technology Officer of Siemens AG. "*The Siemens Xcelerator platform and its solutions are not about us or restricted to us. It's all about making digitalization easy for our customers by providing solutions that work and are open to grow.*"

In this way, Siemens Xcelerator isn't just an extension of the company's existing offerings; it fundamentally transforms Siemens' value proposition by combining its products with a platform for ongoing innovation and digital services. This evolution illustrates how platforms can build upon traditional business models to create entirely new avenues for growth and customer engagement.

AXA Digital Commercial Platform as a platform

AXA, a global insurance leader, created the Digital Commercial Platform to support businesses in managing and mitigating emerging risks, including those related to climate change, cybersecurity, and artificial intelligence.

This platform offers a variety of specialized services provided by third-party companies with expertise in niche areas. By facilitating the exchange between industrial customers and these external providers, this transactional platform enables value creation through efficient matchmaking and service delivery across the ecosystem.

For example, clients can access advanced cybersecurity tools, data analytics for climate impact assessment, and machine learning models for predictive risk analysis—all provided by selected external partners. This approach allows AXA to continuously innovate and provide cutting-edge, customized solutions tailored to the complex needs of its business clients while benefiting from the specialized knowledge and agility of its third-party providers. This setup generates cross-side network effects—more clients on the platform attract more service providers, and vice versa.

But AXA's platform goes far beyond these transactional elements. It also leverages an orthogonal CaaS extension, where it uses data generated by the platform to enhance its risk management capabilities. This data-driven approach provides AXA's internal teams with critical insights to develop better insurance products and risk management services. For example, data on environmental factors collected through the platform—such as real-time climate data, geospatial information, and location-specific risk indicators—enables AXA to tailor insurance offerings based on climate risk forecasts.

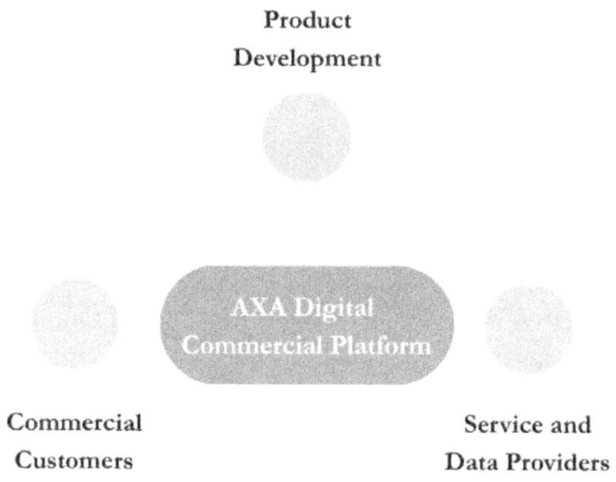

Figure 2.11 – AXA Digital Commercial Platform as a Platform

The orthogonal player here is AXA's product development function, which uses this data to innovate. For instance, the insights derived from client interaction with AI-based risk assessment tools or data-driven cybersecurity monitoring systems could lead to the development of highly specialized insurance products. These products might include tailored cyber-risk insurance policies or custom climate-related coverage that addresses the specific risk profile of a business location. Through this data-informed approach, AXA is able to refine its offerings and deliver services that are not only reactive but also anticipatory, helping clients to manage emerging risks more effectively (Figure 2.11).

This hybrid platform model demonstrates how a traditional industry like insurance can use Platform Thinking to not only facilitate transactions but also leverage the data it collects to enhance its core offerings. The combination of transactional and orthogonal mechanisms allows AXA to serve its customers more effectively while continuously improving its products.

AXA Digital Commercial Platform's Idle Assets

AXA built its Digital Commercial Platform by strategically leveraging a set of idle assets—existing resources already central to its operations but not fully exploited until activated through platform mechanisms. These idle assets gave AXA a uniquely strong foundation to launch and scale its platform, positioning the company far ahead of any potential startup entrant.

First and foremost, AXA's idle brand asset—its global recognition and longstanding reputation as a trusted insurance provider—offered a significant advantage. This deeply rooted trust, built over decades, made it far easier to attract both commercial clients and service providers to the platform—an entry barrier that often proves insurmountable for new platforms starting from scratch.

In parallel, AXA already had a vast idle asset in the form of its existing commercial client base. Spanning industries, geographies, and company sizes, this customer network provided immediate critical mass on the demand side, giving the platform built-in relevance from day one. Most startups face a cold-start problem; AXA, by contrast, could activate a warm, ready-made ecosystem.

Another key idle asset was AXA's deep market knowledge. With decades of experience in assessing and managing complex commercial risks, the company possessed a rich understanding of its clients' needs. This expertise, while historically used to refine insurance products, found new expression on the platform—guiding the design of services that were highly targeted, credible, and valuable.

By orchestrating these idle assets—its brand, client relationships, and domain knowledge—AXA transformed long-standing capabilities into powerful drivers of platform value. What makes this especially noteworthy is that these resources represent a unique source of competitive advantage—deeply embedded in AXA's legacy and extremely difficult, if not impossible, for a startup to build from the ground up.

In this case, being a legacy company was not a limitation—it was the very foundation of AXA's platform opportunity.

AXA's brand, customer relationship, and market knowledge played a crucial role triggering strong cross-side network effects: as more providers joined, the platform became increasingly valuable to clients, and vice versa, leading to continuous growth. The orthogonal CaaS dynamic was built on top of an already existing transaction one, allowing the company to use the data generated from platform interactions to fuel its product development processes. In traditional insurance models, product development can be slow and heavily reliant on historical data. However, with the Digital Commercial Platform, AXA can gather real-time insights from the interactions between commercial clients and service providers, using this data to improve one of its primary activities: risk management and product development.

This orthogonal dynamic allows AXA to anticipate emerging risks and innovate more rapidly than ever before. By feeding platform-generated data into its internal operations, AXA can create more tailored and innovative insurance products that are better aligned with the specific needs of its commercial clients. In this way, the platform doesn't just support AXA's current offerings; it actively drives the evolution of its entire insurance portfolio, ensuring the company remains at the forefront of innovation in the industry.

Open-es as a platform

Open-es, powered by integrated energy company Eni, starts as a more straightforward example of a transactional platform. The initial goal was to increase sustainability in the supply chain and, quite soon many partners joined the initiative and started to improve their supply chains' sustainability. Open-es helps companies find partners who can provide sustainable solutions, certifications, or services to mitigate their supply chain's impact.

The Open-es platform directly facilitates transactions between suppliers (the demand side) and certification bodies or service providers (the supply side). For example, a company seeking to improve its sustainability credentials might connect with a certification agency that verifies its environmental practices or with a service provider offering carbon-reduction technologies. The more suppliers that join the platform, the more valuable it becomes to service providers, and vice versa. This is a classic case of cross-side network effects at work: the platform becomes more attractive to both sides as participation grows.

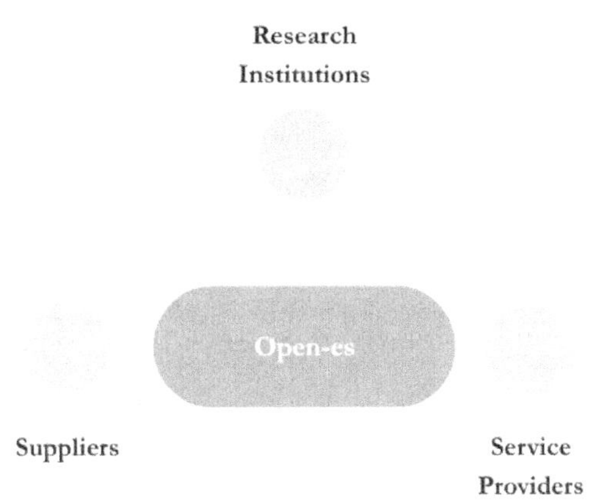

Figure 2.12 – Open-es as a Platform

Still, like AXA's platform, which combines transactional and orthogonal elements, Open-es also has an orthogonal extension that, in this case, serves external actors rather than internal functions. Indeed, one remarkable extension of Open-es is the involvement of research institutions, which can act as *orthogonal players* interested in aggregated data (Client-as-a-Source). These institutions could use the data from the platform to generate sustainability reports and conduct research on industry-wide trends. Although this role is less central to the platform's primary function, it highlights how even an initially purely transactional platform can open new value streams through data-sharing and knowledge generation (Figure 2.12).

Open-es' Idle Assets

Eni, a global leader in the energy sector, launched the Open-es platform by strategically leveraging a set of idle assets—existing resources already in use within the organization but not yet fully activated through platform mechanisms. These idle assets gave Eni a significant advantage in building and scaling a platform with immediate relevance and credibility.

One of the most critical idle assets was Eni's extensive network of suppliers, developed over decades of procurement activities. This existing ecosystem provided a ready-made user base on the demand side of the platform, offering immediate critical mass and engagement. In parallel, Eni's long-standing idle partnerships with key industry players such as Snam and Saipem created a strong foundation for expanding the platform beyond its initial scope. These relationships were not new—they were already active in Eni's traditional operations—but they were reactivated in a new, more scalable way through the platform model.

Another essential idle asset was Eni's brand—an established symbol of industrial credibility and leadership. This brand equity, already known and trusted in the energy and procurement ecosystems, gave the platform instant legitimacy. For suppliers, service providers, and potential partners, joining Open-es meant entering an ecosystem orchestrated by a recognized and reputable player. This significantly reduced the perceived risk of participation—something that new or unknown platforms often struggle to overcome.

Together, these idle assets—existing supplier relationships, strategic partnerships, and a trusted brand—formed the backbone of Open-es' early success. But more than that, they enabled the emergence of strong cross-side network effects. As more suppliers joined to align with trusted companies like Eni, Snam, and Saipem, the platform's value increased for certification bodies, ESG consultants, and other service providers. Their entry, in turn, reinforced the value of the platform for suppliers—offering them tools, support, and recognition to enhance their sustainability journeys. The result was a self-reinforcing ecosystem in which participation on one side directly enhanced the attractiveness and utility of the other.

Crucially, these assets represent a unique source of competitive advantage—rooted in Eni's legacy and industrial history—that would be extraordinarily difficult for a startup to replicate. The ability to activate such deep, pre-existing relationships and trust networks is not something that can be built overnight. In this case too, being a legacy company was not a barrier but a platform advantage: Eni's established position made Open-es possible, relevant, and scalable from day one.

Even though Open-es is now a stand-alone platform that has many established companies as partners and platform providers, it is relevant to highlight how – in its conception - Open-es played a pivotal role in fostering innovation within Eni's broader business model by directly impacting one of its key support activities: procurement.

Open-es transforms procurement relationships, helping to promote a sustainability orientation throughout the entire supply chain.

By using the platform, Eni was able to encourage suppliers to adopt more sustainable practices. In doing so, Open-es not only supported Eni's procurement efficiency and overall corporate sustainable goals but also encouraged similar-sized and established firms like Snam and Saipem to reinvent their approach to supplier relationships. This shift in procurement practices is a key example of how Open-es enables innovation, transforming a critical support activity into a more dynamic, data-driven, and collaborative process across the entire industry.

Platforms as versatile value creation modes

These three cases (Figure 2.13) clearly show that platforms can take many forms, depending on the business's goals and needs. Siemens Xcelerator illustrates how an innovation platform can also function as a marketplace, creating multiple layers of value for both customers and developers, AXA's Digital Commercial Platform shows how transactional and orthogonal elements can combine to create value through direct exchanges and data-driven innovation. Finally, Open-es demonstrates the power of a purely transactional platform to drive sustainability in the supply chain.

Each of these platforms aligns with one or more of the archetypes we discussed—transactional, innovation, and orthogonal—but they also demonstrate how flexible these models can be. Platforms are not rigid structures; they evolve based on the business environment, user needs, and opportunities for value creation. This adaptability is part of what makes Platform Thinking such a powerful tool for established firms looking to innovate and grow in the digital age.

	Siemens Xcelerator	**AXA Digital Commercial Platform**	**Open-es**
Trigger	Digital Transformation	Climate Change	Sustainability
Platform Thinking Benefits		Co-creation with external partners Efficiency Scalability Quasi zero-marginal cost in the operations Opportunities of business expansion	
Idle-Assets	Hardware product portfolio Business customers Data Trust in Siemens' brand	Commercial client base Relationships with service providers Data Trust in AXA's brand	Industrial relationships with suppliers Trust in Value Chain Leaders' brand Procurement know-how

Figure 2.13 – Summary of the three Digital Phoenixes

As we've seen, these real-world platforms do more than just connect users—they create dynamic ecosystems that generate continuous value. To learn more about the nuances of each platform type and how they can be applied to specific business challenges, we refer to our previous work in *Platform Thinking – Read the Past, Write the Future*, as well as our MOOCs on the basis of Platform Thinking.

Main Takeaways

This chapter aimed to clarify the confusion surrounding platforms, offering clear definitions and examples to sharpen our understanding of what platforms truly are and are not. By focusing on the defining characteristics of platforms, we explored how they differ from traditional, linear value chains and examined three core platform archetypes: transactional, innovation, and orthogonal platforms.

Let's recap the key insights and takeaways.

The first crucial takeaway is that not all businesses labeled as platforms actually fit the definition. Platforms have two defining characteristics: They serve two or more sets of interdependent users and generate indirect network effects between these user groups. In other words, platforms create value by facilitating interactions between distinct sides rather than delivering value in a unidirectional way, as in traditional businesses.

We identified three main archetypes of platforms that illustrate the different ways they can create value: transactional platforms, innovation platforms, and orthogonal platforms.

Another key insight from this chapter is that Platform Thinking is not limited to tech startups or digital-native companies. We revisited the real-world examples of Siemens, AXA, and Open-es to show how different platform models can be applied by legacy companies. These examples demonstrate that, even in traditional industries like advanced manufacturing, insurance, and energy, platforms can drive significant innovation by reimagining how value is created and exchanged.

This chapter also shows that different platforms can coexist and reinforce each other, creating hybrid solutions. For example, we saw how Siemens Xcelerator functions both as an innovation platform, facilitating developers' innovation, and as a transactional marketplace, allowing direct exchanges between industrial customers and service providers. Similarly, AXA's Digital Commercial Platform began as a transactional platform to improve business partners' risk management and mitigation but expanded into an orthogonal model to improve the internal new service development process, leveraging the data gathered through the transactions. Finally, the Open-es case combines a transactional platform connecting suppliers and service providers with an orthogonal one to support external research institutions.

These hybrid models highlight the flexibility of Platform Thinking. Platforms can evolve and adapt based on the needs of their users, the data they collect, and the business challenges they aim to solve. This adaptability makes platforms particularly powerful for established firms looking to innovate across different aspects of their operations, whether that means launching new services, transforming core business activities, or optimizing support functions.

Still, there's more. These three stories highlight an important factor in the success of Platform Thinking within established firms: all three companies could count on idle assets that startups would typically struggle to have (Figure 2.14). We can cluster these assets into four categories:

1. **Relationships**: All three companies relied on strong, preexisting relationships within their industries. Siemens' long-standing relationships with business customers provided a ready-made user base that quickly attracted developers and service providers on the Xcelerator platform. For AXA, relationships with commercial clients were central to the AXA Digital Commercial Platform, triggering a similar mechanism. Finally, Eni's industrial connections with suppliers (and also with partners like Snam and Saipem) gave Open-es a crucial head start.
2. **Physical Assets**: Legacy firms often possess significant physical resources that can be strategically positioned at the

core of platform models, becoming critical and hard-to-replace assets. Siemens, for example, leveraged its extensive portfolio of industrial hardware to provide the foundation for developers to build complementary software on Xcelerator. These physical assets acted as the backbone of the innovation platform, adding immediate, tangible value to the ecosystem.

3. **Know-how**: Decades of industry-specific expertise played a major role in developing these platforms. Siemens, with its industrial expertise, knew exactly how to support developers and customers through its platform's technical offerings. AXA's deep understanding of commercial risks allowed it to tailor its platform services to meet the needs of its clients. At the same time, Eni's knowledge of energy supply chains initially enabled Open-es to focus on sustainability in a meaningful way.
4. **Data**: The data that these firms already possessed was another vital asset. AXA's Digital Commercial Platform, built as a transactional system connecting clients with service providers, naturally generated a wealth of data. Initially, this data remained an idle asset—collected but underutilized. By layering an orthogonal, *Client-as-a-Source* architecture on top, AXA activated this data to inform product development. Insights from client behavior and risk interactions were fed back into the business, enabling more targeted, responsive insurance solutions and turning the platform into a continuous engine for innovation.

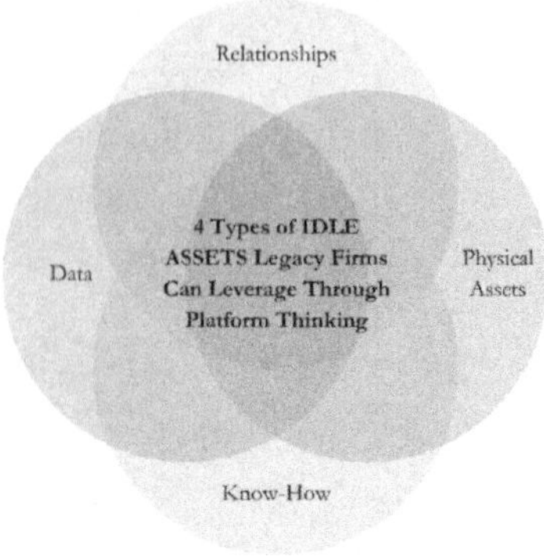

Figure 2.14 – The 4 types of Idle Assets

What's key across these stories is that these assets were often idle (not fully exploited) within the firms—they already existed (and were used for other purposes). Still, they weren't utilized at their maximum until the platforms were launched. These legacy firms were able to put these dormant resources at the center of their platform strategies, allowing them to overcome common challenges faced by platform startups. Leveraging what they already had, these companies completely bypassed the chicken-and-egg paradox responsible for the early death of many platform-based start-ups.

3

The Platform Transformative Framework

Igniting Transformation Through Platform Thinking

Innovation often begins with inspiration, and *The Digital Phoenix Effect* sets out to provide that. This book was created with two primary goals in mind: to inspire managers to drive transformation through Platform Thinking and to equip them with the tools and frameworks necessary to make it happen. It's not just a guide; it's a catalyst for change, encouraging leaders to reimagine their businesses by tapping into the untapped potential of platform models.

In the first part of the book, we aimed to spark that inspiration. Through the stories of Siemens Xcelerator, AXA Digital Commercial Platform, and Eni Open-es, we demonstrated the transformative power of Platform Thinking in action. Each case demonstrated how platform models could address various challenges. These flagship examples provided a glimpse into what's possible when Platform Thinking is embraced within established firms.

Now, as we transition from the first to the second part of the book, our focus shifts from inspiration to action. This chapter serves as a reference tool, designed to help you understand how Platform Thinking is applicable in many different settings. No matter the industry, no matter the specific challenge, platforms hold the potential to solve a variety of business problems. By exploring these possibilities, we aim to empower you to identify opportunities for transformation in your own organization.

The chapter you are about to read marks a pivotal step in your journey. It introduces the *Platform Transformative Framework*—a tool designed to make Platform Thinking actionable within legacy organizations. Its purpose is twofold: to expand your view of where transformation can happen, and to clarify how Platform Thinking can be used to address specific, recurring problems through targeted interventions.

Applying these concepts practically, this framework will serve as your map. You will begin by exploring **WHERE** Platform Thinking can be applied in legacy organizations—not only in customer-facing activities, but also within core internal processes and systems. Next, you will examine **WHAT** kinds of challenges Platform Thinking helps to solve—ranging from innovation blocks and rapidly shifting customer needs to ineffective collaboration models and the underuse of valuable data. Finally, you will uncover **HOW** platforms can be used to tackle these problems through a set of focused, practical interventions: the Platform Thinking Hacks.

The next two parts of the book will help you move from concept to execution—connecting the strategic potential of Platform Thinking with the specific levers of transformation inside your business.

Whether your goal is to enhance existing processes, create new services, or rethink entire business models, the *Platform Transformative Framework* will help you chart your course. It is not just a tool for understanding Platform Thinking—it's a guide for turning insight into action.

As we move towards this new phase of the book, keep in mind the power of the examples you've already seen. Siemens, AXA, and Open-es demonstrate that Platform Thinking is not reserved for digital-native startups; it's a paradigm that can unlock innovation in even the most traditional industries.

Now, let's explore how this framework can illuminate new paths for innovation and help you spark transformation within your organization.

Where can Legacy Organizations apply Platform Thinking?

Legacy companies are typically built around a linear value chain, where inputs are transformed into customer outputs through a sequence of primary activities—such as logistics, manufacturing, and sales—supported by other essential activities like R&D, HR, and IT. Traditional platform models tend to reimagine how customers are served, often bypassing this linear chain altogether. Consider Uber, which orchestrates interactions between riders and drivers without directly owning transportation assets, thus stepping outside the conventional input-to-output framework.

Yet, as our analysis of Siemens, AXA, and Open-es reveals, platforms within established firms can do far more than just reshape customer interactions. They can drive transformation within the company itself, revolutionizing both primary and support processes. In this way, platforms don't only offer new avenues to serve customers; they hold the potential to redefine the fundamental structure of business operations. By applying Platform Thinking internally, established companies can break free from the constraints of a linear model, challenging the traditional "input-transformation-output" structure and unlocking new efficiencies and synergies across the organization. This is where the true, often untapped power of Platform Thinking lies for incumbents.

Our three cases offer a clear example of the different impacts that platforms can have on an established firm's (Porter-based) value chain:

- Siemens built a platform **next to its original value chain**, creating an entirely new service offering through servitization. The Siemens Xcelerator platform allowed developers to build software solutions that enhanced the functionality of Siemens' industrial products, turning what was once a straightforward product business into an innovation-driven ecosystem. Siemens didn't just improve an existing activity—it expanded its business model, creating an open platform that added value beyond its traditional product lines, thereby creating a long-term service model alongside its hardware sales.

- AXA innovated through Platform Thinking within a **primary activity** of its original value chain. The AXA Digital Commercial Platform transformed the company's risk management and price-setting processes by integrating real-time data from its users. This enabled AXA to create more tailored and effective insurance solutions, turning a core function into a source of continuous innovation.
- In contrast, Eni (the initiator of the Open-es initiative) started from the need to improve a specific process within the procurement department, a **support activity** of its value chain. With the Open-es platform, the company digitized and streamlined supplier relationships, fostering collaboration and sustainability across its supply chain. This platform improved the efficiency and transparency of procurement, turning what had been traditionally a back-end function into a driver of innovation. By transforming this support activity, Eni aligned its supply chain with broader sustainability goals, making procurement a more strategic component of its business.

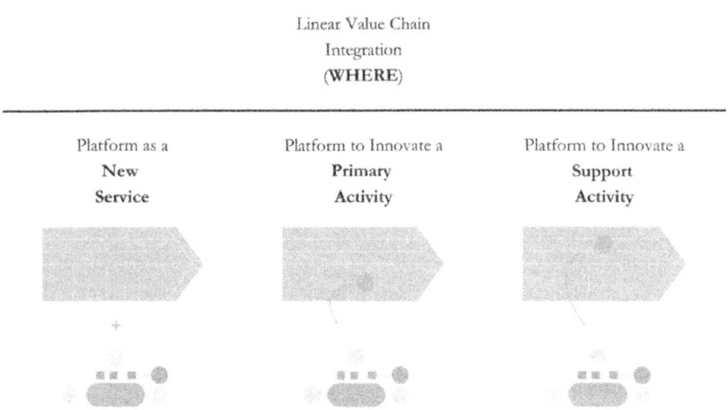

Figure 3.1 – Where – The 3 strategies

These examples clearly demonstrate that platforms, besides being standalone services in the market, can emerge from different parts of a company's existing value chain. The challenges that originated each platform were rooted in distinct parts of their businesses: in a primary activity, in a support activity, or as a new opportunity in the market. These examples show the immense power of Platform Thinking for established firms. They underscore that platforms are not confined to one area of a business—they can be applied to innovate across primary activities and support functions and even to create entirely new business models that extend beyond the traditional value chain.

The ability of platforms to evolve and adapt based on the business's specific needs makes them incredibly powerful tools for fostering innovation along all single aspects of the value chain.

Therefore, the first question as a professional approaching this book should be: Where do you want to foster transformation?

- Platform as a New Service.
- Platform to Innovate a Primary Activity.
    - Logistic, Operations, Marketing & Sales, Services, …
- Platform to Innovate a Support Activity.
    - HR, R&D and Innovation, Knowledge Management and Company Infrastructure, IT, …

What Business Problems can Legacy Organizations solve through Platform Thinking?

The cases of Siemens Xcelerator, AXA Digital Commercial Platform, and Open-es represent distinct examples of how platforms can ignite transformation within legacy firms. While these three cases are emblematic of the transformative power of platforms, they are just a small part of the examples we have studied. They are our flagship cases—stories that inspired us and illustrate the profound potential of Platform Thinking. However, to ensure that the framework we propose is robust and widely applicable, we based this book on a much larger research project.

Our study sought to understand how legacy firms—not startups or native digital companies—are embracing Platform Thinking to solve pressing business challenges. To do this, we focused on all the companies within the S&P 500 list, analyzing initiatives that were explicitly linked to platform models or related concepts, such as data usage or network effects.

We began with the February 2023 list of S&P 500 companies when we gathered data for this research, excluding those that were born as platforms, like Facebook or Google. This left us with 484 firms that primarily operate through linear value chains. Through extensive online research and secondary sources, we identified 796 initiatives. After discarding 23 initiatives due to insufficient information, we classified the remaining.

Of these, 656 initiatives emerged as digital extensions of linear value chain services rather than true platforms (e.g., digital services missing either the second interconnected customer or the cross-side network externalities). Ultimately, we identified 140 platform-based initiatives developed by 108 different firms. These initiatives became the foundation of our analysis, providing rich insights into how Platform Thinking is being applied in non-digital-native established firms (Figure 3.2).

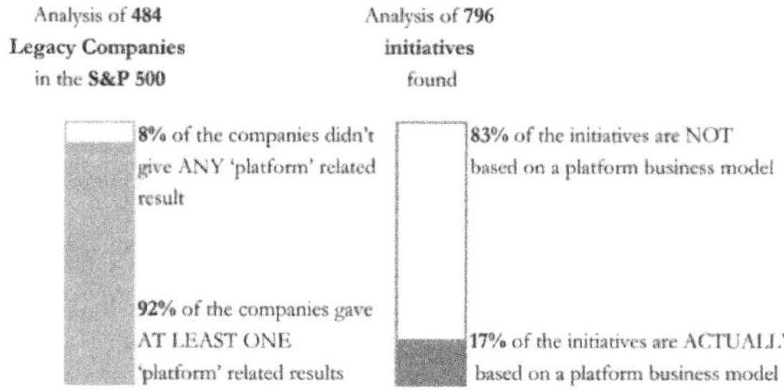

Figure 3.2 – Analysis of the S&P500 cases

Through our research, we not only classified these **140 initiatives** based on their link with the linear value chain (new services, primary activities, or support activities), but we also carefully analyzed them to determine whether it was possible to distill a set of challenges that platforms help address. What emerged was a pattern of five distinct challenges that Platform Thinking can address. Our research revealed that these companies use platforms to solve five recurring business challenges that hinder growth, efficiency, and adaptability:

1. **Missing or Inefficient Transactions** – Established firms often experience slow, costly, or missed interactions between suppliers, partners, and customers, —both externally and within internal provider-customer chains—leading to revenue loss, higher costs or operational friction.
2. **Evolving Customer Demands** – Today's consumers expect seamless, personalized experiences, which rigid, (legacy) product-based business models struggle to deliver.
3. **Innovation Bottlenecks** – Traditional R&D structures limit the speed, the area of application and scalability of innovation, making it difficult to keep pace with fast-moving competitors.
4. **Underutilized Data** – Many firms collect large volumes of data but lack a clear strategy to extract value, optimize decision-making, or create new business opportunities.
5. **Lack of Data for Strategic Insights** – Without timely access to high-quality data, firms struggle to make proactive, market-responsive decisions, but too often they are difficult to be gathered.

How can Legacy Organizations solve those Business Problems applying the Platform Thinking Hacks?

Each of these challenges corresponds to a practical platform-base approach – that we labelled **Platform Thinking Hacks** - that can guide managers and professionals seeking to drive innovation in their organizations (Figure 3.3). Notably, our data clearly show that all these hacks can be leveraged to create new services, innovate primary activities, or enhance support activities:

- Missing or Inefficient Transactions ↔ **Enhance or Enable Transactions Among Existing Stakeholders:** Established firms rely on complex transactions with suppliers, partners, and internal teams, often facing inefficiencies. Platform Thinking streamlines these interactions, creates value for all stakeholders, and even enables new transactions among existing partners to boost collaboration.

- Evolving Customer Demands ↔ **Solving Customers' Needs by Onboarding New Stakeholders:** Customers' needs are constantly evolving and meeting them often requires the involvement of new players in the value chain. Platform Thinking allows firms to innovate by bringing in these new stakeholders, who can contribute unique perspectives and capabilities.
- Innovation Bottlenecks ↔ **Complementing My Products Through Others' Capabilities:** Innovation doesn't always require starting from scratch. Often, the best results come from leveraging the capabilities of others to complement and enhance existing offerings. Platform Thinking breaks down silos, fostering collaboration and scaling impact.
- Underutilized Data ↔ **Data Exploitation:** Established firms generate vast amounts of data through their operations, yet much of this data remains underutilized. Platform Thinking provides a framework for unlocking the hidden value of this information, turning it into a driver of innovation and growth.
- Lack of Data for Strategic Insights ↔ **Data Harvesting:** In some cases, the data a company needs doesn't yet exist. Platform Thinking can enable firms to gather this data by creating value propositions that encourage stakeholders to generate and share information.

The journey begins by asking a simple but profound question: Where in your company do you want to innovate? This continues with the second key question: Which problem are you trying to solve? Once you've identified the challenge you want to address, Platform Thinking can guide you toward a solution that not only solves the problem but also creates lasting value.

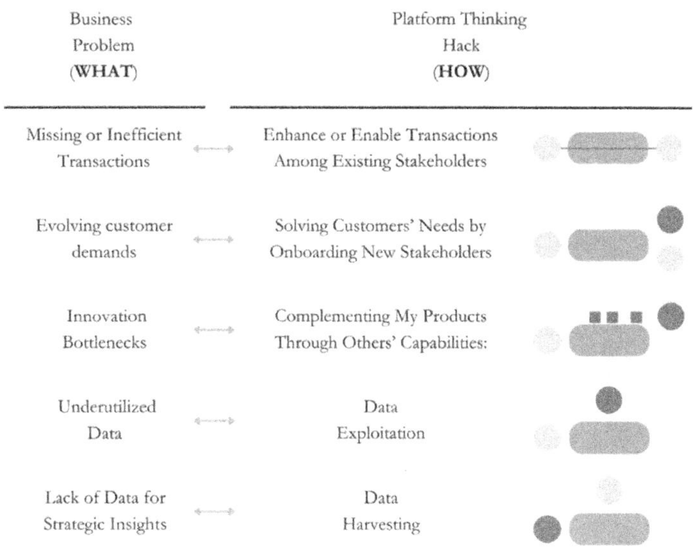

Figure 3.3 – What & How: Business Problems and Platform Thinking Hack

The Platform Transformative Framework: A Guiding Framework for Platform Thinking

Merging the three places where you can apply Platform Thinking (Platform as a New Service, Platform to Innovate a Primary Activity, and Platform to Innovate a Support Activity) and the five hacks you can use to solve the business problems "Enhance or Enable Transactions among Existing Stakeholders", "Solving Customers' Needs Onboarding New Stakeholders", "Complementing my product through others' capabilities", "Data Exploitation", "Data Harvesting"), the reference framework of this book emerges: *The Platform Transformative Framework.*

This compass is more than a theoretical tool. It's a practical guide to help managers and professionals navigate transformation projects by identifying specific "digital phoenixes" that can ignite change. Each "phoenix", each case will see, represents a unique way to apply

Platform Thinking, offering insights into how platforms can solve critical business challenges. At the same time, the *Platform Transformative Framework* serves as a roadmap for this book, the framework can direct readers to inspiring stories that showcase the versatility and power of platform-based mechanisms (see the next chapter for the list of all the cases).

The table (Figure 3.4) below summarizes how the 3 integration strategies with the Linear Value Chain can match with each of the 5 Business Problems and the related Platform Thinking Hack.

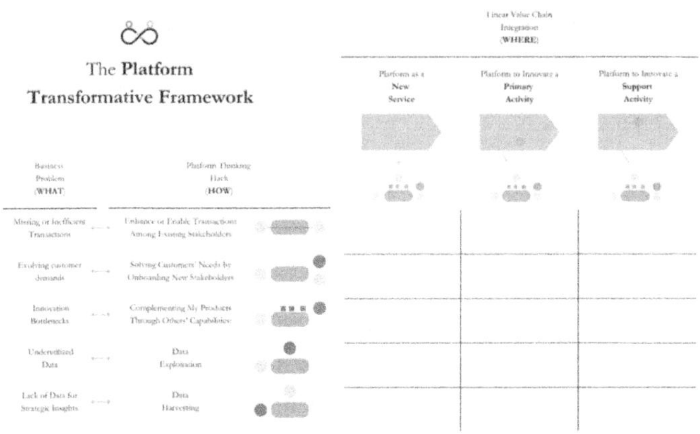

Figure 3.4 – The Platform Transformative Framework

In the following chapters, each match will be explored trough a dedicated case, providing a structured lens through which readers can better understand and apply Platform Thinking in their own organizations.

These five hacks form the basis of the next five chapters in this book. Each chapter will explore a Business Problem and the related Platform Thinking Hack in detail, drawing on real-world examples to illustrate how platforms can be applied effectively.

Whether your goal is to enhance transactions, onboard new stakeholders, complement existing capabilities, exploit data, or harvest new information, Platform Thinking provides a powerful toolkit for transformation. By understanding and embracing these principles, you can unlock new opportunities, drive innovation, and position your organization for long-term success in a platform-driven world.

As you explore the chapters ahead, keep this framework in mind. It will guide you through inspiring stories, practical tools, and actionable insights, ensuring that Platform Thinking becomes a cornerstone of your strategic approach.

PART 2
5 Business Problems to be solved through Platform Thinking

Notes on the structure of Part 2

This second part is based on the analysis of 140 cases which reveal 5 different types of business problems—and the related solutions—that established firms can address through Platform Thinking.

As we highlighted in Chapter 3, Platform Thinking can be used for different strategic innovation goals, from new services to innovation in primary and support activities of established firms. To capture the complexity of the phenomenon we are describing, we will dedicate a chapter to each problem, using different cases. To ensure clarity and actionable insights, each chapter follows the same structure, designed to enhance understanding and relevance for managers.

Framing the Problem:

Each chapter begins by presenting a common problem that organizations face, contextualized through two real-life examples. These examples, anonymized to protect confidentiality, aim to highlight the key business mechanism under scrutiny. In the examples, we first analyze the problem in a concrete setting and then propose two solutions: a linear (traditional) one and a platform-based one, to clarify what it means to apply Platform Thinking to solve a business problem (differently from the classic approach).

Diving into Real-World Cases

The second section of each chapter delves into three real-world cases, each tied to one of the three integration strategies—New Service, Primary Activity Innovation, or Support Activity Innovation. These cases illustrate how Platform Thinking has been successfully applied in diverse contexts, offering readers concrete examples, including platforms designed for internal users responsible for business processes, and not just for external customers, as is typical in startups based on platform business models.

Key Insights from our Research

Drawing on the 140 initiatives identified in our research, this section provides broader insights into the patterns and trends observed across the S&P 500 companies. These findings are complemented by reflections from our direct experience working with established firms, offering a balanced mix of data-driven analysis and practitioner perspectives.

Best Practices for Platform Design

Finally, each chapter concludes with actionable guidance on platform design, grounded in years of academic research and practical experience. While much of the literature on platform design originates from startups, these principles remain highly relevant and valuable for established firms looking to harness the power of platforms.

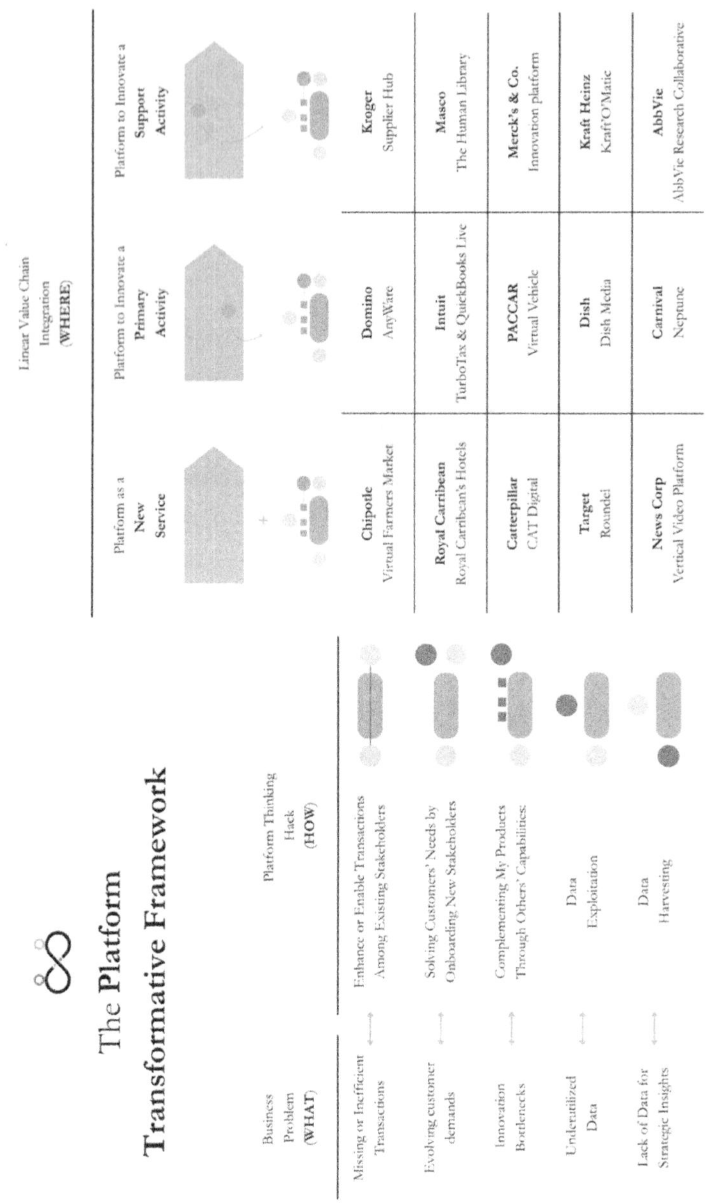

Figure Part 2.1 – The Examples to introduce the Platform Transformative Framework.

4

Missing or Inefficient Transactions

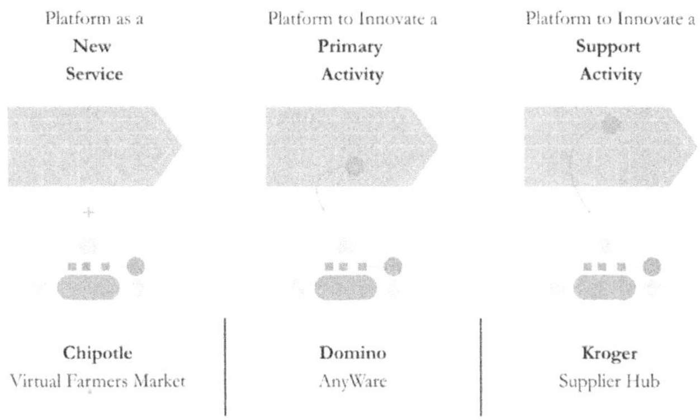

The Nature of Organizations: Efficiency in Transactions

"The firm is essentially a means of reducing the cost of operating the price mechanism."

— Ronald H. Coase, The Nature of the Firm (1937)

In 1937, economist Ronald Coase introduced a groundbreaking idea in his essay "*The Nature of the Firm*": firms exist to reduce transaction costs. They emerge as mechanisms for simplifying interactions that would otherwise be prohibitively complex or expensive in the open market. This insight underpins the structure of traditional organizations, where activities are internalized to achieve efficiencies and competitive advantage. Over the decades, this thinking became the foundation of the linear value chain, a sequence of processes optimized to create value while maintaining control, as well as the basis of any organizational process with activities as an input to reach a defined output.

The traditional linear value chain faces a significant challenge in today's fast-paced and ever-changing business environment. While historically praised for its efficiency, this model increasingly acts as a barrier to innovation. Established firms must now confront a critical question: Is centralizing coordination activities among stakeholders still the most effective way to optimize processes and minimize transaction costs? Or could an alternative approach, building a platform that redistributes some of these coordination activities back to the participants, unlock even greater levels of efficiency and innovation? This shift invites a reevaluation of long-standing assumptions and an exploration of platform-based strategies that empower ecosystem players to drive value creation collaboratively

To give an answer to this question, let's consider a few examples.

Reframing the Role of a Travel Agency - From Gatekeeper to Facilitator

Imagine stepping into a travel agency a decade ago. Rows of glossy brochures showcase pre-packaged vacations that promise convenience and adventure. The travel agent sits at the center of a carefully curated ecosystem. Experience providers—hotels, tour operators, and airlines—are all vying for a spot in the catalog. Travelers seek guidance and inspiration for their next journeys. The agent's role is clear: negotiate deals with providers, bundle experiences, and sell them to travelers, all while managing logistics and offering support.

For years, this model thrived on a simple value proposition: agents could secure better deals and greater convenience than travelers could achieve on their own, while offering the best possible packages. But the world changed. Travelers, armed with smartphones and endless options, began demanding personalization. They no longer wanted generic packages; they craved unique, tailored experiences. Platforms like Airbnb and TripAdvisor stepped in to fill this gap. Suddenly, travelers could connect directly with providers, explore reviews, and craft their own itineraries.

The traditional travel agent, once the gatekeeper of experiences, began to feel like a relic. How can travel agencies adapt to the changing landscape? How can they continue to provide value by helping travelers achieve the personalized experiences they crave while maintaining their relevance? One approach might be to innovate with a linear value chain mindset: working on their own activities. Travel packages could be reimagined as starting points, supported by extensive interviews and iterative processes to craft truly bespoke journeys. However, this approach comes with significant trade-offs: higher operational costs and a slower process in a world where travelers demand near-instantaneous access to options and personalization.

But what if the solution doesn't lie in refining the linear value chain but in embracing Platform Thinking instead?

Now, imagine a travel agency that embraces this shift. Instead of clinging to its gatekeeping role, it reimagines itself as a platform. The agency still leverages its existing relationships with experience providers and travelers, but it focuses on facilitating direct interactions between them. Through an intelligent digital platform, travelers can browse offerings from providers, filtering options based on their interests—be it adventure, relaxation, or cultural immersion. The agency must understand what these interests are, how they evolve, and how to optimise the match between clients and experience providers.

The agency remains vital, but its role has evolved. It now operates as a facilitator rather than a gatekeeper, fostering direct interactions between travelers and experience providers. Previously, the provider interacted exclusively with the agency, as did the client, with the agency serving as the intermediary for both. Now, the interaction occurs directly between the two, with the agency enabling and supporting this relationship.

This change brings a significant shift: providers effectively become clients of the agency. The agency is no longer buying and reselling its activities; it now enables direct transactions between them and the travelers. By empowering providers to differentiate themselves and travelers to craft personalized journeys, the agency still maintains (at least some) relationships with both groups, leveraging its long-standing connections to secure special rates with providers and ensure competitive pricing. Additionally, it offers value-added services like seamless booking and robust customer support, enhancing the overall experience for both providers and travelers. This dual role strengthens the agency's relevance in a rapidly evolving market.

Not just commercial transactions: focusing on knowledge-based interactions within the firm

In the opening of this chapter, we reported Ronald Coase's famous quote, that pushes towards a clear view: the firm, ultimately, is an organizational structure designed to reduce transaction costs. It is through this reduction that a competitive advantage can emerge, and the boundaries of its existence are defined. Building on these ideas, Platform Thinking can go far beyond commercial transactions and extend to virtually all processes within a company. Processes within a company can be viewed as internal chains of customer-provider relationships, where each function or team delivers value to another, creating interconnected exchanges. Platform Thinking isn't limited to external ecosystems; it can also profoundly transform internal dynamics, focusing on any type of exchange managed by a firm, such as knowledge exchanges between internal functions.

Let's see a possible example. In many B2B organizations, a common challenge arises between innovation and sales teams. Innovation teams, responsible for developing cutting-edge use cases, often pass these ideas to sales teams, who must translate them into client-ready solutions. Yet, without a deep understanding of these innovations, sales professionals struggle to communicate their value effectively, leading to inefficiencies and missed opportunities.

How could you solve this issue through a traditional linear process? Procedures, KPIs, and incentives would probably be the first hypotheses. For example, asking salespeople to study new use cases every couple of months, measuring the usage of the various use cases over time with dedicated surveys, or directly incentivizing the usage of new use cases with bonuses and compensation. In all these examples, the solutions may be perceived as an imposition that could create disengagement: the company is controlling and incentivizing me to do something I would not do otherwise.

A completely different approach could be to develop an internal GenAI-based platform that bridges the gap by connecting two internal customers: the sales team and the innovation team. The platform, designed as an interactive chatbot, learns from use case libraries created by the innovation team and from customer insights gathered by the sales team. Sales teams can quickly access relevant resources, ask which use case best fits a specific situation, and get instant answers to their questions. In turn, their interactions generate new knowledge, especially when dealing with unfamiliar industries or client needs, which feeds back into the system. Innovation teams can use this real-time feedback to refine existing solutions and develop better ones. This marks a significant shift: while the sales team was traditionally treated as the end customer in a linear model, the innovation team now also becomes a user of the platform, as they draw on it to stay closely aligned with evolving market needs.

This transformation, from "*I have to do it*" to "*I want to do it*", fosters engagement and aligns internal goals with broader organizational priorities.

Not just efficiency, but also effectiveness

When organizations tackle Missing or Inefficient Transactions, they also achieve improvements in effectiveness, compared to traditional processes. Platforms streamline interactions, reducing the friction and bottlenecks that slow down conventional workflows, while simultaneously creating opportunities for richer, more impactful engagement.

For example, a travel platform that directly connects experience providers and travelers not only makes the transaction smoother by helping travelers to find the experience providers (efficiency) but also enables travelers to discover and personalize experiences tailored to their needs (effectiveness). As these interactions deepen, the ecosystem becomes increasingly valuable: new providers are drawn to the platform to reach an engaged audience, while satisfied travelers amplify the platform's reach by sharing their positive experiences.

The same happens for the internal platform case. Consider the example of connecting innovation and sales teams. An internal platform doesn't just streamline the transfer of use cases from one team to the other (efficiency); it also fosters real-time feedback loops and knowledge sharing, allowing innovation teams to deliver more tailored, effective and innovative use cases for the clients (effectiveness). The platform ensures that innovation teams refine their offerings based on actual market insights, creating solutions that better align with customer needs.

Common Threads: The Platform Power in Action

Both the external example of the travel agency and the internal example of bridging innovation and sales teams highlight three crucial dynamics that emerge when organizations adopt Platform Thinking. These shared traits underline why this approach is transformative across contexts.

1. **Suppliers Become Customers**

In both cases, the traditional role of the supplier is reframed. Experience providers in the travel agency scenario and the innovation team in the internal platform example are no longer just contributors to a process. Instead, they become customers of the platform, deriving direct value from engaging with it. The travel agency empowers experience providers to connect directly with travelers, creating a tailored value proposition that meets their needs. Similarly, the innovation team becomes a customer of the internal platform by gaining actionable feedback from sales, enabling more relevant innovations.

2. **Cross-Side Network Effects**

The platform unlocks cross-side network effects by facilitating interactions between distinct stakeholder groups. For the travel agency, as more travelers engage with the platform, the value for experience providers increases, and vice versa. Internally, the more the sales team utilizes the innovation team's use cases and provides insights and feedback, the more the innovation team's ability to create impactful solutions is enhanced, thereby amplifying value across both teams.

3. **Leveraging Idle Assets**

Platforms excel at unlocking the hidden potential of idle assets. In the case of the travel agency, long-standing relationships with providers become key resources for creating personalized experiences. For the internal platform, the untapped knowledge of the innovation team, often underutilized due to poor communication channels, can be fully leveraged and transformed into a strategic asset. By surfacing and optimizing these assets, platforms create new avenues for value generation.

These commonalities highlight how Platform Thinking redefines roles, relationships, and resources to foster more dynamic ecosystems. Whether external or internal, the shift transforms the organization's ability to unlock untapped potential and scale innovation effectively.

The Business Problem and its Platform Thinking Hack

Legacy firms often experience Missing or Inefficient Transactions: slow, costly, or missed interactions between suppliers, partners, and customers, both externally and within internal provider-customer chains, that result in revenue loss, higher costs, or operational frictions.

The hack to solve it is "*Enhance or Enable Transactions among Existing Stakeholders*":

The message is clear: enhancing or enabling transactions among stakeholders is not just a tactic—it is a transformative strategy. Whether applied to external ecosystems or internal workflows, Platform Thinking challenges organizations to rethink their fundamental purpose. Where do you perceive inefficiency in the process you manage? What are the frictions that reduce the effectiveness of your processes?

In the sections ahead, we will dive deeper into the mechanics of this type of transformation. Through real-world case studies and actionable insights, we will explore how Platform Thinking can help organizations unlock untapped potential, foster innovation, and secure their place in the platform economy.

Three Inspiring Stories: Chipotle, Domino & Kroger

Chipotle's Virtual Farmer's Market: A Platform to Enhance Connections

Chipotle Mexican Grill revolutionized the fast-casual dining industry by championing "Food with Integrity." Founded in 1993, the brand quickly gained a following for its commitment to serving high-quality, responsibly sourced ingredients. Unlike many competitors, Chipotle embraced a farm-to-table ethos at scale, forging close relationships with local farmers and producers to ensure the sustainability of its supply chain. By the 2010s, the company had grown into a global powerhouse, with thousands of restaurants and millions of devoted customers. However, this growth presented challenges. Maintaining deep relationships with local suppliers while scaling operations globally became increasingly complex. The COVID-19 pandemic, in particular, exposed vulnerabilities in traditional supply chains, creating a pressing need for innovative solutions.

The Challenge: A Disrupted Supply Chain

The pandemic brought unforeseen challenges to Chipotle's supplier network. Local farmers, integral to the company's sourcing strategy, faced reduced demand as restaurant operations slowed. Many suppliers lacked the infrastructure or market access to pivot to other revenue streams, leaving them financially vulnerable. For Chipotle, the risk extended beyond supply shortages—it threatened the very ecosystem the company had spent decades cultivating: if they wouldn't survive the pandemic, the whole supply chain to guarantee Chipotle work is at risk.

The Solution: A Transactional Platform for New Service Innovation

In June 2020, Chipotle responded by launching the Virtual Farmer's Market, a transactional platform designed to enhance transactions between two key groups already within its ecosystem: local farmers and consumers. Built in collaboration with Shopify, the platform equipped farmers with personalized e-commerce sites to sell products such as meat, dairy, and grains directly to consumers.

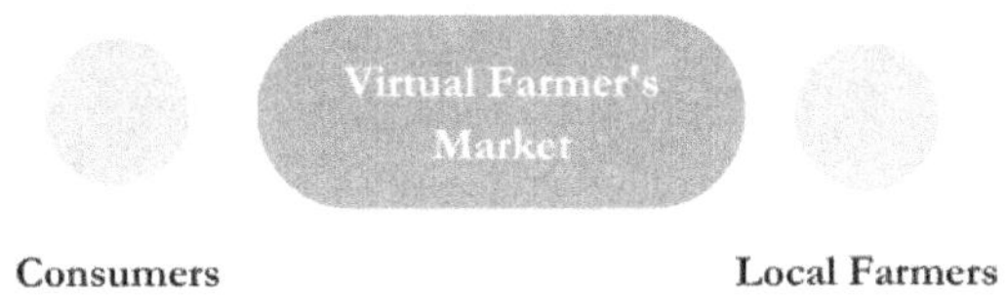

Figure 5.1 – Chipotle's Virtual Farmer's Market

This solution leveraged Chipotle's unique position at the intersection of these two groups. Consumers, already familiar with and loyal to Chipotle's brand values, formed the demand side of the platform. Local farmers, long-standing suppliers, made up the supply side. The transacted good was fresh, sustainable food products, extending the farmers' reach beyond their usual B2B relationships with Chipotle.

Because the platform did not introduce new actors, onboarding challenges were minimal. Farmers were guided through setting up their e-commerce presence, while Chipotle marketed the initiative to its consumer base, driving traffic to the platform. This streamlined process sidestepped the typical chicken-and-egg problem faced by nascent platforms, as Chipotle's existing relationships ensured participation from both sides. The platform also created bi-directional cross-side network externalities: as more farmers joined, the variety and availability of goods improved, enhancing the platform's value to consumers. Conversely, the more Chipotle's customers joined the platform, the more value it offered to the farmers.

The Alternative Linear Path

Had Chipotle relied on a traditional linear value chain approach to solve the problem, it might have directly financed its distribution network or purchased excess produce from struggling farmers. While effective in the short term, this strategy would have required significant capital investment and ongoing operational costs. It also would have failed to create a sustainable, self-reinforcing solution. By introducing a transactional platform, instead, Chipotle unlocked several advantages. First, the Virtual Farmer's Market required less initial investment. Leveraging its existing farmer relationships allowed Chipotle to launch the platform quickly and at scale, externalizing the technical execution to Shopify's infrastructure. Second, the platform generated quasi-zero marginal costs structure, as each additional farmer or consumer added value to the ecosystem without proportionate increases in operational expenses.

The Virtual Farmer's Market not only provided an additional revenue stream for farmers but also deepened Chipotle's connection with its customers. Consumers appreciated the opportunity to support local farmers and participate in Chipotle's mission of sustainability. This strengthened brand loyalty and reinforced Chipotle's identity as a purpose-driven company.

Takeaways

In the Virtual Farmer's Market case, direct transactions between local farmers and consumers weren't just inefficient—they were missing altogether. Looking at the Platform Transformative Framework, Chipotle addressed this gap using the platform Thinking Hack labeled "*Enhance or Enable Transactions among Existing Stakeholders*." Importantly, Chipotle didn't replace its traditional linear value chain. It still sources ingredients, prepares food, and sells final products. The platform is a "*new service*" that expands what the company offers to its customers.

Moreover, as a legacy firm, Chipotle could effectively leverage pre-existing relationships, solving the chicken-and-egg paradox that often plagues platform launches. Local farmers and consumers, both familiar with the brand, were eager to participate. This case illustrates the transformative potential of Platform Thinking in addressing traditional business challenges and creating sustainable solutions. It's a powerful reminder that sometimes the key to innovation isn't building something entirely new—it's unlocking value already present within your ecosystem.

Domino's AnyWare: Redefining Customer Engagement Through Platforms

Domino's Pizza began in 1960 as a small pizzeria in Michigan, distinguished by its commitment to consistency and speed. Over the decades, it grew into a global leader, operating in over 90 countries. Domino's reputation as a delivery innovator was cemented in the 1980s with its bold "30 minutes or less" promise. Yet, innovation didn't stop at logistics. By the early 2010s, as consumer behaviors shifted toward mobile and on-demand convenience, Domino's realized it needed to embrace technology to remain competitive. This commitment to evolution eventually led to one of its most transformative initiatives: the AnyWare platform.

The Challenge: Keeping Pace with Evolving Customer Expectations

Domino's faced a structural challenge as digital transformation redefined how consumers engaged with brands. While customer expectations evolved toward seamless, integrated digital experiences, Domino's operated within a legacy model where the primary transactional relationship was between the customer and the individual restaurant. Domino's corporate role was focused on managing relationships with its franchisees, not with the end customers themselves.

This created a fundamental disconnect. Customers were attributing their experience to the Domino's brand, but the company had limited control over how that experience was delivered, as each store handled orders, service quality, and local execution independently. As digital habits became more embedded—through smart speakers, wearables, and connected vehicles—the gap between what customers expected and what the existing model could deliver widened. Ordering through a basic website or app felt increasingly inadequate. The result was growing friction in the ordering process, inconsistent experiences, fragmented data, and a diminished ability for Domino's to shape or own its customer interactions.

The Solution: Turning Devices Into Transactional Gateways

Domino's launched AnyWare in 2015, a suite enabling customers to order through various digital touchpoints, including smart speakers, smartwatches, smart TVs, social media, text messaging, and in-car systems. This innovation targeted a primary value-chain activity—marketing and sales—by transforming how Domino's corporate connected not just with its franchisees, but now directly with end consumers as well. Rather than creating a new product, Domino's leveraged existing ones—its pizzas and delivery services—and dramatically reduced the friction involved in accessing them.

With AnyWare, Domino's expanded its customer base: from serving only its franchise restaurants to also serving final consumers directly. The platform provides a seamless ordering experience for consumers, while simultaneously offering value to restaurants, which now receive a steady stream of orders without needing to independently manage customer acquisition, digital channels, or marketing efforts. This dual-customer architecture positioned Domino's as a service provider to both sides, coordinating interactions rather than merely supplying brand assets or support.

Figure 5.2 – Domino's AnyWare

AnyWare operates as a transactional platform, bridging end customers with Domino's stores. The "transacted good" in this model is the order—comprising the customer's selection of pizza, sides, and beverages—prepared and delivered from a local

Domino's store. The platform reduces barriers to completing a transaction, making the interaction immediate, digitally enabled, and consistent across contexts. In other words, AnyWare dramatically increases the efficiency of an already existing transaction by centralizing and streamlining the value exchange between two interdependent customer groups.

Domino's achieved this result by capitalizing on idle assets that were already integral to its business. The company utilized its long-standing relationships with the stores and the trust and loyalty of the consumers to the brand. Relationships with loyal customers ensured a strong demand-side base for the platform, while the vast network of physical stores, already optimized for production and delivery, provided the supply-side infrastructure. These assets allowed Domino's to implement AnyWare rapidly without requiring significant new investments in infrastructure and without suffering from the chicken-and-egg paradox. The players on both sides were already part of the company. AnyWare's innovation lies in improving how these existing stakeholders interact, creating a more seamless and efficient process. Technological partners, such as Amazon Alexa and Ford SYNC, were indirectly onboarded to enable the transactions. However, these partners are not actors on the platform itself; their role is limited to providing the technological interface, while the transactions remain exclusively between customers and stores.

This platform approach also harnessed bidirectional cross-side network externalities. As more customers used AnyWare through their devices, Domino's stores saw increased order volumes, encouraging further technological integration and customer satisfaction. The cycle of mutual benefit created a robust, self-reinforcing system.

The Alternative Linear Path

Had Domino's opted for a linear solution, it might have focused on refining its website and mobile app or developing more advanced digital tools for individual restaurants to manage locally. This would have kept customer interactions fragmented and dependent on each store's digital capabilities, leading to inconsistent experiences across the network. It also would have required higher investment in technology deployment, support, and ongoing local marketing, without addressing the growing demand for seamless, omnichannel convenience.

By adopting a platform approach instead, Domino's shifted from enabling stores to sell independently to orchestrating the transaction between consumers and restaurants. This created a unified customer experience, reduced duplication of effort across stores, and significantly lowered customer acquisition and service costs. The real gain came from scale: once the platform was in place, each additional transaction required almost no incremental cost. More importantly, Domino's unlocked cross-side network effects—the more consumers joined the platform, the more value was delivered to restaurants, and vice versa—creating a self-reinforcing system that would have been impossible in a linear model.

Takeaways

In the Domino's AnyWare case, transactions between consumers and restaurants already existed, but they were fragmented, inconsistent, and increasingly misaligned with digital expectations. Looking at the Platform Transformative Framework, Domino's addressed this gap using the Platform Thinking Hack labeled "*Enhance or Enable Transactions among Existing Stakeholders.*" Importantly, Domino's didn't replace its traditional linear value chain. Local stores still prepare food and fulfill orders. The platform is not a new service, it redesigns a "*primary value-chain activity*": marketing and sales. Before AnyWare, Domino already supported this activity by providing brand assets, advertising campaigns, and promotional services aimed at helping individual restaurants attract and convert customers locally. With the platform, Domino's magnified the effectiveness of this function by taking direct control of the customer interface.

Moreover, as a legacy firm, Domino's was able to leverage its strong relationships with both consumers and franchisees, solving the chicken-and-egg paradox that often hinders platform launches. Customers already trusted the brand, and stores were ready to fulfill demand. This case illustrates how Platform Thinking can transform a primary value-chain activity by improving the efficiency and reach of interactions between existing actors.

Kroger's Supplier Hub: Revolutionizing Procurement for Agility

In the highly competitive world of retail, Kroger Co. has long been recognized as a leader in leveraging innovation to maintain operational excellence. Founded in 1883, the company grew from a single grocery store in Cincinnati to one of the largest supermarket chains in the United States. Known for its focus on efficiency and customer satisfaction, Kroger has consistently sought ways to enhance its supply chain and procurement processes. In 2018, Kroger faced a pressing need to modernize its supplier interactions, a challenge that led to the creation of the Supplier Hub—a centralized vendor management system designed to transform how the company managed its procurement activities and supplier relationships.

The Challenge: Navigating Procurement Complexity

Kroger's procurement system was facing inefficiencies that hindered its ability to maintain accurate supplier data, ensure compliance, and streamline interactions. With thousands of suppliers and an ever-growing need for agility in the supply chain, the company needed a scalable solution to manage vendor relationships effectively. Adding to the complexity was the sheer number of internal buyers operating across multiple categories, departments, and stores. Each category had its own specific needs, and every store required precise coordination to meet local demands. The challenge was clear: how could Kroger enhance its procurement activities to better serve its stakeholders while maintaining trust and compliance?

The Solution: Centralizing Procurement with the Supplier Hub

In April 2018, Kroger introduced the Supplier Hub, a transactional platform that centralized vendor management and redefined the company's procurement process. This innovation was not about creating a new product or service for end consumers but about transforming a critical support activity—procurement—within the company's value chain.

The Supplier Hub acts as a transactional platform connecting two distinct stakeholder groups: buyers on the demand side (internal Kroger teams responsible for procurement and compliance) and suppliers on the supply side (external vendors providing goods and services). The transacted "good" in this ecosystem is vendor information, from compliance documentation to certifications and performance metrics, essential for maintaining a reliable supply chain.

Figure 5.3 – Kroger's Supplier Hub

A fundamental shift in perspective underpinned the platform's design: suppliers, while still supply the Kroger supermarket, are treated as customers of the platform. The Supplier Hub was explicitly crafted to solve their problems, offering them tools, resources, and support to enhance their compliance, efficiency, and overall experience. Suppliers were provided with job aids, videos, and a dedicated Supplier Engagement Group to ensure their success within the ecosystem. By addressing supplier needs and streamlining their interactions with Kroger, the platform not only improved supplier performance but also created value for the entire supply chain.

The platform's design fostered bi-directional network externalities, meaning that suppliers see more value if they are exposed to more buyers and vice versa. Suppliers benefited from better tools and resources, such as job aids and dedicated support teams, which improved their efficiency and compliance. In turn,

Kroger's internal teams gained higher-quality data and reduced friction in vendor interactions, creating a virtuous cycle of enhanced performance on both sides. It is relevant to note that both stakeholder groups already existed within Kroger's ecosystem: buyers, who are internal to the company, and suppliers that were already providing goods to the company.

The platform's success was also driven by Kroger's existing relationships. Unlike a startup attempting to launch a similar solution, Kroger could pivot its deep, established connections with suppliers and internal teams to create immediate value. By leveraging these idle assets—existing relationships and trust—the Supplier Hub was able to bypass the chicken-and-egg paradox typically associated with platform launches, ensuring early adoption and long-term sustainability.

The Alternative Linear Path

Had Kroger opted for a linear value chain approach, the company might have invested in building a larger internal team dedicated to manually managing supplier data, compliance tracking, and vendor communications. Alternatively, it could have developed multiple siloed software tools, customized for different departments or procurement categories. While such options were feasible, they would have introduced significant operational complexity and ongoing coordination challenges. Every improvement in the supplier onboarding or compliance process would have required corresponding increases in staffing, training, and systems integration—creating a direct correlation between performance gains and rising costs.

This linear approach would have also increased the risk of data fragmentation, inconsistencies across departments, and delays in responding to supplier needs. Maintaining accuracy and compliance at scale would require constant manual oversight, reducing agility and limiting Kroger's ability to adapt quickly to supply chain disruptions or regulatory changes.

Takeaways

In Kroger's Supplier hub case, the relationship between internal buyers and external suppliers was already existing, but the many frictions forced the company to have a full department to facilitate and manage these transactions. Looking at the Platform Transformative Framework, Kroger addressed this gap using the platform Thinking Hack labeled "*Enhance or Enable Transactions among Existing Stakeholders.*" It is important to see that Kroger did not replace its business model nor created a new service. The platform is transparent for the final customers of the supermarket as it innovate a "*support value-chain activity*": the procurement.

By focusing on procurement, Kroger streamlined its supply chain, reduced friction, and fostered stronger supplier relationships. The platform model's efficiency stemmed from leveraging existing relationships and treating suppliers as customers, providing them with tools and resources to enhance their performance. This case highlights the power of Platform Thinking in addressing operational challenges and underscores how companies can unlock value by reimagining interactions within their ecosystems.

Looking Across Missing or Inefficient Transactions Cases

In exploring how companies can solve "*Missing or Inefficient Transactions*" by applying the Platform Thinking hack "*Enhance or Enable Transactions among Existing Stakeholders,*" we analyzed three distinct cases that showcase how established organizations can drive innovation by reimagining interactions within their existing ecosystems. Each case demonstrates the transformative potential of Platform Thinking, where companies leverage their current relationships and assets to create new forms of value without the need to onboard entirely new stakeholders.

Despite operating in different industries, these cases share a common strategy: they recognized untapped potential within their existing networks. In some instances, the transactions already existed and were significantly improved, enhancing efficiency and reducing friction. In other cases, transactions were enabled from scratch, creating entirely new avenues for value exchange—but always among stakeholders already embedded within the organization's ecosystem. By fostering more efficient and dynamic connections, these organizations not only strengthened their operational resilience but also deepened stakeholder engagement, proving that sometimes, the greatest opportunities lie in optimizing the relationships you already have.

Each example illustrates the versatility of this hack:

Chipotle's Virtual Farmer's Market showcases the transformative power of Platform Thinking by enabling new transactions from scratch between local farmers and consumers. By leveraging idle assets such as its long-standing relationships with trusted suppliers and the strong loyalty of its customer base, Chipotle created a new service that extended beyond its traditional restaurant model. This approach generated cross-side network effects—more farmers increased product variety, while more consumers enhanced demand—resulting in a resilient, value-rich ecosystem that reinforced Chipotle's sustainability mission.

Domino's AnyWare exemplifies how enhancing existing transactions can significantly boost customer engagement. By capitalizing on its idle assets—deep-rooted relationships with a global network of stores and a loyal customer base—Domino's integrated multiple digital touchpoints, such as smart devices and connected cars. This reduced friction in the ordering process, making it more convenient for customers. This innovation didn't alter the core product but transformed how the company's primary value-chain process of sales and marketing can be innovated to support their restaurant sales, creating seamless, omnichannel experiences that strengthened brand loyalty while driving incremental sales with minimal additional costs.

Kroger's Supplier Hub highlights how a platform approach can completely reshape a support value-chain activity like procurement. The platform leveraged Kroger's idle assets, including its extensive network of supplier relationships and internal procurement processes, to streamline vendor management. By treating suppliers as platform participants rather than mere vendors, Kroger enhanced compliance, improved data accuracy, and fostered stronger supplier relationships. The platform created bi-directional network effects—better supplier tools improved operational efficiency, while robust supplier engagement enriched Kroger's supply chain resilience and agility.

These cases demonstrate how this Platform Thinking Hack adapts to different interactions within the value chain. Chipotle and Domino's operate entirely outside the organization, connecting suppliers and customers or restaurants and consumers. In contrast, Kroger employs a hybrid model, with one side internal and the other external to the firm.

Considering the whole dataset, we gathered through the S&P500 cases, we found **60 initiatives** applying Platform Thinking to solve Missing or Inefficient Transactions. More in detail:

- **2 out of 60 (3.3%)** initiatives introduced new services
- **51 out of 60 (85.0%)** targeted primary value chain activities, such as operations, marketing, sales, or after sale services.
- **7 out of 60 (11.7%)** focused on support activities like R&D, innovation and procurement.

Breaking down these 60 initiatives further reveals their structural differences:

- **37 out of 60 (61.7%)** are open platforms, with both sides external to the organization.
- **5 out of 60 (8.3%)** are closed platforms, connecting only internal stakeholders.
- **18 out of 60 (30.0%)** are hybrid platforms, linking internal and external stakeholders.

These figures underscore a dominant focus on external platforms, which are often more visible in the market. However, the data doesn't tell the whole story.

Interestingly, while external platforms dominate public discourse internal platforms are much more appreciated and developed in practice than what emerge from the dataset. Our direct experience working with companies shows that closed platforms—where both sides of the transaction are internal—frequently drive critical improvements, particularly in areas like internal collaboration and knowledge sharing.

For example, a closed platform might connect R&D teams with sales functions, ensuring smoother transitions from innovation to market delivery (as in the early example of this chapter). These platforms may not receive the same visibility as customer-facing initiatives but are just as crucial in enabling efficiency and effectiveness within organizations.

The cases of Chipotle, Domino, and Kroger highlight platforms' adaptability and impact. Chipotle focuses on sustainability and transparency, Domino's focused on convenience and loyalty, while Kroger on process optimization and alignment. Together, they show that the true power of platforms in tackling Missing or Inefficient Transactions lies in their ability to align with organizational goals while transforming relationships into dynamic ecosystems.

As more companies adopt Platform Thinking, the lines between stakeholders blur. Suppliers become partners. Customers become collaborators. Transactions evolve into opportunities for co-creation. By enhancing and enabling these interactions, organizations not only streamline their processes but also position themselves for long-term growth and innovation.

Best Practices from Transactional Platform Design

Transactional platforms represent one of the most prominent and extensively studied categories in the platform economy. Over the years, a substantial body of research has been developed, providing deep insights into how these platforms operate and succeed. Rather than starting from scratch, businesses and innovators can leverage the wealth of knowledge accumulated by studying the best practices of industry-leading transactional platforms. By examining the strategies of these successful developers, we can uncover actionable lessons and proven approaches to addressing market needs, reducing transaction costs, and creating value for all stakeholders involved. The key lies in building upon what already works while tailoring it to specific contexts and opportunities.

Take Booking.com, for example. Before its inception, travelers faced significant challenges in finding the ideal hotel. Options were fragmented, reviews were scarce, and booking processes were inconsistent. Similarly, hotels struggled to connect with a global audience, relying on traditional channels that limited their reach. Booking.com emerged as a platform to address these dual frictions. By aggregating hotel options, offering verified reviews, and simplifying the booking process, it transformed how travelers and hotels interact, creating a thriving ecosystem.

For decades, research on transactional platforms—largely driven by startups—has revealed critical insights. Here are the key lessons for managers in established firms seeking to adopt the "Enhance or Enable Transactions Among Existing Stakeholders" hack.

1. **Implement Robust Trust Mechanisms**

Trust is the foundation of any transactional platform. In a system where parties may have little prior interaction, mechanisms like verification systems, reputation scores, and dispute-resolution tools are critical for ensuring smooth and reliable transactions.

Take BlaBlaCar, a ride-sharing platform. It addresses the inherent trust gap between drivers and passengers by implementing robust systems such as profile verifications, user ratings, and mutual feedback. These mechanisms create a sense of safety and reliability, encouraging more users to participate. Managers must design platforms that actively build and sustain trust, as it directly impacts stakeholder engagement and transaction frequency.

2. **Design a Specific Value Proposition for Each Stakeholder and Empower Them**

For a transactional platform to succeed, every stakeholder must be seen as a customer who freely decides to onboard because of a clear and compelling reason to join. Each side—whether suppliers, customers, or internal teams—must feel that the platform is designed to serve their needs. This involves more than just connecting parties; it requires creating tools and services that empower them to thrive within the ecosystem.

Consider OpenTable. To attract restaurants, it didn't just promise access to more customers. Instead, it offered a robust table management system, helping restaurants optimize seating arrangements and reduce inefficiencies during peak hours. This value proposition addressed a specific pain point for restaurants while simultaneously improving the customer experience.

Managers should ask themselves: "Why would each stakeholder want to join and actively participate?". By addressing this question, they can create platforms that foster innovation, engagement, and co-creation among stakeholders.

3. **Focus on Platform Health Metrics**

The success of a transactional platform isn't just about the number of users; it's about the quality of the interactions and the volume of transactions. Network health metrics—such as transaction volume, participant retention, and engagement quality—are better indicators of a platform's vitality.

BlaBlaCar's success illustrates this point. The platform's focus isn't just on adding users but on ensuring that drivers and passengers find a match for every ride. Empty seats are its version of perishable inventory, and the platform's effectiveness lies in minimizing these. By focusing on matching users and optimizing transactions, BlaBlaCar ensures its network remains healthy and valuable, encouraging organic growth on both sides.

Managers should prioritize creating value through transactions first, trusting that the user base will expand as a natural result.

4. **Start Small with a Core Transaction**

Launching a successful platform doesn't require advanced technology or a fully developed ecosystem. Instead, the focus should be on addressing a single, critical transaction and iterating based on feedback.

Airbnb exemplifies this approach. The platform's early version was little more than a basic website connecting hosts and guests. Its success didn't stem from sophisticated features but from solving a simple problem: matching travelers with affordable, local accommodations. By focusing on the core transaction, Airbnb built trust, refined its model, and gradually expanded its offerings.

For managers, the lesson is clear: Start with the matching process. Technology and additional features can follow once the core transaction proves its value.

Key Questions to Evaluate the Hack's Fit

Before adopting the "Enhance or Enable Transactions Among Existing Stakeholders" hack, managers should reflect on the following questions:

1. Can you identify a process that involves a transaction with significant friction or that is not enabled yet?
   Is there inefficiency in how your stakeholders find and engage with one another?
2. Is the process multi-stakeholder? Does it involve multiple parties with different needs that could benefit mutually from a more dynamic interaction model?

If the answer to both questions is yes, the next step is to imagine reinventing your role: Can you move from being a gatekeeper to an orchestrator? Instead of controlling interactions linearly, can you create a platform that serves all stakeholders and empowers them to engage and co-create?

By addressing these questions and applying the insights from transactional platforms, managers can unlock the transformative potential of the "Enhance or Enable Transactions Among Existing Stakeholders" hack, driving innovation and growth in their organizations.

5

Evolving customer demands

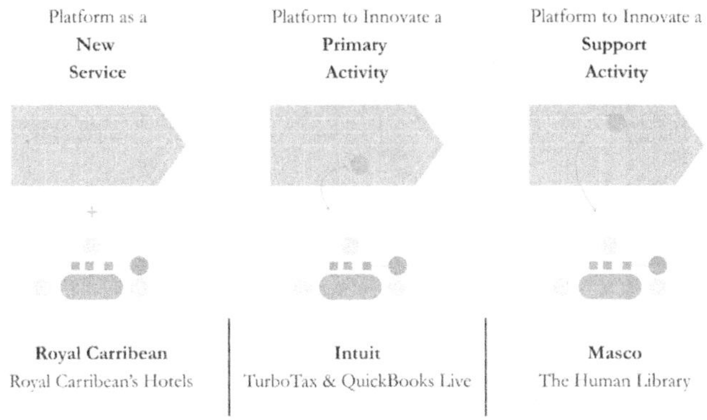

The Age of Customer Centricity

"Customer centricity isn't a strategy; it's a culture that prioritizes understanding and serving customer needs better than anyone else."

— Don Peppers, co-author of *The One to One Future.*

Over the past few decades, customer centricity has evolved into a foundational principle for businesses seeking to enhance efficiency and effectiveness. By deeply understanding customer needs, organizations have successfully optimized their transactions—internally and externally—creating better products, improved services, and more seamless processes. This focus has fueled innovation, minimized waste, and fostered loyalty, allowing firms to differentiate themselves in an increasingly competitive marketplace.

But customer centricity should not be limited to external customers. For process owners, it is equally a guiding principle for serving internal stakeholders. Take a Human Resources (HR) department, for example. Employees are its internal customers, relying on HR to provide services like payroll management, recruitment, and travel support. When HR adopts a customer-centric approach, it doesn't merely process requests—it anticipates employee needs, enhances their experience, and seeks innovative ways to support them.

Whether addressing the needs of external clients or internal stakeholders, customer centricity is a powerful lens through which process owners can refine their operations and deliver value. However, as customer expectations evolve, so too must the approaches organizations use to meet them.

Customer needs are evolving faster than ever, and organizations often find themselves stretched thin trying to meet these demands. While traditional approaches to customer centricity emphasize honing internal expertise or building partnerships, they can lead to inefficiencies, high costs, or diminishing returns.

Consider this: Is your organization inherently the best suited to solve every customer need, whether internal or external? Or could others, equipped with the right tools, expertise, and incentives, step in to provide solutions more effectively, efficiently, and at scale? This raises an intriguing question: how can platforms help? By facilitating connections and fostering collaboration, platforms offer a pathway to enhance transactions through the involvement of new stakeholders, unlocking opportunities that might otherwise remain untapped. Let's explore some examples to see how this works in practice.

A Journey into the Highway Payment Industry

To illustrate this shift, let's step into the shoes of a company that manages highway payments. For years, the mantra of customer centricity guided the organization's efforts to provide a seamless and pleasant experience. The focus was on making the core offering—highway toll payments—fast, reliable, and user-friendly.

But as competitors began introducing add-on services, the company sought to improve its value proposition. What if it could go beyond toll collection and help customers manage parking once they exited the highway?

Approaching this idea through a linear value chain mindset led to obvious solutions:

- Buying parking lots across the country to ensure availability.
- Partnering with select providers to secure reserved spots for customers.

Both options would pose significant challenges. The first requires massive investments in infrastructure and operational overhead, with no guarantee that these parking facilities would align perfectly with customer needs. The second demands numerous, costly partnerships that could dilute profitability without ensuring comprehensive coverage.

What if the company reframed its role? Instead of entering the parking lot business, it could act as an enabler. By building on its promise of convenience and leveraging its existing customer relationships, it could create a platform connecting drivers with parking lot managers.

Take municipalities as an example. Historically, many have struggled with parking management, relying on outdated systems like park meters or kiosk-sold paper tickets. By integrating these services into the highway payment app, the company could facilitate a seamless experience for travelers—allowing them to pay for parking in cities through the same system they use for highway tolls.

The result? A win-win(-win) scenario:

- **Customers** gain a seamless, convenient solution for managing their journeys.
- **Municipalities** solve long-standing inefficiencies in parking management.
- The **company** generates a new revenue stream from municipalities while enhancing its value proposition.

By onboarding municipalities as new platform clients, the organization transforms its ecosystem into one where new participants help meet customer needs more effectively than the company could on its own.

Extending the Logic: Internal Stakeholders as Customers

The power of onboarding new stakeholders isn't limited to external ecosystems. It can profoundly impact internal workflows by addressing the evolving needs of employees—the "internal customers."

Consider a Human Resources (HR) department tasked with supporting employee welfare services. Employees often face frustrations when accessing wellness programs, childcare, or cultural services, while HR struggles to negotiate competitive rates with a wide range of suppliers. Tackling this challenge through a linear value chain mindset involves striking direct partnerships with a limited number of providers, offering fixed discounts. But such arrangements rarely provide comprehensive solutions and often result in significant costs and inefficiencies for HR.

Now, imagine a platform approach. An internal welfare platform could allow welfare service providers to offer their services directly to employees. With a critical mass of employees using the platform, providers would see a clear market opportunity, offering competitive rates and tailored solutions. These providers are not preselected by the HR department, but compete openly within the platform, guaranteeing continuous quality, innovation, and competitive pricing.

One Italian insurance company took this approach to great success. What began as an internal welfare initiative for its employees expanded into a platform serving external customers, transforming a support function into a revenue-generating business.

From Customer Centricity to Continuous Improvement

In the examples above, customer centricity doesn't lose its relevance—it evolves into something far more dynamic and impactful. By welcoming new customers into the ecosystem, organizations achieve more than simply meeting customer needs. At the same time, by looking at them as customers and not partners and providers, they unlock the potential for continuous improvement, bringing fresh perspectives, complementary capabilities, and novel opportunities for collaboration. These new elements catalyze innovation, enabling businesses to scale their impact while maintaining relevance in a rapidly shifting marketplace.

However, this approach requires a fundamental shift in how traditional organizational boundaries are perceived. First, companies must confront the reality that they are not always the best equipped to address every customer requirement. Even with the most dedicated teams and resources, gaps may remain that others—better positioned or more specialized—can fill with greater precision and efficiency.

Second, organizations need to reconsider how they perceive their relationships with stakeholders. Stakeholders, whether external providers or internal departments, are not merely suppliers of input or recipients of output. Instead, they must be seen as customers in a dynamic and interconnected ecosystem. This shift in perspective transforms stakeholders into co-creators of value, unlocking opportunities for richer interactions and more innovative solutions.

By embracing this broader perspective, organizations can reimagine how they meet evolving customer needs, creating ecosystems that not only adapt to change but thrive on it.

Common Threads: The Platform Power in Action

Three dynamics underscore the transformative power of onboarding new stakeholders:

1. **Suppliers Become Customers**

Onboarding new stakeholders often involves reframing their role. Parking lot managers, municipalities, and travel service providers shift from being peripheral actors to active customers of the platform. By offering them value—such as access to new users or operational efficiencies—platforms create a mutually beneficial relationship.

2. **Cross-Side Network Effects**

Platforms thrive on network effects. As more stakeholders join, the value of the platform increases for all participants. For instance, more parking lot managers mean greater choice for travelers, attracting more users, which in turn draws more parking lot managers. The same logic applies to the HR welfare platform: as more employees engage, providers see greater opportunities and expand their offerings.

3. **Leveraging Idle Assets**

Platforms unlock value by activating resources the company already controls. In the highway toll example, the existing customer base—already onboarded with payment details—becomes an asset to attract municipalities, avoiding the chicken-and-egg paradox. Similarly, in the welfare case, a company can onboard providers like gyms or childcare centers by offering immediate access to its employees. These pre-existing relationships enable platforms to scale quickly with minimal friction.

The Business Problem and its Platform Thinking Hack

All the companies are experiencing a clear problem: Evolving customer demands. Today's consumers expect seamless, personalized experiences, which rigid, product-based business models struggle to deliver.

The hack to solve it is "Solving Customers' Needs Onboarding New Stakeholders".

Organizations often take pride in knowing their customers. But truly meeting all their needs often exceeds the company's core capabilities, capacity, or mission. While it may be possible to develop or acquire the missing competencies, doing so typically adds complexity, drives up costs, and results in subpar outcomes—especially when the need falls outside the company's core focus.

But in a platform-driven world, the real opportunity lies in recognizing the broader ecosystem of stakeholders who can contribute to solving customer needs. By orchestrating these relationships, firms can scale their impact, optimize their resources, and foster continuous improvement.

The message is clear: customer centricity, when paired with Platform Thinking, isn't just about being the best solution provider. It's about enabling the best solutions to emerge through collaboration, innovation, and the onboarding of new stakeholders (and see them as customers).

Three Inspiring Stories: Royal Caribbean, Intuit & Masco

Royal Caribbean: Sailing into Platform Innovation

Royal Caribbean International is a global leader in the cruise industry, known for its innovative approach to providing unforgettable experiences at sea. The company's story reflects decades of excellence in hospitality and a commitment to pushing the boundaries of what a cruise can offer. From state-of-the-art ships to cutting-edge entertainment and dining, Royal Caribbean has continuously raised the bar for the industry. However, in March 2022, the company made a notable leap beyond its traditional offerings, launching a platform called Royal Caribbean Hotels. This move demonstrated the company's willingness to embrace Platform Thinking, not only enhancing its value proposition but also creating new opportunities for growth in a digital-first world.

The Challenge: Simplifying the Journey

As Royal Caribbean expanded its global reach, the complexity of the travel experience for its customers increased. Travelers often needed accommodations before and after their cruises, whether near the departure port or their final destination. While some customers relied on external booking sites, this fragmented approach created inconvenience and increased costs. Despite not being part of its core offering, pre- and post-cruise accommodations remained a critical part of the customer journey. If handled poorly—through inconsistent quality, lack of availability, or support issues—these experiences could negatively impact overall customer satisfaction and damage the brand. Royal Caribbean faced the challenge of addressing this unmet need: simplifying the travel planning process for its cruise passengers while maintaining control over the customer experience.

The Solution: Redefining Travel Through a Platform

Royal Caribbean Hotels emerged as a great solution, leveraging Platform Thinking to address customer needs while onboarding a new stakeholder group—hotels. This platform marked a significant departure from the traditional cruise business model. Rather than merely offering cruises, Royal Caribbean expanded into the broader travel ecosystem, delivering an integrated experience for its customers. By enabling travelers to access exclusive rates and book accommodations tailored to their itineraries, the platform streamlined what was once a disjointed process, ensuring greater convenience and value for its users.

Royal Caribbean Hotels operates as a transactional platform at its core, connecting two distinct sides: travelers, who represent the demand side, and hotels, which form the supply side.

Figure 6.1 – Royal Caribbean's Hotels

The transacted good is hotel accommodations, selected specifically to complement the cruise experience. While travelers were already part of Royal Caribbean's ecosystem, hotels represented new stakeholders. The company worked to onboard these new actors by providing them with access to a platform that offered significant benefits, such as increased visibility and direct access to a ready-made customer base.

The success of Royal Caribbean Hotels lies in its ability to generate bi-directional cross-side network effects. As more hotels join the platform, the value proposition for travelers increases due to greater choice and flexibility. Similarly, the influx of cruise passengers booking accommodations enhances occupancy rates for participating hotels, making the platform increasingly attractive to both sides. This dynamic highlights how the platform not only addresses an immediate customer need but also creates a thriving ecosystem where all parties benefit from participation.

The Alternative Linear Path

If Royal Caribbean had chosen a traditional linear value chain approach, the solution might have involved contracting with a limited number of hotels or managing bookings directly. This would have required significant upfront investment in scouting, infrastructure, and personnel. Specifically, the company would need to negotiate and maintain multiple individual agreements, manage inventory and pricing, handle customer support for lodging issues, and ensure quality standards across a fragmented set of partners. These activities fall far outside Royal Caribbean's core competencies in cruise operations and hospitality at sea, and would risk diverting focus and resources from its main business.

Instead, by adopting a platform strategy, Royal Caribbean minimized initial investments and benefited from quasi-zero marginal costs per additional transaction. Moreover, its strong customer relationships—an idle asset from the linear model—enabled a seamless transition to the platform, something a startup would struggle to replicate.

Takeaways

In the Royal Caribbean Hotels case, the company responded to a growing challenge: "*Evolving customer demands*" for a more seamless, end-to-end travel experience. Looking at the Platform Transformative Framework, Royal Caribbean addressed this need using the Platform Thinking Hack labeled "*Solving Customers' Needs Onboarding New Stakeholders.*" Importantly, the company didn't alter its traditional linear value chain—it still designs, operates, and markets cruise vacations as its core business. Instead, it launched a "*new service*" adjacent to that core, creating a platform that connects travelers with hotel providers. This move expanded the company's value proposition without disrupting its main operations and successfully integrated hotels into the ecosystem as active participants—treated not just as suppliers, but as customers of the platform.

In this case, hotels are not mere suppliers; they are customers of the system, participating in a mutually beneficial exchange. This transformation exemplifies how established firms can harness Platform Thinking to create lasting value and maintain a competitive edge.

Intuit: Turning Expertise into a Scalable Platform Solution

Founded in 1983, Intuit began as a small software company aiming to simplify financial tasks for individuals and small businesses. Initially, the company gained traction with Quicken, a personal finance management tool that resonated with users seeking better control over their financial lives. By the 1990s, Intuit had established itself as a major player in the software industry, diversifying its portfolio to include solutions for small business accounting and tax preparation. This success was driven by a deep understanding of customer needs, continuous innovation, and a user-friendly approach that made financial management accessible to millions. Over time, Intuit's commitment to empowering its customers through intuitive technology cemented its reputation as a trusted leader in the financial software space.

The Challenge: Bridging the Expertise Gap

Financial management and tax filing can be daunting tasks, especially for small business owners and individuals without a background in finance. This challenge was compounded by two growing trends: the increasing complexity of financial situations—driven by the rise of gig work, self-employment, and non-traditional income sources like ridesharing or freelance platforms—and the reality that many users had limited financial literacy. Customers often faced complex decisions and lacked confidence in their ability to file taxes correctly or maintain accurate records.

This gap in expertise created a real risk for Intuit. Users might exit the software experience in search of external help—whether through friends, local consultants, or online forums. Such behavior not only reduced the perceived value and completeness of Intuit's offering, but also opened the door for other service providers to insert themselves into the customer journey. Over time, these alternatives could erode loyalty and evolve into viable competitors. Intuit needed a way to keep users within its ecosystem while empowering them with the expert guidance they increasingly required.

The Solution: Embedding Expertise Through Transactional Platforms

Intuit's solution was both innovative and practical: integrate live assistance from certified tax professionals directly into its TurboTax software. TurboTax Live offered users three key features: real-time help during tax preparation, the option to have tax returns reviewed by a professional, and full-service preparation where an expert handled the filing process. This innovation didn't alter TurboTax's core product functionality; instead, it enhanced customer experience by overlaying expert guidance and marked a significant transformation in how customer care activities were delivered.

Similarly, QuickBooks Live addressed the bookkeeping challenges of small and medium-sized enterprises (SMEs). Users were paired with dedicated bookkeepers who could categorize transactions, reconcile accounts, and ensure accurate financial records. By embedding these services into the existing QuickBooks software, Intuit provided a seamless and accessible way for businesses to manage their finances and significantly improved the customer care process.

Both offerings leveraged a transactional platform model, connecting two distinct user groups: SMEs (or individuals) on the demand side and certified professionals on the supply side.

Figure 6.2 – Intuit's Turbo Tax Live & QuickBooks Live

These professionals—new to Intuit's ecosystem—had to be onboarded through rigorous training and certification processes to ensure consistent service quality. Intuit verifies expert eligibility by requiring professional credentials (like CPA, EA, or attorney status) and proven experience preparing tax returns over multiple seasons.

Despite these requirements, Intuit positions these experts as customers of the platform, offering them a suite of services including flexible remote work, the ability to choose when and how much to work, access to Intuit's tools and resources, ongoing training through Intuit Academy, and opportunities to grow their client base through the platform.

Intuit's existing Professionals and SME user base, a significant idle asset, provided a ready-made demand side, reducing the typical challenges associated with launching a transactional platform.

This platform transacts professional services, delivered virtually through Intuit. This generates bi-directional cross-side network effects: more certified experts meant better availability and response times for users, while a growing user base attracted more professionals eager to join and monetize their expertise.

The Alternative Linear Path

In a traditional linear value chain, Intuit might have opted to create a separate consulting division or partner with external firms to offer expert services. This approach, while viable, would have required significant upfront investments in infrastructure and personnel. While the service is crucial to ensure a delightful customer experience, delivering it directly would have marked a shift from Intuit's core identity as a software company—requiring changes to its organizational DNA to manage service operations at scale.

Moreover, it would lack the flexibility and scalability of a platform model—especially important for services like tax preparation, where demand spikes seasonally and fluctuates year to year. A linear model would tie resources and costs to fixed capacity, while the platform approach allows Intuit to scale expert support up or down dynamically, without carrying unnecessary overhead.

Takeaways

The case of Intuit demonstrates how established companies can address the challenge of "*Evolving customer demands*" by applying the Platform Thinking Hack labeled "*Solving Customers' Needs Onboarding New Stakeholders*." TurboTax Live and QuickBooks Live showcase how Platform Thinking can drive innovation in a "*primary value-chain activity*"—specifically, customer support and after-sales service—without altering the company's core software products. The onboarding of certified experts, while complex, was made feasible by leveraging Intuit's existing customer base, allowing the company to bypass the typical chicken-and-egg paradox associated with launching new platforms.

By framing experts as customers rather than suppliers, Intuit unlocked a scalable, high-value offering that deepened its market presence and strengthened customer loyalty.

Masco and the Human Library Platform: A Case of Transformative Collaboration

Masco Corporation, a leader in home improvement and building products, has long been recognized for its commitment to innovation and corporate responsibility. The company operates a diverse portfolio, ranging from plumbing products to decorative architectural elements, and serves millions of customers globally. However, Masco's leadership also emphasizes an internal commitment to fostering a positive and inclusive organizational culture. In recent years, this focus on inclusion led Masco to an extraordinary partnership with the Human Library, an initiative aimed at breaking down stereotypes through open dialogue.

The Challenge: Cultivating a Culture of Empathy

Like many large organizations, Masco faced challenges in fostering a truly inclusive workplace. With employees spread across geographies and cultural contexts, the company needed an effective way to address unconscious biases and create a deeper understanding among its workforce. The traditional tools available—training sessions, workshops, and policy revisions—offered some value but fell short of delivering a transformative cultural shift. Employees needed a way to connect on a personal and empathetic level, transcending the boundaries of formal HR programs.

The Solution: A Platform to Transform Human Resources

Recognizing the opportunity to address this challenge through innovation, Masco partnered with the Human Library to create a new digital platform. This initiative took a transactional platform approach, connecting two distinct groups: employees (as the demand side) and Human Library volunteers (as the supply side). The platform facilitated meaningful one-on-one or small-group conversations, where employees could "check out" human "books" and engage in discussions on diversity, inclusion, and prejudice.

Figure 6.3 – Masco and the Human Library

The platform represented an innovation in Masco's support value-chain activities, specifically within its human resource management function. It went beyond traditional HR practices by introducing a dynamic, interactive model that fostered direct exchanges. In this model, both employees and Human Library volunteers are treated as customers, each receiving tailored services.

Employees, already part of the company's ecosystem, were provided with access to a diverse range of personal narratives, facilitating meaningful one-on-one or small-group conversations. This service aimed to enhance their understanding of diversity, inclusion, and prejudice, aligning with Masco's commitment to fostering an inclusive workplace culture.

Human Library volunteers, new stakeholders in Masco's ecosystem, received support in preparing for digital interactions, including training and access to a platform that connected them with engaged listeners. This setup allowed volunteers to share their stories in a structured environment, contributing to the platform's goal of challenging stereotypes through open dialogue.

The platform leveraged bi-directional cross-side network effects: as more employees joined, the value of participation for volunteers increased through enriched discussions. Simultaneously, as the diversity of volunteers expanded, employees gained greater opportunities to explore different perspectives. The system's transactional nature ensured that these interactions remained structured, impactful, and scalable.

The Alternative Linear Path

Had Masco relied solely on a traditional, linear HR strategy, the solution might have involved rolling out a global training program on unconscious bias. While such an approach could offer consistency, it would require significant upfront investment in materials, facilitators, and logistics. Another option might have been to identify external providers or partners to deliver live testimonials or awareness sessions across locations. However, both approaches tend to be resource-intensive and often lack the personal engagement and sustained impact necessary to drive real cultural change. Moreover, they scale poorly—addressing more types of bias or reaching more employees would only increase complexity and cost.

In contrast, the platform approach offered distinct advantages. First, it minimized initial investments by building on existing partnerships and leveraging digital tools. Second, it benefited from near-zero marginal costs, as additional interactions between employees and volunteers required no significant additional resources. Finally, Masco's existing relationship with its employees provided a critical idle asset—trust—that a startup attempting to replicate the model would struggle to establish.

Takeaways

The Human Library platform exemplifies the Platform Thinking Hack "*Solving Customers' Needs Onboarding New Stakeholders*." Looking at the Platform Transformative Framework, Masco addressed the challenge of "*Evolving customer demands*" by innovating within a "*support value-chain activity*"—specifically, training and development, with the HR department as the platform orchestrator. The platform allowed the company to meet the growing need for a more empathetic and inclusive workplace culture by connecting employees with external Human Library volunteers. While onboarding these new stakeholders posed challenges, Masco's existing employee base served as a strong foundation, helping the company avoid the typical chicken-and-egg paradox often associated with platform launches.

Crucially, this case demonstrates how volunteers are not suppliers in a linear sense but participants whose presence enhances the platform's value. For them, the platform offers an opportunity to share their stories and connect with listeners who care about the same issues.

Looking Across Evolving Customer Demands Cases

In exploring how companies can face "*Evolving customer demands*" by applying the Platform Thinking Hack "*Solving Customers' Needs Onboarding New Stakeholders*," we've seen three diverse cases that illuminate its potential across various contexts. Royal Caribbean, Intuit, and Masco each took a unique approach, addressing challenges in their operational and stakeholder relationships through Platform Thinking. Despite their differences, these cases share a common goal: Instead of developing internal competencies or securing new providers and partners, they address their internal or external customers' needs by seeking out new customers. This means they develop a transactional platform that can scale quickly, utilize external assets, and focus on achieving a win-win-win outcome for the demand side, supply side, and the company itself.

Each example illustrates the versatility of this approach:

Royal Caribbean Hotel: Royal Caribbean Hotels is a platform that onboards hotels to offer cruise passengers tailored accommodation options. Instead of focusing on securing new providers, it addresses customer needs by attracting new customers and creating a scalable transactional ecosystem. This allows the creation of a new service for the existing customers and enhances convenience for the demand side (travelers), generates value for the supply side (hotels), and drives customer excellence for the company (Royal Caribbean) itself.

Intuit's TurboTax & QuickBooks Live: TurboTax Live and QuickBooks Live connect professionals and small businesses with certified tax and accounting professionals. Instead of focusing on hiring or finding new service providers, they address customer needs by attracting new customers and creating scalable transactional ecosystems. This approach reinforces the post-sales services (primary activity) and enhances convenience for the demand side (individuals and businesses), generates value for the supply side (tax and accounting professionals), and drives growth for the company (Intuit) itself.

Masco's Human Library Platform: Masco's Human Library connects employees with volunteers from the Human Library organization to enhance workplace inclusion. The HR department through the platform innovates a support value-chain activity: training and development. Instead of focusing on expanding partnerships to support HR activities, it serves both employees and volunteers as customers, fulfilling their needs through meaningful interactions. This approach strengthens engagement for the demand side (employees), creates value for the supply side (volunteers), and supports growth for the company.

Considering the whole dataset we gathered through the S&P500 cases, we found 37 initiatives working on this hack. A broader analysis offers deeper insights into how this Platform Thinking Hack is applied across the various integration strategies:

- **21 out of 37 (56.8%)** initiatives introduced new services.
- **11 out of 37 (29.7%)** targeted primary value chain activities, such as operations, marketing, sales, or services.
- **4 out of 37 (10.8%)** focused on support activities, including 4 in R&D/innovation and 1 in procurement.
- **1 out of 37 (2.7%)** is a hybrid platform introducing a new service and serving a primary activity at the same time.

Breaking down these 37 platforms further reveals their structural differences:

- **34 out of 37 (91.9%)** are open platforms, with both sides external to the organization.
- **1 out of 37 (2.7%)** is a closed platform, connecting only internal stakeholders.
- **2 out of 37 (5.4%)** are hybrid platforms, linking internal and external stakeholders.

The numbers reveal a predominant trend: the majority of platforms fall into the category of open platforms, where stakeholders from outside the firm play a critical role. This observation is consistent with prior findings and aligns with market visibility—open platforms often attract greater attention due to their direct customer impact and more frequent public disclosure by firms.

However, just as in the previous chapter, the dataset may not tell the whole story. Companies are far more likely to share details about customer-facing initiatives rather than internal projects, as the latter often lack the same marketing appeal. This bias in reporting inevitably skews our results toward external platforms, even though significant innovation is occurring internally.

Yet there's more to consider. The very nature of this Platform Thinking Hack—"*Solving Customers' Needs Onboarding New Stakeholders*"—inherently drives a focus on external interactions. The hack revolves around identifying new stakeholders to address the needs of existing ones. Naturally, this leads to initiatives that extend beyond organizational boundaries, leaving little room for purely closed platforms. Among the dataset, only one instance stands out: a platform where employees play a new role by leveraging non-professional skills to drive social sustainability, embodying a shift in responsibilities rather than onboarding external stakeholders.

Interestingly, hybrid platforms appear to be underrepresented despite their logical fit for this hack. Hybrid platforms bridge internal needs with external solutions, setting up ecosystems that combine resources from within the firm with capabilities sourced externally. The welfare platform initiative discussed in the opening is a prime example of this approach, where a program initially designed for internal employees successfully evolved into a broader market-facing solution.

The Platform Thinking Hack "*Solving Customers' Needs Onboarding New Stakeholders*" is as versatile as the organizations adopting it. Whether focused on connecting external stakeholders, internal teams, or hybrid ecosystems, this approach fundamentally reshapes how businesses address stakeholder needs and unlock untapped potential.

This adaptability is evident in diverse applications across industries. Royal Caribbean leveraged its platform to simplify and enhance the travel experience for its cruise customers by integrating external hotel partners, creating a seamless pre- and post-cruise journey. Intuit simplified the use of its digital solutions, connecting customers with certified tax experts and improving the accuracy and convenience of financial services. Masco, on the other hand, extended its platform approach to foster inclusion and empathy in the workplace, engaging employees and external volunteers in meaningful interactions that drive cultural transformation.

These examples demonstrate the transformative power of onboarding new stakeholders. Suppliers evolve into partners, customers become collaborators, and traditional transactions are redefined as opportunities for co-creation. By adopting this hack, organizations not only streamline their interactions but also position themselves for long-term growth, innovation, and resilience.

As more companies embrace Platform Thinking, the boundaries between stakeholders blur. Platforms foster ecosystems where value flows freely between participants, creating new opportunities to solve existing challenges and scale innovation across markets and industries.

Best Practices from Transactional Platforms Design

Transactional platforms thrive on facilitating value exchanges among stakeholders, making the insights from the previous chapter highly relevant here. Managers should revisit the foundational strategies for building robust platforms seen in the previous chapter: implementing trust mechanisms, designing value propositions for each stakeholder, focusing on platform health metrics, and starting with a core transaction. These principles remain critical also for ensuring the success of the Platform Thinking Hack "*Solving Customers' Needs Onboarding New Stakeholders.*"

Still, this hack demands a unique focus on customer centricity as a driver for identifying new opportunities. Onboarding new stakeholders to serve existing customers requires additional layers of strategy. Let's explore the key critical success factors that managers must consider to apply this hack effectively.

1. **Addressing the Chicken-and-Egg Paradox**

One of the most common challenges in launching transactional platforms is the chicken-and-egg paradox—which side should you onboard first? While this is a familiar issue for platforms starting from scratch, organizations applying this hack are in a favorable position: one side of the transaction is already onboard (travelers for Royal Caribbean, customers for Intuit, and employees for Masco). The focus now shifts to identifying and onboarding the complementary stakeholders who can fulfill unmet needs.

Even so, onboarding the new side isn't without its challenges. A classic tactic to address the chicken-and-egg paradox is to incentivize one side to join by demonstrating clear benefits derived from the other side's presence. When BlaBlaCar launched, it faced the classic chicken-and-egg paradox: drivers wouldn't join without passengers, and passengers wouldn't join without drivers. To solve this, BlaBlaCar turned to a creative solution during a nationwide public transportation strike in France. They seized the opportunity to buy advertisements in newspapers, targeting stranded passengers and encouraging drivers to offer rides. This clever tactic not only generated awareness but also attracted both sides of the marketplace simultaneously.

This type of creativity is equally valuable when onboarding just one side of a platform. Managers should identify unique, context-specific opportunities to attract new stakeholders, ensuring that their participation feels both valuable and low-risk. Such approaches can spark the initial momentum needed to build a thriving ecosystem.

2. **Treating New Stakeholders as Customers**

One of the most transformative aspects of this Platform Thinking Hack lies in viewing newly onboarded stakeholders as customers, and not as providers. This mindset shift ensures that you don't simply treat them as passive participants but actively design your platform to create value for them.

Take Uber as an example. When the company launched Uber Eats, it wasn't just about expanding its offering to customers. Uber treated restaurants—the new stakeholders—as critical customers of the platform. Beyond providing access to a growing pool of app users, Uber offered restaurants valuable services like delivery logistics and transaction insights. These tools empowered restaurants to optimize their menus and streamline operations, creating a meaningful incentive to join and remain engaged with the platform.

For managers, this means rethinking the onboarding process for new stakeholders. It's not enough to simply connect them to existing users—you must also provide tools, services, or insights that enable them to derive independent value from the platform. In a nutshell: it means treating them as new customers. This ensures sustained engagement and creates a virtuous cycle of transactions that benefits all parties involved.

3. **Ensuring Coherence with the Value Proposition**

While customer centricity drives this hack, coherence with your organization's overarching value proposition is essential. Just because a customer need exists doesn't mean your organization is the right one to address it. Success comes from identifying opportunities that align with your mission and values and reinforce your core strengths.

Telepass, the Italian company that facilitates the payment of highway tolls, for instance, mirrors the example discussed earlier about highway payment companies. Its core promise is to provide customers with a seamless, comfortable experience while moving around. Expanding into grocery delivery, for example, would stretch this promise too far and dilute its identity. Instead, Telepass focuses on initiatives that align with its mission, such as giving customers access to parking lots (by onboarding municipalities) or ski passes (by onboarding ski resorts).

Managers should ask themselves: Does onboarding this new stakeholder align with our purpose and add value to the existing ecosystem? Coherence strengthens trust and ensures that the platform's evolution remains meaningful and credible to all participants.

Key Questions to Evaluate the Hack's Fit

For managers considering whether this Platform Thinking Hack can work in their context, a series of critical questions can provide clarity:

1. Do your (internal or external) customers have emerging needs coherent with your value proposition that you can't directly solve?
2. Is answering that specific need far from the strategy and the DNA of your company?

3. Can you spot someone who can address those needs better than you? Can you treat them as customers?

If the answers are yes, no, yes, the final question is this: Can you imagine reinventing your role as an orchestrator rather than a gatekeeper? Could your organization create a platform to connect these new stakeholders to existing ones, enabling value creation for all parties?

As we've seen, the path to success lies in balancing customer-centricity with strategic coherence, ensuring that every new stakeholder brings value to the ecosystem while receiving value in return. The organizations that master this approach will not only enhance their existing offerings but also position themselves at the forefront of platform-driven innovation.

6

Innovation Bottlenecks

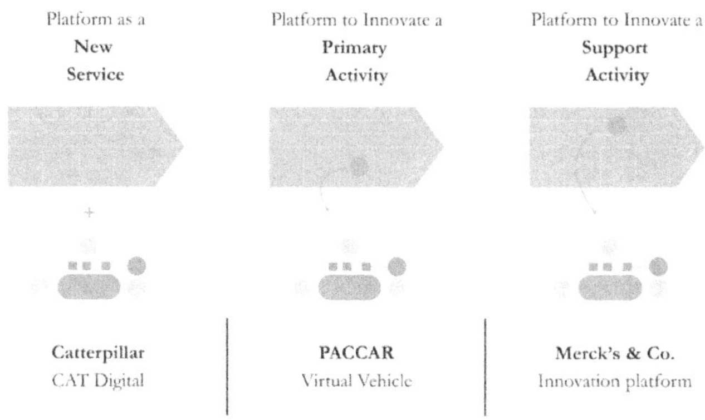

The power of Open Innovation at large

> "*If I have seen further, it is by standing on the shoulders of giants.*"
> — Isaac Newton

This timeless quote by Isaac Newton underscores the essence of human progress: building on the contributions and capabilities of others. Newton's insight was not merely about science; it reflects a broader truth about innovation and collaboration. Today, his words find resonance in modern business strategies, particularly in the context of platforms and open innovation.

This idea connects to another provocative statement: "*No matter who you are, most of the smartest people work for someone else.*" Spoken by Bill Joy, co-founder of Sun Microsystems, this sentiment sparked a revolution in how companies approach innovation. Joy's statement wasn't about undermining internal talent but acknowledging the vast potential of tapping into external expertise. One of the clearest examples of this philosophy in action is Procter & Gamble's groundbreaking Connect + Develop initiative. Recognizing that its internal R&D alone couldn't sustain its innovation pipeline, P&G opened its doors to external collaborators, seeking ideas and solutions from partners worldwide. This shift exemplifies the principles of open innovation, a concept popularized by Henry Chesbrough, which argues that organizations can and should leverage external knowledge to complement their internal capabilities.

However, embracing openness is easier said than done. Innovation is inherently a high-stakes area for businesses—one that requires careful decision-making. Firms often hesitate to cede control over innovation processes, fearing risks to quality, integration, or intellectual property. Yet, as the examples in this chapter will illustrate, when done right, opening innovation silos through platforms can yield transformative results.

From Gatekeeper to Platform Enabler: A Video Game Company's Evolution

Imagine a video game company that recently launched a groundbreaking virtual reality (VR) device. The company achieved viral success thanks to a quirky, beloved game starring a cheerful snowman, capturing the hearts of millions on social media. Sales of the VR device skyrocketed, fueled by the snowman game's popularity. But the company now faces a daunting question: how can it sustain and scale this success?

The obvious answer is to release more games. A traditional, linear approach would involve assembling the in-house creative team, brainstorming new characters and storylines, and launching additional titles. This approach could certainly yield results. However, the risks are substantial: high development costs, long timelines, and uncertain reception in a competitive market. For a firm looking to scale rapidly, relying solely on internal resources may limit its potential.

Now imagine an alternative. Instead of trying to develop every game in-house, the company adopts a platform approach. It opens its VR device to third-party developers by providing a Software Development Kit (SDK) and clear guidelines to ensure compatibility. Developers from around the world can now create their own games for the device, introducing new characters, stories, and experiences. The company retains control over a few key in-house titles, maintaining its creative identity, but shifts its focus to building an ecosystem.

This shift transforms the business model. Instead of bearing the full cost and risk of game development, the company offers to external customers a revenue-sharing model: they develop the games, they get paid, and they pay a fee to the company for building their offering on top of the VR device. This arrangement benefits everyone involved: developers gain access to a ready market of device users, players enjoy a constantly expanding library of games, and the company scales its offering without scaling its cost structure. Over time, the VR device becomes more valuable, not because of the snowman game alone but because of the ecosystem of diverse games it supports.

Rethinking Internal Processes: The Power of GenAI

Consider another scenario, this time inside the efficiency department of a multinational corporation. The department's mandate is to drive process improvement across the organization, and the emergence of Generative AI (GenAI) presents an exciting opportunity. The team partners with a tech provider to integrate AI into everyday workflows, envisioning applications such as smart project scoping and intelligent document searches.

A linear approach might involve the department identifying a few high-priority use cases, customizing the AI tools to address them, and rolling out the solutions. While feasible, this approach presents familiar challenges: high development costs, slow implementation, and limited scalability. Worse, the department may face resistance from internal teams who perceive the project as an imposed burden rather than a valuable resource.

Now consider a platform alternative. Instead of dictating use cases, the efficiency department creates a GenAI-based platform where employees across the organization can design their own tools.

Using low-code interfaces and pre-trained AI models, teams can build customized GPTs tailored to their specific needs, such as automating routine tasks or generating insights from historical data. The platform serves as an enabler, turning employees into innovators and fostering a culture of collaboration.

This approach amplifies the department's impact. By enabling and decentralizing innovation, the organization benefits from the collective creativity of its workforce. At the same time, the platform provides real-time feedback loops, enabling the department to refine its offerings based on user input. The result is not only greater efficiency but also a stronger sense of ownership and engagement among employees.

The power of Open Innovation through Complementors

In previous chapters, we explored how Platform Thinking can enhance efficiency, effectiveness, and stakeholder engagement. This chapter extends those principles into the realm of innovation. Specifically, it examines how organizations can "*complement their products through others' capabilities*" by creating platforms that externalize some innovation activities.

This Platform Thinking Hack offers two critical benefits. The first is leveraging external visions and competencies. Platforms enable organizations to access fresh perspectives and ideas from external collaborators, whether they are independent developers, academic researchers, or internal workforces.

The second is empowering customers through ecosystems. Platforms foster interactive ecosystems where users, developers, and other contributors co-create value. For instance, the VR device ecosystem benefits both players and developers, while the GenAI platform transforms employees into empowered innovators.

As with all platform strategies, success hinges on thoughtful execution. Organizations must identify stakeholders who can contribute to innovation and ensure seamless integration between their solutions and the core product. This often requires developing tools like SDKs or APIs to facilitate collaboration.

Common Threads: The Platform Power in Action

Solving *Innovation Bottlenecks* by leveraging the Platform Thinking Hack: *Complementing my product through others' capabilities* reveals three key dynamics that drive its transformative potential across different contexts. These elements highlight why Platform Thinking redefines innovation processes and relationships.

1. **Innovators Become Customers**

Platform Thinking repositions external developers or internal (developer) teams as customers of the platform. Instead of merely contributing, these innovators derive direct value from engaging with the ecosystem, whether through tools like SDKs, APIs, or other resources that enable their work. This shift ensures mutual benefit: innovators see the platform as an enabler, while the organization scales its innovation capacity through their contributions.

2. **Cross-Side Network Effects**

The value of the platform grows exponentially through interactions between different groups of stakeholders. As external contributors or internal teams produce more solutions, the ecosystem becomes increasingly valuable for all participants. These network effects are the engine for scale and engagement, driving innovation and adoption simultaneously.

3. **Leveraging Idle Assets**

Platforms unlock underutilized resources—whether physical, like devices, or intangible, like internal expertise. By activating these idle assets through collaboration, organizations transform fixed investments into scalable enablers of innovation. This ensures assets generate exponential value rather than being confined to their original purposes.

The Business Problem and its Platform Thinking Hack

The Problem to be solved is "*Innovation Bottlenecks*": traditional R&D structures limit the speed and scalability of innovation, making it difficult to keep pace with fast-moving competitors. Established organizations need to innovate in both new and existing products and processes. However, the best innovation often emerges when external contributors or internal stakeholders—who are not directly in charge of the process—build upon a foundation provided by the company, complementing and enhancing it rather than starting from scratch.

The hack to solve it is "*Complementing my product through others' capabilities*". Platform Thinking breaks innovation silos by leveraging the capabilities of others to scale impact, foster collaboration, and unlock untapped potential.

Why is Platform Thinking necessary? The answer lies in the limitations of traditional innovation models. Established organizations need to innovate not only in new products but also in existing ones. However, the best innovator isn't always the company itself—it may be an external partner or even an internal stakeholder from a different department. Platform Thinking offers a structured approach to breaking down innovation silos and creating a broader impact.

Complementing your product through others' capabilities isn't just a hack—it's a transformative strategy.

Three Inspiring Stories: Cat, Paccar & Merck

Caterpillar: From Heavy Machinery to High-Tech Ecosystem

Founded in 1925, Caterpillar Inc. has long been synonymous with industrial strength and engineering precision. Its iconic yellow machines are fixtures on construction sites and mining operations worldwide, trusted by professionals to perform the toughest jobs under the harshest conditions. Beyond their durability, Caterpillar machines have become a cultural symbol of resilience and capability, featured in films, documentaries, and even children's toys. Their unmistakable design, marked by bold yellow and black branding, evokes a sense of reliability and power that resonates globally. Over the decades, Caterpillar earned its reputation through a linear value chain—designing, manufacturing, and distributing heavy equipment to businesses needing reliable tools for their projects. People admire Caterpillar not just for its products but for the brand's unwavering commitment to innovation and its ability to adapt to changing industrial demands, making it a beloved name across generations of workers and industry leaders.

The Challenge: Customization Meets Complexity

Beyond durable machinery, customers began seeking integrated solutions that could enhance productivity, optimize workflows, and reduce downtime. Equipment monitoring, predictive maintenance, and enhanced fleet management were becoming essential. However, developing bespoke solutions for every customer was not scalable. The complexity of such a task threatened to overwhelm Caterpillar's operations and dilute its focus. Moreover, digital transformation was reshaping customer expectations. Competitors were also exploring connected technologies, putting pressure on Caterpillar to evolve rapidly while maintaining its core strengths.

The Solution: Building a Digital Ecosystem

To address this challenge, Caterpillar turned to Platform Thinking, creating Cat Digital, a division dedicated to blending technology with heavy equipment. At the heart of this transformation was the Cat Digital Marketplace, an online hub enabling external developers to complement Caterpillar's offerings. Through APIs provided on the marketplace, developers could build tailored software solutions, ranging from fleet optimization tools to niche applications addressing unique industry needs.

One example of this approach is a fleet management platform developed in collaboration with partners. This platform offers customers real-time insights into their equipment—tracking location, monitoring health, and optimizing utilization. Another example is an app designed to streamline maintenance scheduling and parts ordering, ensuring machines stay operational longer. These tools, while leveraging the company's machinery, showcase the innovation potential unlocked by empowering external developers to contribute to the ecosystem.

The platform itself is an innovation platform, designed to foster creativity and growth by connecting two distinct groups: Caterpillar's established customer base on the demand side and external Developers on the complementor side.

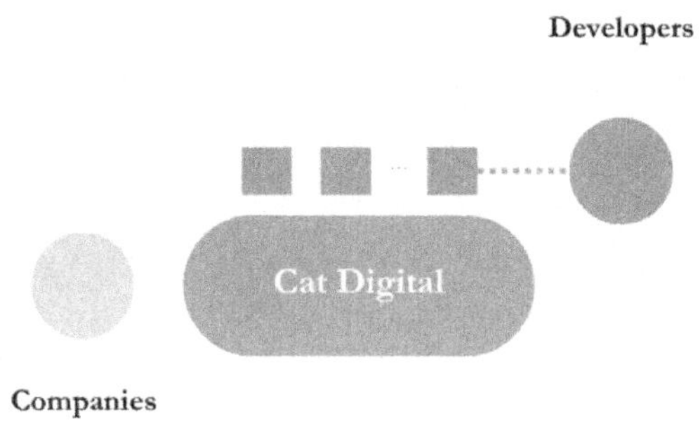

Figure 7.1 – Caterpillar's Cat Digital

Developers, many of whom were new to Caterpillar's ecosystem, became customers of the Cat Digital Marketplace, accessing APIs and datasets to create high-value applications. This dynamic highlights an important shift—developers are no longer seen as mere providers but as co-creators in Caterpillar's digital ecosystem.

To onboard these new stakeholders, Caterpillar simplified the process of accessing tools by emphasizing technical integration through APIs. These APIs allowed developers to seamlessly connect with the company's systems, enabling the creation of tailored solutions while ensuring compatibility with Caterpillar's existing infrastructure. As a result, strong cross-side network effects emerged: the more developers joined the platform, the richer the pool of solutions for Caterpillar's customers. Conversely, the growing customer base incentivized more developers to participate, creating a virtuous cycle of growth.

The Alternative Linear Path

Had Caterpillar chosen to address these challenges through a traditional value chain approach, it would have faced significant hurdles. For instance, the company would have needed to build a specialized digital solution for each customer segment, requiring massive investments in R&D and IT infrastructure. This is not Caterpillar's core business, and it would never be as effective as companies focused solely on this kind of digital development. This linear model would not only have been costly but also slow, risking customer dissatisfaction and allowing competitors to seize the advantage.

By leveraging Platform Thinking instead, Caterpillar minimized its initial investment and reaped the benefits of quasi-zero marginal costs. Developers absorbed much of the innovation burden, while Caterpillar focused on enabling and scaling the ecosystem. Moreover, by engaging external complementors who compete with one another, Caterpillar benefits from a steady flow of increasingly customized and specialized solutions—something that internal teams alone could not easily deliver. Additionally, Caterpillar's established relationships with its customers ensured trust in third-party solutions—a significant edge over a hypothetical startup entering the same space. Most importantly, Caterpillar's physical assets—the machines themselves—remained the foundation of its business. The digital solutions developed by others enhanced their value, reinforcing Caterpillar's market leadership.

Takeaways

The case of Cat Digital exemplifies the Platform Thinking Hack "*Complementing my product through others' capabilities.*" Looking at the Platform Transformative Framework, Caterpillar addressed the problem of "*Innovation Bottlenecks*" by launching a "*new service*" adjacent to its traditional linear value chain. Rather than attempting to develop every digital solution in-house, the company created an innovation platform that empowered external developers to build tailored applications on top of its core machinery. The success of this approach hinged on two key assets: a robust base product—

Caterpillar's equipment—and a digital marketplace that delivered clear value to both developers and customers.

While developers captured part of the value created, Caterpillar benefited immensely. Enhanced digital solutions improved customer satisfaction, solidifying Caterpillar's reputation as an industry leader. Moreover, the integration of cutting-edge technology with its machinery made its brand more relevant and admired in a rapidly digitizing world. The result? A virtuous cycle where every participant—Caterpillar, developers, and customers—gained value, highlighting the transformative potential of Platform Thinking.

The PACCAR Story: Driving Innovation Through Virtual Vehicle

PACCAR, the globally recognized manufacturer of Kenworth, Peterbilt, and DAF trucks, has been a cornerstone of the trucking industry since its founding in 1905 in Seattle, Washington. Originally known as the Pacific Car and Foundry Company, PACCAR began its journey by producing railway and logging equipment before transitioning into truck manufacturing. The company earned a stellar reputation for engineering excellence, with its trucks celebrated for their durability, performance, and innovation. Over the decades, PACCAR has consistently set benchmarks in the heavy-duty vehicle market, becoming a trusted partner for fleet managers worldwide. Its iconic brands, Kenworth and Peterbilt, are synonymous with quality and reliability, making PACCAR a name that inspires confidence and loyalty in the transportation sector. These achievements underscore PACCAR's legacy as a pioneer in heavy-duty trucking, an industry leader firmly rooted in its commitment to innovation and customer satisfaction.

The Challenge: Meeting a Diverse Array of Needs

Fleet managers increasingly demanded tailored digital ecosystems to manage their operations with greater precision, tracking vehicle health, optimizing routes, and addressing an ever-growing list of unique business needs. The work of fleet management was becoming more personalized, as companies sought solutions that could adapt to specific operational demands and environments. This shift highlighted the need for PACCAR to provide flexible and innovative tools that could keep up with this level of customization. Yet, the diversity of use cases posed a formidable challenge. Creating bespoke solutions for every customer would have required immense resources and a highly inefficient approach. PACCAR realized that addressing this demand for personalized systems would require a scalable and adaptable strategy, one that could complement its core strength of manufacturing world-class trucks.

The Solution: Building a Digital Ecosystem

To address this challenge, PACCAR partnered with Platform Science to create Virtual Vehicle, an open OEM platform that enhances the fleet management experience. This platform integrates factory-installed telematics hardware directly into its trucks, providing a seamless connection between vehicles and fleet managers. What sets Virtual Vehicle apart is its ability to include third-party developers, transforming the ecosystem into a vibrant hub for innovation.

This three-sided platform brings together fleet managers, truck drivers, and developers as distinct but interdependent customers. This hybrid platform enabled a dual transformation by integrating two key dynamics. First, the trucks became valuable data sources, turning drivers into active producers of information. Importantly, this data is generated as a byproduct of their core activity—driving—not as a dedicated data production task. These data points were aggregated and analyzed to deliver services specifically designed for fleet managers, establishing an orthogonal platform where one side—truck drivers—contributed the data needed to benefit the other side—fleet managers. At the same time, the platform delivers value back to drivers through services such as duty-aware application interfaces, integrated ELD tools, truck-specific navigation, and safety features like fatigue alerts—enhancing compliance, focus, and operational ease.

Second, the platform operated as an innovation hub by inviting external developers to customize and tailor solutions that maximized the value of this data. These developers, as the third customer group, both serve fleet managers by addressing their operational needs and deliver services to drivers to enable data generation—creating a virtuous loop of real-time, data-fueled innovation

As PACCAR aptly stated, "*The platform allows fleets to create a software experience tailored to individual business needs through a growing pipeline of developer-created innovations.*"

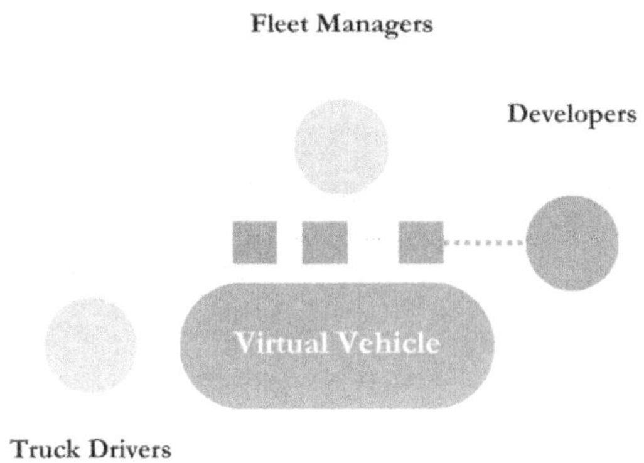

Figure 7.2 – PACCAR's Virtual Vehicle

Virtual Vehicle exemplifies the power of a hybrid platform. It combines two platform models in one: an innovation platform and an orthogonal "*Client-as-a-Source*" (CAAS) platform. As an innovation platform, it enables third-party developers to build new software solutions for fleet managers by giving them access to tools, data, and APIs. At the same time, it functions as an orthogonal CAAS platform, where truck drivers generate valuable data as a byproduct of driving—data that powers the solutions built for fleet managers. By combining the trucks' role as data sources with an open environment for external innovation, PACCAR created a dynamic ecosystem. Fleet managers and drivers, already central to PACCAR's operations, reaped the benefits of tailored solutions, while third-party developers were empowered to bring their innovations to market. These developers were not merely suppliers but valued participants in the ecosystem, incentivized to contribute and expand the platform's offerings. This approach fostered a virtuous cycle of innovation, where each new application increased the platform's appeal and usability.

The Alternative Linear Path

Had PACCAR adhered to a traditional linear approach, the challenges would have been formidable. Meeting fleet managers' growing demands for tailored digital ecosystems would have required PACCAR to take on entirely new responsibilities—analyzing operational workflows, defining technical requirements for different fleet profiles, and delivering customized digital services. While not impossible, this would have gone far beyond PACCAR's core mission and expertise as a truck designer and manufacturer.

Developing, maintaining, and updating a portfolio of fleet management solutions internally would have required building an entirely new business unit focused on software and service delivery—something fundamentally different from PACCAR's long-standing industrial capabilities. The result likely would have been a narrower set of offerings, less responsive to the full range of fleet needs, and slower in terms of innovation. Without external developers contributing their expertise and competing to create the best possible tools, the ecosystem would have lacked the richness, variety, and precision that today's Virtual Vehicle platform enables.

Moreover, PACCAR's established relationships with fleet managers and the trust associated with its trucks provided a competitive advantage that a startup could not easily replicate. The trucks, long a symbol of PACCAR's excellence, became the foundation for a broader digital ecosystem that strengthened customer loyalty and expanded the company's value proposition.

Takeaways

The Virtual Vehicle case underscores the transformative potential of the Platform Thinking Hack "*Complementing my product through others' capabilities.*" Looking at the Platform Transformative Framework, PACCAR addressed the problem of "*Innovation Bottlenecks*" by innovating within a "*primary value-chain activity*"—service management—an area where the company was already offering digital fleet management solutions as a complement to its core truck manufacturing business. By leveraging its trucks as a foundation and empowering external developers to create tailored solutions, PACCAR not only enhanced its value proposition but also established a thriving ecosystem. While developers shared in the value creation, PACCAR's primary business of selling trucks remained the biggest beneficiary. The innovative solutions developed through the platform made PACCAR's trucks indispensable to fleet managers, reinforcing loyalty and solidifying its market position

This case illustrates how platforms can transform primary value-chain activities, demonstrating that even established companies can thrive by embracing collaboration and external capabilities. PACCAR's ability to complement its core offering with cutting-edge digital solutions exemplifies the immense potential of Platform Thinking in an evolving industry.

Merck: Harnessing Collaboration to Accelerate Drug Discovery

Merck & Co., Inc., founded in 1891, is one of the world's leading pharmaceutical companies, recognized for its groundbreaking contributions to healthcare. Headquartered in New Jersey, USA, the company has a storied history of innovation, from the development of the first measles vaccine to pioneering treatments for cancer, diabetes, and infectious diseases. Merck is renowned not only for its life-saving drugs but also for its commitment to scientific research and its role in shaping modern medicine. Over the decades, its major successes, such as the introduction of antibiotics like streptomycin and vaccines for diseases like HPV, have cemented its reputation as a global healthcare leader. Today, Merck continues to push the boundaries of medical science, addressing some of the most challenging health issues of our time.

The Challenge: Scaling Innovation Beyond Internal Capabilities

Merck's R&D teams faced a dual challenge: the pressing need to innovate under the immense time pressure characteristic of the pharmaceutical industry, and the realization that building the advanced tools required internally wasn't feasible. Drug discovery involves massive investments and lengthy development and approval cycles, making efficiency crucial. While new technologies like cheminformatics, machine learning, and sophisticated analytics hold transformative potential, their specificity and complexity make it impossible for any single company to develop them all. To overcome this, Merck needed a way to let other stakeholders incorporate their specialized solutions into a collaborative platform, while ensuring a robust ecosystem for internal innovation.

The Solution: An Innovation Platform for Drug Discovery

Merck's solution was its cloud-based research platform—an innovation platform designed to accelerate drug discovery by bridging internal expertise with external innovation. On one side, the platform serves Merck's own researchers and R&D teams. These internal users gain access to a unified digital environment where they can aggregate, access, and analyze vast volumes of scientific data. The platform streamlines workflows and enables integration with advanced tools such as cheminformatics applications for molecular modeling or machine learning models capable of processing unstructured biomedical data. This improves the speed and quality of Merck's internal research without requiring every tool to be developed in-house.

On the other side, the platform welcomes third-party developers—from specialized startups to technology providers—who contribute innovative tools and applications. These developers are equipped with open APIs and integration pathways that allow them to build directly onto Merck's infrastructure. In return, they gain access to a ready market of expert users and the opportunity to co-create high-value solutions that directly address the complex challenges of pharmaceutical research.

In this model, both sides are treated as customers. Merck's researchers benefit from a growing library of tailored solutions, while developers are supported with onboarding resources and exposed to a live, high-value user base. The more developers join, the richer the ecosystem becomes for internal users. At the same time, as more researchers rely on the platform, it becomes increasingly attractive for developers to contribute—creating a strong bidirectional network effect that fuels continuous innovation.

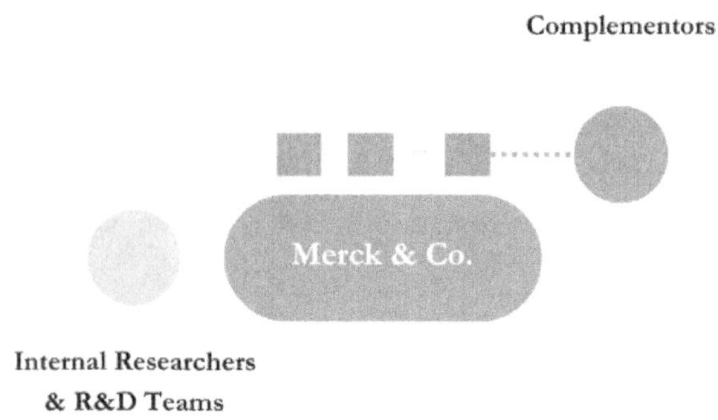

Figure 7.3 – Merck & Co.'s innovation Platform

For instance, one developer provides cheminformatics tools for molecular analysis, while another employs deep learning to process unstructured biomedical data. These complementors are new actors within Merck's ecosystem, transitioning from external providers to co-creators and even customers of the platform. Merck ensured seamless onboarding for these new stakeholders by offering robust developer support and clear pathways for integrating their tools into the platform. This collaborative model generates bidirectional cross-side network effects. As more developers join, they enrich the ecosystem with innovative tools, increasing its value for internal teams. In turn, the platform's growing user base attracts more developers, creating a virtuous cycle of collaboration and innovation.

The Alternative Linear Path

Had Merck taken a linear value chain approach, it would have faced the daunting task of building all these capabilities in-house—a time-consuming and costly endeavor. While partnering with external providers or contracting specialized vendors could have offered some relief, this model posed its own serious challenges. Managing a growing network of external tools through traditional partnerships would have introduced high coordination costs, increased contractual complexity, and limited Merck's ability to integrate diverse solutions into a unified research workflow.

Moreover, relying on discrete vendors would have forced Merck to prioritize only a narrow set of technologies, limiting experimentation and agility. Each new integration would require bespoke arrangements, technical alignment, and governance oversight, making the overall system slower, costlier, and harder to evolve. This increased the risk of missing out on breakthrough innovations—whether due to limited capacity to onboard new tools or the inability to see and evaluate emerging technologies quickly.

In contrast, the platform model enabled a flexible, scalable ecosystem. Developers could integrate rapidly using open APIs, and Merck could tap into a wide array of cutting-edge tools without absorbing the full cost or operational risk. The result was not only greater efficiency but a richer, more dynamic pipeline of innovation—one that ensured the next big idea wasn't left on the outside.

Takeaways

Merck's case exemplifies the Platform Thinking Hack "*Complementing my product through others' capabilities.*" Looking at the Platform Transformative Framework, Merck addressed the problem of "*Innovation Bottlenecks*" by introducing an innovation within a "*support value-chain activity*"—specifically, research and development (R&D). By offering a foundational collaboration platform and a ready market of internal researchers, Merck created a fertile ground for external contributors to thrive.

Crucially, this platform strategy unlocked significant idle assets within Merck's ecosystem. The company's extensive network of internal researchers, vast repositories of scientific knowledge, and state-of-the-art laboratory equipment were leveraged more effectively. These resources, previously underutilized, became central to a dynamic, collaborative R&D environment.

While developers capture part of the value, the primary beneficiary remains Merck, whose improved R&D performance drives its core business of developing and selling life-saving drugs.

This success highlights the potential of innovation platforms to enhance support functions like research and development, enabling organizations to meet complex challenges with greater agility and creativity.

Looking Across Innovation Bottlenecks Cases

In exploring how companies can solve the "*Innovation Bottlenecks*" business problem by applying the Platform Thinking Hack: "*Complementing my product through others' capabilities*", we analyzed three distinct cases—Caterpillar, PACCAR, and Merck—that showcase how established organizations can amplify their value propositions by leveraging external capabilities. Each case highlights the transformative power of Platform Thinking, demonstrating how businesses can create ecosystems where third-party contributors play a vital role in enhancing the core offering.

Though they operate in diverse industries, these cases share a common thread: each company recognized that its growth potential could be significantly expanded by opening its ecosystem to external innovators. This realization enabled them to tap into complementary strengths, fostering collaboration with developers, partners, and specialized contributors who added new layers of value to their foundational products and services.

Each example illustrates the versatility of this hack:

Caterpillar's Cat Digital Marketplace: Caterpillar's Cat Digital exemplifies the transformative power of Platform Thinking, complementing its core heavy machinery business with a dynamic innovation platform. Through the Cat Digital Marketplace, Caterpillar enabled external developers to act as complementors, creating tailored new services that enhance the value of its equipment. Leveraging its trusted brand and extensive machinery base, the platform fosters cross-side network effects—more developers mean richer applications for customers—delivering scalable value without altering Caterpillar's core operations. Everybody wins: developers expanded their reach through new business opportunities, customers benefited from customized digital tools, and Caterpillar unlocked new growth by enhancing its existing offerings.

Paccar's Virtual Vehicle: PACCAR's Virtual Vehicle demonstrates the transformative potential of Platform Thinking, extending its core truck manufacturing business through a hybrid platform that transforms existing fleets and trucks from physical idle assets into data-driven value generators. By innovating a "primary value-chain activity"—services to fleet managers that complement the main product offering (trucks)—PACCAR enabled third-party developers to act as complementors, creating customized fleet management solutions that enhance the value of its trucks. Leveraging its trusted brands and built-in telematics, the platform fosters cross-side network effects—more developers mean more tailored applications for fleet managers—delivering scalable value without disrupting PACCAR's core operations. This created a win-win-win dynamic: developers accessed new markets, fleet managers benefited from personalized digital tools, and PACCAR strengthened customer loyalty while expanding its value proposition.

Merck's Merck & Co: Merck's Innovation Platform demonstrates the potential of Platform Thinking, turning its vast research infrastructure from physical idle assets into a collaborative ecosystem for accelerated drug discovery. By innovating a "support value-chain activity"—R&D—Merck enabled external contributors to act as complementors, creating specialized tools and applications that enhance the efficiency of its internal research teams. Leveraging its extensive data resources and scientific expertise, the platform fosters cross-side network effects—more developers mean richer solutions for researchers—delivering scalable value without disrupting Merck's core pharmaceutical operations. This created a win-win-win dynamic: developers gain new opportunities within Merck's ecosystem, researchers benefited from cutting-edge tools, and Merck accelerated innovation while optimizing its R&D capabilities.

These cases demonstrate how this Platform Thinking Hack adapts to different interactions within the value chain. Caterpillar and Paccar target creating more value for end customers by welcoming developers. In contrast, Merck works internally on the R&D process.

Considering the entire dataset we gathered from the S&P 500 cases, we identified 24 platforms. A broader analysis of these cases provides deeper insights into how this Platform Thinking Hack is applied across industries:

- **16 out of 24 (66.7%)** initiatives introduced new services.
- **5 out of 24 (20.8%)** targeted primary value chain activities.
- **1 out of 24 (4.2%)** focused on support activities.
- **2 out of 24 (8.3%)** are a hybrid platform introducing a new service and serving a primary or support activity at the same time.

Breaking down these 24 platforms further reveals their structural differences:

- **23 out of 24 (95.38%)** are open platforms, with both sides external to the organization.
- **1 out of 24 (4.2%)** is a closed platform, connecting only internal stakeholders.
- **0 out of 24 (0%)** are hybrid platforms, linking internal and external stakeholders.

These figures underscore a dominant focus on external platforms, which are often more visible in the market. However, the data doesn't tell the whole story.

It is important to highlight how this hack has historically been linked with certain fields. Perhaps the most well-known application of this hack lies in the seamless integration of hardware and software. Game consoles like the Xbox, PlayStation, and Nintendo Switch exemplify how platforms can catalyze innovation by empowering external developers. These companies focus on producing high-quality hardware and a few in-house titles, but the true magic lies in their ability to attract third-party developers.

Through development kits, APIs, and revenue-sharing agreements, they transform their consoles into vibrant ecosystems brimming with diverse gaming experiences.

This hack extends beyond gaming. Operating systems for computers and smartphones—such as Windows, macOS, Android, and iOS—operate on the same principle. By enabling third-party developers to create applications that integrate with the core platform, these operating systems increase their value exponentially. Each new app enriches the ecosystem, drawing in more users, which in turn attracts even more developers.

Even though this hack is considered almost a standard in these fields, our results show great potentialities also in other, less explored, industries.

Indeed, the same logic applies to collaborative platforms, which have transformed workplace productivity by encouraging integration with third-party tools. Take Microsoft Teams and Zoom, for example. These platforms started as communication tools, but their integration capabilities have made them indispensable hubs for workplace collaboration. By enabling tools like Miro, Trello, and Salesforce to plug directly into their ecosystems, they've shifted from being standalone products to central nodes in an interconnected web of workplace solutions.

This approach allows users to tailor their experiences by combining the core functionalities of the platform with specialized tools that address unique needs. The approach fosters efficiency and effectiveness by turning the platform into a one-stop shop for a variety of use cases, reducing friction and increasing engagement.

The open-source movement represents another powerful application of this approach, emphasizing community-driven innovation. In open-source platforms, the "product" often starts as a foundational set of tools or code that anyone can personalize and build upon. Popular examples like Linux and Python have grown into global ecosystems where contributions from thousands of developers create value far beyond the original offering.

But the impact of this model isn't limited to the software industry. Consider scientific research or education platforms, where knowledge is shared and expanded collaboratively. The same principles apply: individuals contribute enhancements or innovations, which are then shared with the broader community. This creates a collective knowledge base that grows organically, much like a platform ecosystem.

Best Practices from Innovation Platform Design

Innovation platforms, at their core, embody the idea of building on top of existing foundations to enable creativity, collaboration, and value creation. As Isaac Newton's famous quote reminded us, great progress is achieved by "standing on the shoulders of giants." This principle is central to how innovation platforms operate—they provide a solid base (often in the form of a product, software, or system) upon which external stakeholders, or complementors, can innovate. These complementors expand the ecosystem by contributing their capabilities, ultimately enriching the platform for all participants.

A hallmark example of an innovation platform is Microsoft's decision in the 1980s to open its operating system to third-party developers. By providing Software Development Kits (SDKs), Microsoft empowered developers to create applications that complemented its Windows operating system. This move didn't just enhance the value of Windows itself; it spurred the creation of a vast ecosystem of software solutions that transformed how businesses and individuals interacted with computers. Developers gained access to millions of Windows users, while users benefited from a growing library of applications.

This strategic openness became a template for innovation platforms and a reminder that organizations don't have to do everything themselves to succeed. Instead, they can focus on creating the conditions for others to innovate.

In this case, it is important to note that innovation platforms often coexist with transactional platforms, creating an intertwined ecosystem. Apple's iOS ecosystem offers a perfect example. The App Store, a transactional platform, enables customers to find and purchase apps. However, the apps themselves exist because Apple provides an innovation platform (iOS) that equips developers with the tools—SDKs, APIs, and design guidelines—to create and distribute those apps.

This symbiotic relationship shows that a thriving ecosystem depends on both aspects: the ability to create (innovation) and the ability to transact (find and exchange). For organizations looking to adopt this hack, understanding this integration is crucial. Complementors need tools to innovate and a channel to reach customers, while customers need trust mechanisms and seamless access to the offerings created by complementors.

For these reasons, many lessons from earlier chapters on transactional platforms apply here, even though with unique nuances that demand additional attention. In particular, we would recall

1. **Implement robust trust mechanisms**

Trust here mainly refer to quality check. Quality assurance mechanisms, such as clear guidelines, certifications, and review systems, help build trust across the ecosystem.

2. **Design a specific value proposition for each stakeholder and empower them**

Complementors need clear incentives to participate. Whether through revenue-sharing models, creative freedom, or access to proprietary tools, platforms must empower complementors to innovate while providing tangible benefits.

3. **Focus on Platform Health Metrics**

Successful innovation platforms prioritize the number and quality of interactions over sides' volume. Metrics like the number of active developers, successful integrations, and app usage rates often serve as better indicators of long-term health than total downloads or registrations.

4. **Start Small with a Core Transaction**

Focusing on a specific group of early complementors can set the stage for broader adoption. For example, identifying developers who align closely with the platform's core audience allows for targeted support and more impactful initial contributions. Early successes generate momentum and encourage others to join.

5. **Address the Chicken-and-Egg Paradox**

Platforms must balance the needs of both developers and users. Offering incentives such as funding, reduced fees, or technical support for early developers can help bootstrap the ecosystem.

In addition, innovation platforms also require technical tools to bridge the gap between the complementors and the core offering. SDKs, APIs, and other developer resources are essential to ensuring smooth integration and success.

6. **Design effective**

SDKs and APIs: Unlike other platforms, innovation platforms require technical tools to bridge the gap between the complementors and the core offering. SDKs, APIs, and other developer resources are essential to ensuring smooth integration and success. For example, Microsoft's SDKs for Windows revolutionized the personal computing space by simplifying application development. Similarly, Apple's APIs have become the backbone of its app ecosystem, providing developers with tools to leverage hardware features like Face ID or Siri. A particularly innovative approach is OpenAI's platform for custom GPTs, which allows users to create bespoke AI solutions through a conversational interface rather than traditional programming. This streamlined approach eliminates barriers to entry, enabling a broader range of participants to innovate.

Key Questions to Evaluate the Hack's Fit

Before adopting the Platform Thinking Hack of "Complementing my product through others' capabilities," organizations must assess whether it aligns with their strategic goals. Consider the following questions:

1. Do you have a product or software that would benefit from external integrations or extensions?
2. Can you identify complementors who can actively contribute probably more and better than what you could do?

If the answer to these questions is "yes," then the opportunity to solve your innovation bottleneck problem with this hack is clear. This will require shifting from being a direct producer or consumer of contributions to serving as an enabler. Can you design a system that supports complementors as customers, fostering collaboration and value creation in an innovation ecosystem?

The challenge lies not in doing everything yourself but in empowering others to build on the foundation you've created.

7

Underutilized Data

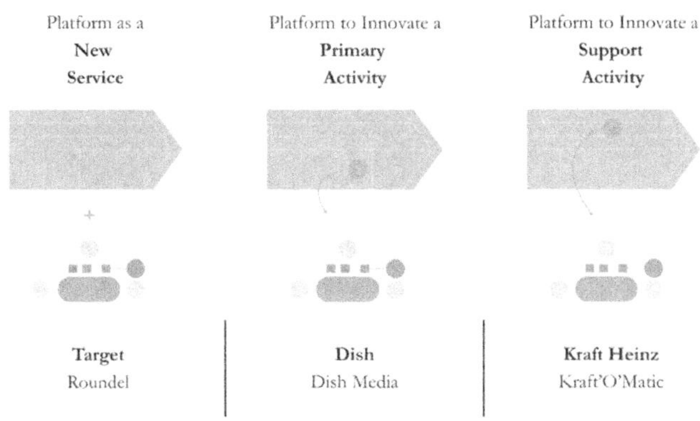

Turning Data into a Catalyst for Transformation

"*Data is the new oil.*"
— Clive Humby.

These are the words of Clive Humby, the British mathematician and architect of Tesco's Clubcard, in 2006. This statement has since become a mantra, repeated in boardrooms and business schools worldwide. Much like oil, data has little intrinsic value until it is refined, processed, and used. And just as oil powered the industrial revolution, data is now the driving force behind the digital revolution.

Over the past few decades, data has evolved into a foundational asset for businesses seeking to enhance efficiency and effectiveness. By deeply understanding and exploiting data, organizations have optimized their transactions—internally and externally—creating better products, improved services, and more seamless processes. This focus has fueled innovation, minimized waste (of data and information), and fostered loyalty, allowing firms to differentiate themselves in an increasingly competitive marketplace.

The point is that while everyone agrees on the power of data, there remains a significant lack of awareness on how to effectively harness and utilize it.

Whether addressing the needs of external customers or internal stakeholders, *Data Exploitation* is a powerful lens through which process owners can refine their operations and deliver value. However, as data availability expands, so too must the approaches organizations use to harness it.

The Efficiency Play: Data Optimization in Agricultural Machinery

Let's consider a company manufacturing agricultural machinery. Over the years, they have equipped their machines with advanced sensors, generating streams of real-time data. These sensors monitor performance metrics like fuel efficiency, engine health, and operational output. With this data, the company has achieved significant improvements across multiple areas. Predictive maintenance has allowed them to reduce equipment downtime, ensuring machines remain operational for longer periods. Optimization algorithms have enhanced machine performance, making operations more efficient and cost-effective.

Through this approach, the company manufacturing agricultural machinery creates a virtuous cycle. Data gathered from machines feeds directly into production and maintenance processes, ensuring continuous improvement. This linear perspective aligns with traditional value chain thinking, where data serves as an input to enhance the same function that generated it.

However, while effective, this approach has limitations. It overlooks data's potential to create entirely new opportunities by involving additional stakeholders. What if he data of the company manufacturing agricultural machinery could transcend its original purpose and unlock new sources of value?

One example of how Data Exploitation can transcend linear value chains involves creating a digital platform that serves two distinct customer groups. On one side, the platform provides actionable insights to farmers by aggregating and analyzing data from agricultural machines. These insights enable farmers to monitor field conditions, track machine status, and anticipate maintenance needs in real time. By using this data, they can make informed decisions to enhance productivity and access tailored recommendations for improving crop yields.

On the other side, the aggregated data can be anonymized, aggregated, and shared with third-party providers, such as seed producers, fertilizer producers, and other suppliers of farming materials. These stakeholders gain valuable insights that help them optimize their products and services for the agricultural market. This dual-customer approach creates a win-win situation: farmers benefit from improved operational insights, while the company generates new revenue streams and strengthens its ecosystem by selling data insights to external stakeholders. By doing so, the platform unlocks additional value and fosters collaboration across the agricultural supply chain.

Internal Stakeholders: Unlocking Potential Within Streaming Services

The value of Data Exploitation isn't limited to external ecosystems. Within organizations, data can become a powerful enabler of collaboration and innovation. Take the example of a streaming service that collects vast amounts of data on user behavior. Initially, this data was used to improve recommendation algorithms and the user interface.

However, by adopting a platform perspective, the streaming service discovered new opportunities. By sharing viewing data with internal content production teams, the company unlocked a range of benefits. For instance, data on audience preferences guided production decisions, helping to identify emerging trends and align content creation with viewer demand. Behavioral insights also reduced risks associated with launching new content, allowing the company to make informed choices about which projects to pursue. Additionally, the process fostered greater collaboration between data scientists and creative teams, sparking innovation and enabling the development of content that resonated deeply with audiences.

In this scenario, data doesn't just optimize existing processes—it becomes a catalyst for organizational transformation. By involving internal stakeholders in the data ecosystem, the company expanded its capacity for innovation and growth.

From Data to Ecosystems

In previous chapters, we explored how efficiency, effectiveness, customer centricity, and innovation can fuel platform-based transformations and eventually drive value creation. The Platform Thinking Hack: *Data Exploitation* builds on these principles by reimagining how data can generate value beyond its original context. Organizations often overlook the potential of their data to benefit stakeholders beyond those who generate it. However, a platform mindset enables firms to unlock this untapped value.

Common Threads: The Platform Power in Action

Three dynamics underscore the transformative potential of Data Exploitation:

1. **Customers as Co-Creators**

In digital services, customers generate data through their interactions. This data, in turn, becomes a valuable resource for the organization, transforming customers into active participants in value creation. Customers remain customers, but they also can be seen as data providers.

2. **Uni-directional Cross-Side Network Effects**

The more data a platform gathers, the greater its value to all participants. For example, as the company's manufacturing operations center for agricultural machinery grows, additional data allow the creation of value in two different ways: on the one hand, they enhance predictive capabilities, attracting more users and reinforcing the platform's utility for end-users. On the other side, when all the data collected is considered together, it unlocks more value also for another customer (e.g., seed producers). This second customer perceived much more value when the number of users increased because the information extracted from them became more and more accurate.

3. **Framing Data as Idle Assets**

Data is often an underutilized resource within organizations. The reason is quite simple. A linear company is accustomed to focusing its attention on a single customer. In many cases, data can have value for this customer, and the company is already extracting using it. The idea of data being an idle asset means that there might be additional value in the data, but for a different customer that the company is not trained or accustomed to satisfying. In the case of the company manufacturing agricultural machinery, this "new customer" was already in the company ecosystem as a provider. The mindset change (once again) is turning a provider into a customer, pretty much as we saw in the previous chapters.

The Business Problem and its Platform Thinking Hack

Legacy firms gather and store incredible amounts of data through many processes. These data are normally already used but they can be valuable not only for those who create them but also for other (internal or external) stakeholders. This is what we can call an *Underutilized Data* business problem.

The hack to solve it is "*Data Exploitation*". To implement it, firms must rethink their approach to data. Instead of treating data as the property of a single department, they should view it as a shared resource within a broader ecosystem. This shift requires new frameworks, technologies, and cultural changes to support collaboration and transparency. The examples of the company manufacturing agricultural machinery and the streaming service highlight a critical truth: data's value lies not only in its ability to enhance existing processes but also in its potential to create new opportunities. By adopting a platform perspective, organizations can unlock this value, involve new stakeholders and foster continuous improvement.

Data Exploitation isn't just about refining operations—it's about reimagining how data can drive innovation, collaboration, and growth. For organizations willing to embrace this mindset, the reward is a dynamic ecosystem where data fuels progress and stakeholders become co-creators of value. In the age of platforms, data's potential is boundless, waiting to be unlocked by those with the vision to see beyond the obvious.

Three Inspiring Stories: Target, Dish & Kraft

Target's Roundel: Harnessing Data to Drive Innovation

Target, founded in 1902, has grown to become a cornerstone in American retail, renowned for its wide range of consumer goods and commitment to affordable quality. But like many established companies, it was facing growing competition from digital-native companies. What made Target different, though, was its deep understanding of customer behavior—an asset built over years of customer interactions both online and offline. This customer data, combined with Target's longstanding reputation, became the foundation for the company's expansion into a new strategic direction.

The Challenge: Unlocking New Value from Existing Data

Target was facing growing pressure from digital-native retailers—agile competitors known for deep discounts, massive product selections, and highly personalized online experiences. To remain competitive, Target needed to find new ways to differentiate itself and strengthen its value proposition beyond traditional retail strategies. One powerful but underutilized resource was already within reach: the company's vast trove of customer data, gathered through years of transactions across physical stores, loyalty programs, and e-commerce. The challenge was clear: how could Target transform this data into a new source of competitive advantage—ideally, a service that would create value beyond its core retail operations—while maintaining customer trust and adhering to strict privacy standards?

The Solution: Roundel, Target's Retail Media Network

To answer this question, Target launched Roundel, marking a pivot from being just a retailer to exploring new strategic opportunities. This is an orthogonal platform with a "*Client-as-a-Source*" strategy. In this setup, customers sit on the demand side, providing data through their interactions, while vendors occupy the orthogonal side, using this data to create targeted advertising campaigns. The transacted good here is the actionable insights derived from customer data, which vendors purchase to enhance their marketing efforts. The image shows this dynamic: with customers generating the demand for insights on one side and vendors leveraging these insights on the other.

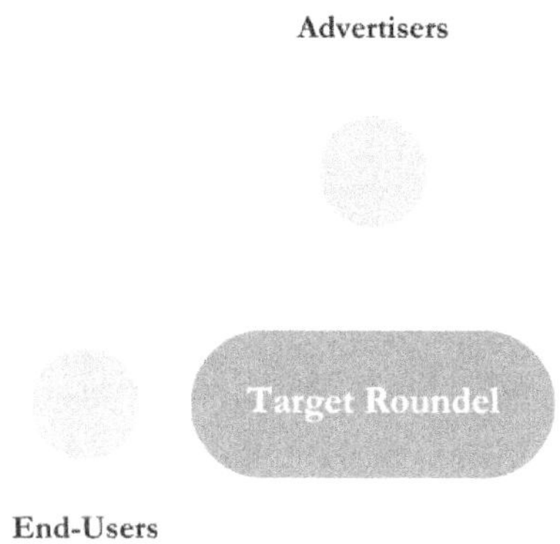

Figure 8.1 – Target's Roundel

The power of Roundel's platform model lies in its ability to capitalize on cross-side network effects. On one side, you have Target's customers—existing shoppers who provide data through their interactions with Target's retail ecosystem. Although they continue to be regular customers, they are now viewed as data providers, supplying insights that fuel the advertising engine. On the other side, you have external brands and advertisers—companies looking to reach specific consumer segments through targeted ads. By joining, these brands gain access to rich customer insights, which allows them to craft advertising campaigns that resonate deeply with their intended audiences. This system benefits from uni-directional network externalities: the more customers who provide data, the more valuable and accurate the insights for brands. However, the reverse is not true, as an increase in brands does not directly enhance value for customers.

Beyond targeted advertising, Roundel offers a suite of services to brands, including influencer partnerships, in-store marketing opportunities, and access to premium placements across Target's digital platforms and over 150 external publishers. These services enable brands to create cohesive, omnichannel marketing strategies that leverage Target's extensive first-party data and customer reach.

This new platform served as a "*Platform as a New Service*" innovation for a new customer (brands and advertisers). It didn't require a massive overhaul of Target's core retail business but rather repurposed existing assets in a novel way to create value. The advertisers (vendors) benefit from the increasing pool of consumer data, while Target, by offering these insights as a service, transforms itself into a key player in this new strategic arena. In a sense, Target used its own data as a new product to sell—creating a win-win scenario for both sides.

Target was uniquely positioned to do so, thanks to its idle assets. Chief among these was its data, which could be analyzed to extract actionable insights. Furthermore, Target's longstanding relationships with customers meant it didn't have to work to build trust or convince them to provide more data—that trust was already established. Finally, the company's existing e-commerce infrastructure allowed it to seamlessly publish special offers and deliver value back to its clients, thereby driving additional revenues. These idle assets made it exceptionally easy to onboard vendors: Target already had something valuable to sell, could guarantee continuously updated insights, and provided a ready-made channel for vendors to monetize those insights.

The Alternative Linear Path

Had Target pursued a traditional, linear approach to monetizing its assets, it might have attempted to collaborate with external advertising agencies or third-party platforms to utilize its customer insights. However, this would have introduced complexities in data sharing, potential privacy concerns, and challenges in maintaining the integrity and security of customer information. Moreover, outsourcing such a critical function might have put Target under the spotlight for direct data selling, receiving potential critiques.

By contrast, the platform approach used by Roundel offers a range of benefits, including lower marginal costs and the ability to scale with minimal upfront investment. The platform's success lies in its ability to tap into data and relationships that were already in place—Target didn't need to invest heavily in new infrastructure or convince customers to join the platform; they were already part of the ecosystem. This data-driven approach also enables Target to create new revenue streams with quasi-zero marginal costs, something that would have been impossible with a traditional linear value chain approach.

Takeaways

Target's Roundel platform is a prime example of the Platform Thinking Hack "*Data Exploitation*," where existing assets—in this case, consumer data—are used to unlock new sources of value. Looking at the Platform Transformative Framework, Target addressed the problem of "*Underutilized Data*" by launching a "*new service*" targeted at a new set of customers. While advertisers may have already been part of Target's ecosystem, brands were traditionally suppliers in its linear retail value chain—not customers of a data-driven service. Through Roundel, Target repositioned these brands as paying customers of a media offering powered by insights from shopper behavior. This shift enabled Target to transform itself into a retail media platform, generating scalable, high-margin revenue while delivering value to partners eager for access to rich, first-party data. The ease of onboarding these actors—already integrated into the ecosystem—further demonstrates the strategic power of Platform Thinking when paired with a trusted brand and a deep reservoir of latent data.

Dish Media

Dish Network Corporation, founded in 1980, is a leading provider of satellite television services in the United States. The company is widely recognized for its innovative approach to delivering high-quality programming, competitive pricing, and exceptional customer service. Over the years, Dish has built a reputation for being a trailblazer in leveraging technology to enhance its offerings, from pioneering DVR technology to its commitment to expanding connectivity in underserved areas. This adaptability has enabled Dish to remain a trusted and influential leader in the satellite TV industry.

The Challenge: Turning Data into Opportunity

Dish's core challenge revolved around staying competitive in an advertising landscape increasingly dominated by digital-native platforms like Google, Facebook, and streaming services. These players had reshaped advertiser expectations by offering hyper-targeted campaigns, real-time analytics, and clearly measurable ROI. In contrast, traditional linear TV advertising—Dish's home turf—was becoming less attractive, seen as broad, inflexible, and harder to justify in data-driven marketing plans. If Dish couldn't offer similar capabilities, it risked losing relevance and revenue in one of its most critical business areas.

At the same time, Dish had a powerful but under-leveraged asset: a vast reservoir of viewer data generated through millions of set-top boxes. This data had long been used to personalize content and improve service delivery—but its broader strategic potential remained untapped. The strategic challenge was to convert this data into a scalable, advertiser-facing service—without compromising customer trust or disrupting its core service model.

The Solution: Exploiting Data to Boost a Platform

Dish Media provided the answer by transforming operations into a value-driving platform. It offers advertisers a unified, data-driven solution that combines the reach of linear TV with the precision of digital targeting. Through advanced data analytics, Dish could harness information on demographics, viewing habits, and household characteristics while respecting viewer privacy. Advertisers were now offered precision targeting comparable to that of Google or Facebook, but with expanded reach to traditional TV screens. For instance, two households watching the same prime-time program could receive entirely different ads relevant to their profiles.

This innovation didn't create a new revenue stream but enhanced an existing one by making ad space significantly far more valuable. Advertisers gained higher returns on investment, reducing wasted ad spend and enabling targeted campaigns with measurable outcomes.

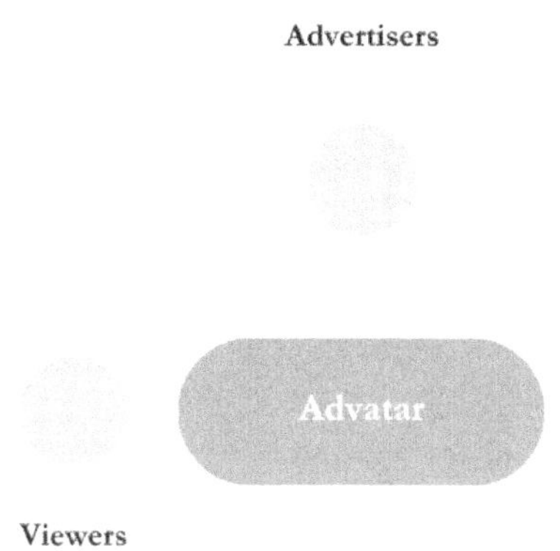

Figure 8.2 – Dish's Dish Media

The model represents an orthogonal platform, where viewers, initially customers of the television service, became providers of behavioral data. On the other side, advertisers acted as the orthogonal participants, leveraging this data to reach tailored audience segments. The transaction revolved around audience insights, now transformed into a vital good. It generates unidirectional network effects: more viewers meant higher quality data, directly benefiting advertisers. While advertisers gained more precise targeting, the value did not flow back to viewers in a reciprocal manner. Importantly, this was not a shift into a new service or market; advertising was already part of Dish's business model. Dish Media represented a platform-driven innovation within a primary value-chain process. It made operations smarter, more scalable, and more valuable.

The Alternative Linear Path

Had Dish chosen a more traditional, linear approach, it might have attempted to close the gap with digital ad platforms by building internal capabilities around audience segmentation and targeting. For instance, it could have developed a proprietary ad tech solution that used viewer data to segment households and package ad inventory accordingly—offering advertisers predefined audience groups (e.g., "sports enthusiasts" or "young families") through internal sales teams.

This would have allowed for some level of targeting, but advertisers would still have been passive clients buying pre-configured segments, not active participants shaping or optimizing campaigns in real time. Without self-serve tools, dynamic integrations, or developer access, the system would have lacked flexibility and speed. Moreover, every new targeting capability would require Dish to develop and maintain the underlying infrastructure—limiting innovation and driving up operational costs. In a fast-moving ad tech space, this could have quickly made Dish appear outdated—sacrificing long-term relevance for short-term control.

Takeaways

The Dish Media case is a powerful example of the Platform Thinking Hack "*Data Exploitation*" to innovate within a "*primary value-chain activity*": operations. Looking at the Platform Transformative Framework, Dish addressed the problem of "*Underutilized Data*" by transforming how it engaged with advertisers—customers it already served—through a dramatically improved, data-driven advertising operation. Rather than launching a new service or entering a new market, Dish used Platform Thinking to unlock the untapped potential of its existing viewer data. The result was a more targeted, scalable, and effective advertising offering that redefined how value was delivered to advertisers, reinforcing Dish's relevance in an increasingly digital ad landscape.

What made this transformation especially powerful was the set of idle assets Dish was able to activate. It already had a massive customer base, a set-top box in every home capable of collecting data, deep behavioral insights on its viewers, and long-standing relationships with advertisers. The core elements were all in place—it was simply a matter of unlocking them.

Kraft Heinz: A Legacy Reinvented

The roots of Kraft Heinz date back to the late 19th century, when J.L. Kraft began selling cheese from a horse-drawn wagon and Henry John Heinz was revolutionizing food preservation with his glass-bottled ketchup. Over the decades, the two companies grew into household names, renowned for their iconic products like Kraft Macaroni & Cheese, Heinz Ketchup, and Oscar Mayer hot dogs. Their ability to capture the hearts (and taste buds) of millions worldwide has made Kraft Heinz a symbol of consistency and innovation in the food industry, firmly embedded in the collective memory of consumers everywhere.

The Challenge: Making Sense of Data

The challenge Kraft Heinz faced was twofold. On one side, its R&D and marketing teams were struggling to understand and anticipate market needs in an industry where the failure rate of new products often exceeds 80%. This high-stakes environment underscored the need for a more data-driven approach to innovation. On the other side, the company had amassed vast amounts of untapped data from sources like point-of-sale records, consumer panel feedback, and marketing analytics. The pressing question was how to harness this treasure trove of information to create actionable insights that could transform their innovation pipeline and maintain their competitive edge.

The Solution: Kraft-O-Matic and the R&D Revolution

To address this challenge, Kraft Heinz, in collaboration with Google Cloud, developed Kraft-O-Matic—a cutting-edge proprietary platform leveraging artificial intelligence and machine learning to analyze vast amounts of data in real time. At its core, Kraft-O-Matic exemplifies a platform designed to innovate a support value-chain activity, like R&D.

The platform operates as an orthogonal one with a "*Client-as-a-Source*" strategy. Consumer data serves as the input on the demand side, and internal functions like R&D and marketing form the orthogonal side. In this model, the main good is actionable insights derived from aggregating and analyzing diverse data sources, including point-of-sale data, consumer panel responses, and marketing metrics. Kraft Heinz had a wealth of data—from store sales, consumer surveys, and marketing campaigns—but it was scattered and primarily used for basic tasks, such as tracking inventory or reviewing past performance. R&D and marketing teams couldn't easily turn that data into insights for innovation. For example, they couldn't predict emerging trends or tailor product ideas to specific consumer segments. With the new platform, all data is connected and analyzed in real time. Now, teams can spot upcoming trends, test product ideas more precisely, and launch highly targeted, data-backed campaigns—capabilities that simply weren't possible before.

The actors in this ecosystem are both familiar and newly empowered. End users—existing customers of Kraft Heinz—remain a core part of the ecosystem but shift roles to become data providers. This shift is seamless because of the trust built over decades of consistent product quality. On the orthogonal side, R&D professionals represent internal actors who use the insights generated to enhance innovation pipelines. While no new actors were introduced to this ecosystem, the real value came from reimagining the roles of existing ones, leveraging Kraft Heinz's idle assets: trusted customer relationships and a wealth of historical data.

This approach strengthened cross-functional collaboration and unlocked synergies between aggregating and analyzing data and decision-making.

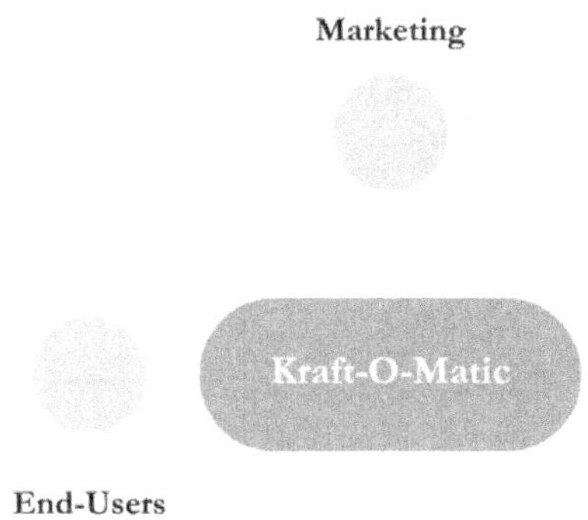

Figure 8.3 – Kraft's Kraft-O-Matic

Uni-directional network externalities further amplify the platform's impact. The more end users contribute data, the more precise and valuable the insights become for R&D. However, the reverse—R&D driving direct value for end users—does not occur, maintaining a unique focus on supporting internal processes rather than directly influencing consumers.

The Alternative Linear Path

Had Kraft Heinz pursued a linear approach, its strategy might have focused on incremental improvements within siloed R&D departments. Insights would be derived manually through traditional methods such as focus groups, in-field research, ethnography, and other tools to investigate customers' needs. These methods often rely on limited sample sizes or delayed analyses of market trends, making such an approach costly, time-consuming, and likely to yield less precise results.

By adopting a platform-based model, Kraft Heinz avoided the significant upfront investments typically associated with building extensive market research infrastructures. Instead, it achieved quasi-zero marginal costs in analyzing additional data streams once the platform was established. Additionally, the company's legacy assets—trusted consumer relationships and a wealth of historical data—offered an advantage that a startup could not replicate.

Consumers, already engaged with Kraft Heinz's products, were more willing to share behavioral data, ensuring a steady flow of high-quality insights.

Takeaways

The Kraft-O-Matic case illustrates the transformative power of the Platform Thinking Hack "*Data Exploitation*." Looking at the Platform Transformative Framework, Kraft Heinz addressed the problem of "*Underutilized Data*" by introducing an innovation within a "*support value-chain activity*"—specifically, how insights are generated for R&D and marketing. Instead of relying on fragmented data used in isolated ways, the platform enabled the company to look at customers as data sources and extract insights more accurately, quickly, and at scale. This redefined how innovation and brand strategy are informed. The platform did not just enhance efficiency; it enabled Kraft Heinz to move from reactive decisions to proactive, data-driven leadership.

What made this transformation especially powerful was Kraft Heinz's ability to activate a set of idle assets that most companies would struggle to match. It already had trusted, long-term relationships with millions of consumers, vast historical data from sales, surveys, and marketing campaigns, and a strong presence across retail channels. These assets—previously used in limited or siloed ways—became the foundation for a more dynamic and predictive approach to innovation. Unlike a startup, Kraft Heinz didn't need to build trust or collect new data from scratch. It had everything in place—it simply needed a platform to unlock the full potential.

Looking Across Underutilized Data Cases

By examining how legacy companies can address the "*Underutilized Data*" problem by leveraging on the Platform Thinking Hack "*Data Exploitation*," we analyzed three distinct cases—Target, Dish, and Kraft Heinz—that illustrate how established organizations can drive innovation by utilizing existing data for purposes that vastly differ from the original reasons for its collection. Each case highlights the transformative power of Platform Thinking, showing how businesses can leverage their existing assets to create ecosystems that deliver value for multiple stakeholders.

Though they belong to diverse sectors, these cases exhibit a common strategy: they experienced a realization and recognized the potential value in the data they had already gathered. This realization also correlates with identifying both internal and external, as well as existing and new customers who could benefit from the insights derived from that data.

Target's Roundel: Target's Roundel showcases the transformative power of Platform Thinking, adding a platform-based service to its linear retail operations. By leveraging customer data, Roundel provides advertisers with actionable insights, turning vendors into orthogonal clients. Leveraging customer trust and historical data, it creates unidirectional network effects—more shoppers mean richer insights—delivering scalable value without disrupting Target's core business. This created a win-win-win dynamic: advertisers gained targeted insights, vendors benefited from enhanced campaign effectiveness, and Target unlocked new value from its existing operations.

Dish Media by Dish: Dish Media exemplifies Platform Thinking as an innovation within its primary value chain operations. By recognizing that viewers were already data providers through set-top boxes, Dish enhanced the value of its ad operations. The platform avoided costly infrastructure investments, leveraging existing assets like its customer base, and created unidirectional network effects—more viewer data enriched advertiser offerings. This orthogonal platform created a win-win win dynamic: advertisers gained targeted insights, viewers received more relevant content, and Dish unlocked new value from existing operations.

Kraft-O-Matic: Kraft Heinz utilized its proprietary platform, Kraft-O-Matic, to analyze consumer data for real-time insights into market trends and product development. This orthogonal platform redefined R&D, a key support activity, by integrating customer-provided data with machine learning capabilities. By leveraging existing assets like trusted consumer relationships and historical data—originally collected for other purposes—Kraft Heinz minimized costs while accelerating innovation and breaking down internal silos. This created a win-win-win dynamic: consumers influenced product development, R&D teams gained data-driven insights, and Kraft Heinz enhanced its innovation efficiency.

These cases demonstrate how this Platform Thinking Hack adapts to different interactions within the value chain. Target Roundel & Dish Media operate entirely outside the organization**,** connecting advertisers and end-users. In contrast, Kraft-O-Matic employs a hybrid model, with one side internal and the other external to the firm.

After reviewing the entire dataset collected from the S&P 500 cases, we identified 16 platforms applying Data Exploitation. A broader analysis offers deeper insights into how this Hack is applied across industries:

- **8 out of 16 (50%)** introduced new services.
- **4 out of 16 (25%)** targeted primary value chain activities, such as operations, marketing, sales, or services.
- **3 out of 16 (18.8%)** focused on support activities, including R&D/innovation and procurement.
- **1 out of 16 (6.3%)** was a hybrid platform introducing a new service and serving a support activity at the same time.

Breaking down these 16 initiatives further reveals their structural differences:

- **9 out of 16 (56.3%)** are open platforms, with both sides external to the organization.
- **1 out of 16 (6.3%)** is a closed platform, connecting only internal stakeholders.
- **6 out of 16 (37.5%)** are hybrid platforms, linking internal and external stakeholders.

The analysis reveals a striking trend: there are relatively few documented cases of orthogonal platforms focused on *Data Exploitation*. This scarcity contrasts with the abundance of companies used to more linear applications of data, such as improving customer interactions or streamlining operational processes. While this observation aligns with the broader landscape of platform studies, it also suggests an underexplored area of innovation.

One possible explanation lies in the nature of research and case reporting. Many studies and datasets focus on platforms that leverage data in traditional, linear ways, which often yield clearer and more immediate results. Orthogonal platforms, which involve using data in ways unrelated to the original purpose, remain less studied and, consequently, less covered in the literature.

Another explanation stems from a cultural and reputational challenge. In the wake of high-profile scandals like Cambridge Analytica and increasing privacy concerns, companies may be hesitant to share how they exploit data, even anonymously. Fear of backlash or reputational damage likely discourages public disclosure, limiting the availability of insights into these platforms. We will address these concerns in the next section, drawing lessons from the rise of orthogonal platforms among leading platform makers.

Despite these challenges, our analysis shows that most documented cases in this category focus on new services and external stakeholders. It is common for firms to onboard new external stakeholders who can benefit from aggregated or anonymized data. However, similar to previous Platform Thinking Hacks, there are fewer examples of *Data Exploitation* aimed at primary or support activities within the firm. Internal initiatives often remain unpublicized, further contributing to the apparent gap in the dataset.

This gap in visibility does not necessarily reflect reality. Our experience with companies adopting Platform Thinking suggests that internal applications of Data Exploitation can have a strong impact on managers. Platforms designed to optimize internal processes, enhance employee collaboration, or unlock new efficiencies represent a significant opportunity for innovation within firms.

This adaptability is evident in diverse applications across industries, as the three stories highlight.

As with other hacks, *Data Exploitation* is versatile across industries. While external platforms dominate the narrative, internal and hybrid applications offer unique potential for firms willing to explore them. By embracing orthogonal approaches to *Data Exploitation*, organizations can transform how they meet stakeholder needs, whether by creating new external services or reimagining internal processes.

The examples and insights discussed underline this hack's adaptability. Platforms that leverage *Data Exploitation* blur the boundaries between stakeholders, fostering ecosystems where value flows freely. This dynamic creates opportunities to address existing challenges, unlock untapped potential, and scale innovation across industries. As companies continue to adopt Platform Thinking, the rise of orthogonal platforms may well represent the next frontier of transformative business strategies.

Best Practices from Orthogonal Platform Design

Exploiting data's value lies at the heart of orthogonal platforms, particularly when viewing clients as a source of opportunity. As Clive Humby famously stated, "*Data is the new oil.*" But like oil, data in its raw form is not immediately valuable. Data must be processed, refined, and matched with the right customers who can extract its potential value. A vivid example of this is Strava Metro, a platform that highlights how *Data Exploitation* can create entirely new markets and customer relationships.

Strava Metro was born from the data generated by Strava's core users: cyclists and runners tracking their activities. By aggregating and anonymizing this data, Strava created a product that helps urban planners and city officials design safer and more efficient transportation infrastructures. Strava Metro demonstrates how a platform can transform data initially collected for personal fitness into insights with significant societal impact. Initially, Strava Metro generated revenues for Strava by selling this aggregated data to city planners and organizations. Over time, it evolved into a corporate social responsibility initiative, now offered free of charge to support safer and more efficient urban development. It also underscores the importance of identifying non-obvious stakeholders who can benefit from refined data products.

The rise of orthogonal platforms, often spearheaded by startups, offers valuable lessons for managers in established firms. The following best practices can help guide the process of designing platforms that unlock new value through Data Exploitation.

1. **Leverage Design Thinking to Identify Possible Customers**

Finding potential customers for aggregated data is rarely straightforward. Established firms must move beyond traditional brainstorming approaches to explore opportunities they might not initially envision. Design thinking—with its emphasis on divergent and convergent thinking—is a powerful tool for this purpose. Divergent thinking encourages exploring a broad array of possibilities, while convergent thinking focuses on narrowing down to the most promising opportunities.

Consider how X, when still Twitter, tapped into this principle. By aggregating tweets and making them available to research institutions and universities, Twitter created a new revenue stream while contributing to academic and market research. This example illustrates how exploring unconventional uses of data can reveal entirely new customer segments.

2. **Don't Overlook Stakeholders Already in Your Ecosystem**

While selling aggregated data to external customers is often appealing, many companies find immense value in keeping these insights within their ecosystem. For instance, Spotify's creation of Spotify for Artists offers a compelling case. By analyzing user listening habits, Spotify provides artists with granular insights into their audiences—where they're located, what they listen to, and how often. This service not only enhances artist engagement with the platform but also strengthens Spotify's ecosystem by creating a deeper alignment of interests.

For managers, this insight emphasizes the importance of leveraging data to enrich relationships with existing stakeholders. Platforms can thrive when they focus on creating mutual value for the participants already within their network.

3. **Prioritize Privacy and Data Ethics**

The importance of privacy cannot be overstated when designing orthogonal platforms. All successful examples studied in the platform world stress the need for anonymized and aggregated data to ensure user privacy. The Cambridge Analytica scandal serves as a cautionary tale. Facebook, the platform at the center of this controversy, faced significant backlash for its role in enabling the misuse of personal data. This event underscores the necessity of maintaining trust by prioritizing transparency and adhering to strict privacy standards.

Managers should treat privacy not as a constraint but as an opportunity to differentiate their platforms. By emphasizing ethical data practices, firms can build stronger trust with their stakeholders while mitigating potential risks.

4. **Integrate *Client-as-a-Source* and *Client-as-a-Target* Strategies**

An important consideration in *Data Exploitation* is integrating *Client-as-a-Source* and *Client-as-a-Target* strategies. Many successful platforms have demonstrated how data generated by one group of users can be leveraged to create highly personalized relationships with another. Facebook's hybrid model is a prime example of this approach. By analyzing user interactions and preferences, Facebook provides advertisers with tailored insights, enabling them to deliver highly targeted campaigns. This integration creates a self-reinforcing cycle in which data from end-users not only enhances their experience but also fuels the platform's advertising revenue.

For managers, this dual strategy highlights the importance of aligning the interests of different stakeholder groups. Platforms that seamlessly connect client-generated data with targeted services can create value across their ecosystem, ensuring both user engagement and commercial success.

Key Questions to Evaluate the Hack's Fit

To determine whether the Platform Thinking Hack of *Data Exploitation* is viable for your organization, consider the following critical questions:

1. Do you have access to large volumes of data?
2. Are your data robust, accessible, and reliable?
3. Can you imagine needs that this data could address, apart from its original purpose?

The hallmark of orthogonal platforms is their ability to address entirely new problems. Identify these opportunities by looking beyond your current customer base and exploring non-obvious stakeholders who might benefit from your data.

If the answers to these questions are affirmative, the next step is to apply Platform Thinking to reimagine the value of your data. By doing so, you can create ecosystems where data becomes a catalyst for innovation, collaboration, and growth.

8

Lack of Data for Strategic Insights

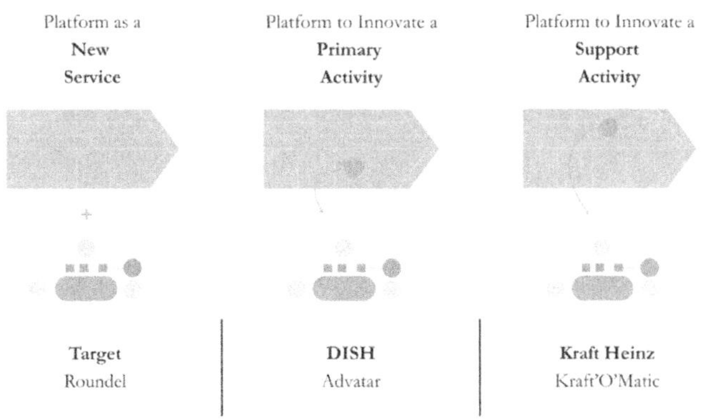

Turning a Pain into an Opportunity

> "*Without data, you're just another person with an opinion.*"
> — W. Edwards Deming.

These words, attributed to W. Edwards Deming, the statistician and management consultant, resonate now more than ever in the data-driven era. When Deming first said this, it was during a time when statistical process control and lean manufacturing were reshaping industries, particularly in post-war Japan. The quote encapsulated a shift toward evidence-based decision-making—a principle that has grown into a mantra for countless organizations today. Peter Drucker makes an even greater point with the claim, "*You can't manage what you can't measure*," and agile methodologies (and Lean Startup) emphasize it with the insistence on data-based decisions over intuition. Nonetheless, it remains a frequent scenario for managers to require specific data that has yet to be gathered.

Initiating a data collection campaign or establishing new *Data Harvesting* processes tends to be a slow endeavor, often met with resistance from employees who view this initiative as an added burden and, occasionally, as a means of oversight and evaluation. Discovering clever and efficient methods to gather the necessary data poses a significant challenge for numerous managers and organizations.

The Hidden Complexity of Gathering Data: connecting caffeine and sleep patterns

Some people can drink an espresso just before going to sleep and enjoy a relaxing night. Others, however, will have a terrible night if they consume a canned soda after 2 PM. This variability in caffeine sensitivity posed a significant problem for a soda company. Their evening sales were dropping because consumers feared caffeine's impact on their sleep. The company needed to understand the correlation between caffeine consumption and sleep patterns to address this issue, but they lacked the tools and data to do so.

They turned to an activity tracker company, known for tracking behavioral habits like calories burned, steps taken, and, of course, sleep patterns. At first glance, the solution seemed simple: collaborate with the bracelet company to gain access to aggregated sleep data. However, the bracelet company didn't track beverage consumption, which meant they couldn't provide the specific insights the soda company needed.

In a linear world, the bracelet company might have attempted to collect this additional data directly by adding beverage-related questions to their app or distributing customer surveys. These approaches, however, are limited by low response rates and static, episodic data collection. Moreover, they treat users merely as data providers, offering little incentive for active participation.

Approaching this challenge with a platform mindset led to a transformative solution. Instead of directly asking for data, the bracelet company designed a new app feature that invited users to log their daily beverage consumption. In return, users received personalized insights about how caffeine affects their sleep patterns. This new service started with creating a 'Caffeine Persona Profile,' helping users understand their unique sensitivity to caffeine. The app then linked caffeine intake to sleep quality and finally offered tailored suggestions on how to improve sleep based on individual data.

This approach created a win-win-win dynamic. The soda company gained valuable, continuous insights to inform product development and marketing strategies. Users (the demand side) benefited from personalized health information that enhanced their well-being. Meanwhile, the bracelet company expanded its value proposition by delivering meaningful, engaging services, with data collection becoming a natural by-product of this engagement.

The key takeaway is that the process began with a specific data need—understanding caffeine's impact on sleep—and evolved into a platform-based solution that generated this data as a natural outcome of user engagement. This shift from viewing customers as data sources to valuing them as active participants in a data-driven ecosystem exemplifies the power of Platform Thinking in transforming business challenges into opportunities for innovation and growth.

Engaging Internal Stakeholders: The case of Diversity data

The value of *Data Harvesting* isn't limited to external ecosystems. Within organizations, it can be a powerful tool for fostering collaboration and driving cultural change. Consider an HR department seeking to promote diversity and inclusion by highlighting not just the most common differences, such as gender or ethnicity, but also behavioral and cognitive diversity, including being intrinsically or extrinsically motivated, or having a visual rather than factual learning approach. In a linear model, HR might ask employees to complete questionnaires and attend webinars on the topic. While well-intentioned, this approach risks treating employees as mere data providers, with little incentive for them to engage meaningfully.

A platform-based approach, however, flips the script. Imagine partnering with a university to develop a digital learning program featuring short, weekly video lessons on topics like motivational drivers, or behavioral styles. Integrated into the program is a diagnostic tool that allows employees to assess their own behavioral tendencies and compare them against aggregated organizational data. After several weeks, participants receive a personalized report that not only fosters self-awareness but also reveals the rich diversity within their organization. In this model, employees aren't just passive participants; they become active customers of the learning experience, gaining insights that enhance their professional growth.

The Key Shift: From Data Exploitation to Data Creation

In previous chapters, we discussed how organizations can exploit existing data to drive innovation and efficiency. *Data Harvesting*, however, focuses on creating new data points by designing value propositions that incentivize stakeholders to contribute information actively. This shift requires rethinking traditional roles: data providers must also be seen as customers, with clear value delivered to them in exchange for their participation.

While opportunities for data creation abound, engagement remains a critical hurdle. Simply having the infrastructure to collect data doesn't guarantee participation. To overcome this, organizations must craft compelling value propositions that resonate with data providers. The examples above—a personalized app for caffeine-sleep analysis and an engaging digital learning program—illustrate how aligning incentives with stakeholder needs can transform passive data collection into an active, mutually beneficial process.

Common Threads: The Platform Power in Action

Several dynamics underpin the effectiveness of *Data Harvesting* as a hack:

1. **Data Providers Become Customers**

To gather meaningful data, organizations must offer stakeholders a compelling reason to participate. This could be a personalized service, actionable insights, or enhanced learning opportunities.

2. **Uni-Directional Cross-Side Network Effects**

The value of data increases as more stakeholders contribute. For example, the sleep data app becomes more accurate and useful as additional users participate, benefiting all parties in the ecosystem.

3. **Leveraging Idle Assets**

Relationships and existing infrastructure often serve as untapped resources for data collection. Whether it's leveraging a trusted customer base or integrating new capabilities into an existing app, these assets can be key enablers of *Data Harvesting*.

The Business Problem and its Platform Thinking Hack

Legacy firms want to support their strategic decisions by leveraging data, but in many cases, that data is not collected yet. We name this problem "*Lack of Data for Strategic Insights*".

The hack to solve it is "*Data Harvesting*": those data can be gathered by designing value propositions that incentivize stakeholders to actively generate and share data. Platform Thinking is an effective tool to transform data providers into customers and enabling new forms of value creation.

This approach emphasizes collaboration, engagement, and the reimagining of relationships within and beyond organizational boundaries. By adopting a platform mindset, firms can unlock the full potential of data, not just as a resource to be exploited but as a catalyst for innovation, growth, and transformation.

In the next sections, we'll dive deeper into how *Data Harvesting* can be implemented across different industries and organizational functions. From leveraging digital platforms to designing engaging value propositions, the possibilities are vast for organizations willing to embrace this transformative hack. By understanding the principles outlined here, you'll be better equipped to turn data from a static asset into a dynamic driver of success.

Three Inspiring Stories: News Corp, Carnival & AbbVie

News Corp and Vertical Video Data Harvest Platform

News Corp, a global media and information services giant, has long held a distinguished position in the news and entertainment industry. Known for its array of digital and print platforms, the company has built its reputation on delivering tailored news, analysis, and entertainment to diverse audiences worldwide. News Corp has built its success upon a robust portfolio of traditional media services, including iconic newspapers like The Wall Street Journal and The Times, which have set benchmarks in journalistic excellence. Its network of television stations and print publications, such as The New York Post, has long catered to diverse audiences with trusted news and compelling stories. These cornerstone offerings solidified News Corp's reputation as a leader in delivering content to its target globally.

The Challenge: Competing in a New Ecosystem

But the world of media is fast changing, with advertisers demanding more than broad reach—they seek granular insights and engagement metrics to precisely target audiences. Platforms like TikTok, YouTube Shorts, and Instagram Reels have quickly come as dominant forces in this space, particularly among younger, mobile-savvy users. In this new landscape, News Corp's traditional formats—banner ads and horizontal video—faced tough competition from the immersive nature of vertical, interactive video ads. The company recognized it needed to adapt quickly to avoid losing significant advertising revenue to these new platforms.

The Solution: A Vertical Video Platform Powered by Data Harvesting

In response, News Corp launched its Vertical Video Platform in 2022—a mobile-first initiative designed to compete directly with the likes of TikTok and YouTube Shorts. At its core, this platform redefined the company's value proposition, creating a new service for advertisers and end users alike.

The innovation wasn't just about adopting a new format; it fundamentally shifted the nature of engagement. The platform offered mobile-optimized, full-screen vertical videos tailored to users consuming content on the go. More importantly, it integrated "shoppable video ads," allowing users to purchase products directly from the content without leaving the platform. This seamless integration bridged inspiration and transaction, boosting engagement while retaining users within News Corp's digital ecosystem.

The platform's true competitive edge, however, came from its integration with Intent Connect, News Corp's proprietary data capability. By analyzing over 2 billion monthly first-party data signals, Intent Connect enabled the platform to deliver hyper-personalized ad experiences. Advertisers could now target micro-segments based on user behaviors, such as reading preferences or shopping habits, ensuring that every ad reached the right person at the right moment.

This wasn't merely a service enhancement; it was a shift in strategy. By incentivizing users to engage with interactive, shoppable content, News Corp transformed its audience from passive viewers into active data providers. This approach epitomized *Data Harvesting:* designing a platform that not only engaged users but also extracted rich, actionable insights as a byproduct of that engagement.

Vertical Video Platform is a quintessential example of an orthogonal platform, starting from the orthogonal actor, advertisers, and their data needs, the platform was designed with the precise intent to transform data producers into customers. On the demand side, it attracts end users—mobile-first consumers seeking short-form, engaging content.

While end users were newcomers to News Corp's ecosystem—competing directly with platforms like TikTok and Instagram—the advertisers were pre-existing stakeholders. The platform leveraged its deep relationships with advertisers, an idle asset, to understand their shifting needs and deliver new forms of value, all while building engagement with a younger demographic. This dynamic also introduced unidirectional cross-side network effects: the more users the platform attracted, the more valuable it became to advertisers. However, the reverse was not true, reinforcing the need for strong user engagement strategies.

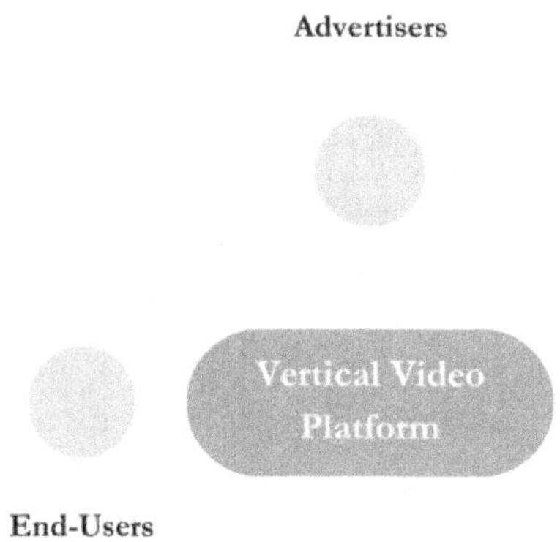

Figure 9.1 – News Corp's Vertical Video Platform

The Alternative Linear Path

Had News Corp pursued a traditional linear value chain approach, the standard alternative would have been to invest a lot of money to investigate this new segment and create content for them on traditional channels. This would have required significant upfront costs and yielded only marginal gains in advertising revenue. A linear approach would also have failed to capitalize on the potential of data to enhance ad targeting, leaving advertisers dissatisfied with generic insights.

By adopting a platform approach, News Corp minimized initial investment. The vertical video format—coupled with interactive features—ensured quasi-zero marginal costs as the platform scaled.

Takeaways

The News Corp case highlights the transformative power of the Platform Thinking Hack "*Data Harvesting*" when integrated into a platform model. Looking at the Platform Transformative Framework, News Corp addressed the problem of a "*Lack of Data for Strategic Insights*" by creating a "*new service*" specifically designed for a new audience segment—mobile-first, short-form content consumers. The goal wasn't just to reach these users with content but to generate meaningful behavioral data through their interactions. This shift allowed News Corp to offer advertisers hyper-targeted, data-rich ad solutions, while simultaneously engaging a younger, previously underrepresented audience.

This approach underscores a fundamental mindset shift: starting with the data advertisers need and building a service that makes users want to provide it. News Corp was uniquely positioned to do this by activating several idle assets—its strong brand, established audience reach, and long-standing relationships with advertisers. These assets gave it credibility, scale, and access that a startup would struggle to build from scratch. As a result, News Corp could move quickly, turning its media legacy into a platform-driven, data-rich advantage.

Carnival's Neptune Platform: Harvesting Insights to Power the Fleet

Carnival Corporation, the world's largest cruise company, has long been synonymous with unforgettable travel experiences. Operating over 100 vessels across the globe, Carnival has built a reputation for excellence in hospitality, entertainment, and customer service. Behind the scenes, however, lies an immense challenge: ensuring that this vast fleet operates safely, efficiently, and in compliance with evolving environmental regulations. For Carnival, achieving this level of operational excellence required more than technological upgrades—it demanded a strategic approach to *Data Harvesting*, ensuring the operational departments had access to the critical insights they needed to optimize the fleet.

The Challenge: Meeting Operational Demands for Better Data

Managing a fleet of cruise ships is no small feat. Each vessel generates complex data from its navigation systems, engine performance, fuel usage, emissions, and water management processes. Operational departments across Carnival—ranging from sustainability teams to fleet managers—faced an urgent need to access and interpret this data to ensure compliance, improve safety, and enhance overall efficiency. However, traditional systems left valuable insights fragmented, making it nearly impossible to gather and analyze data at scale.

This was not a question of exploiting existing data for secondary gains. Instead, the operational departments explicitly sought a system capable of capturing the critical information they required to streamline operations and meet environmental standards. Carnival needed a platform that could provide these departments with the right data at the right time, enabling them to drive meaningful change.

The Solution: Neptune, A Data-Harvesting Platform

Carnival's solution came in the form of Neptune, an advanced fleet management platform designed to address the specific data needs of its operational departments. Neptune is a cloud-based Internet of Things (IoT) solution that connects all 100+ vessels in Carnival's fleet, harvesting operational data to provide actionable insights.

At its core, Neptune's purpose is to serve the needs of the operational departments, which act as the orthogonal side of the platform. These teams required real-time access to metrics like engine conditions, fuel efficiency, emissions levels, and navigational data to ensure safety, optimize performance, and support compliance initiatives. On the supply side, the vessels themselves became active data providers.

Previously, ship crews were responsible for manually collecting and reporting operational data—a process that was time-consuming and often disconnected from immediate operational benefits. This manual reporting was seen as an additional burden, offering little direct value to the crew's day-to-day responsibilities.

With the implementation of Neptune, this dynamic changed significantly. The platform automated data collection through IoT sensors, reducing the manual workload on the crew. More importantly, it provided crews with real-time insights into their vessel's performance, such as fuel consumption and engine efficiency, enabling them to make informed decisions that improved operational outcomes. This immediate feedback loop transformed data collection from a burdensome task into a valuable tool for enhancing the crew's operational effectiveness.

By collecting and transmitting operational data through IoT sensors, the vessels played a pivotal role in generating the information that operational departments needed. Carnival's Neptune platform collects real-time data from individual vessels and combines it with aggregated insights from across the fleet to deliver more robust solutions. By analyzing data from multiple ships, Neptune identifies patterns, trends, and opportunities for optimization that transcend individual operations. For example, the platform can recommend strategies to improve fuel efficiency, reduce emissions, and enhance energy usage fleet-wide by learning from the performance of all vessels. It also enables predictive capabilities, helping operational teams foresee maintenance needs or potential safety concerns before they arise. Additionally, the system benchmarks performance metrics, allowing Carnival to implement universal best practices and drive continuous improvement across the fleet. This multi-vessel approach enables Carnival to achieve broader operational efficiency, compliance, and safety improvements on a scale that would be impossible by focusing on individual ships alone.

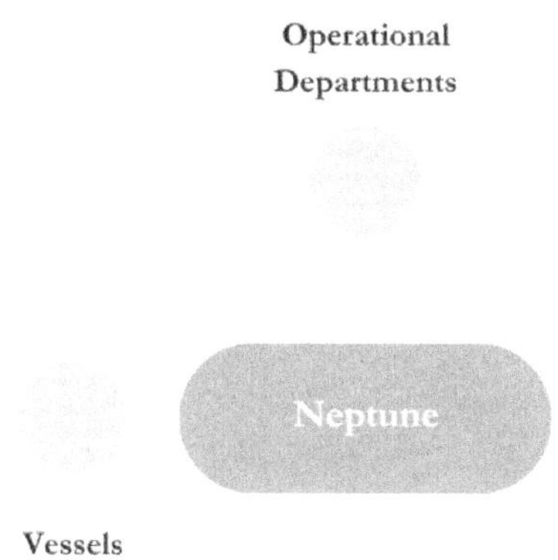

Figure 9.2 – Carnival's Neptune

Importantly, the vessels were not exploited only for their data. Instead, Neptune created tangible value for them as participants in the ecosystem. The platform's real-time monitoring capabilities delivered direct benefits to the vessels by improving navigational safety and energy efficiency, ensuring smoother operations and more informed decision-making by onboard crews.

The Alternative Linear Path

Had Carnival tackled the problem with a traditional linear approach, it likely would have developed isolated tools and manual reporting systems tailored to each operational department. Departments like sustainability, engineering, and maintenance would have worked independently, relying on crews to manually collect and submit data. This approach would have led to duplicated efforts, slow response times, and inconsistent data quality. Valuable insights would have taken longer to surface, reducing the company's ability to act quickly on critical safety or efficiency issues. The cost of building and maintaining multiple disconnected systems—and training personnel for each—would have been significantly higher. Most importantly, without centralized, real-time visibility, Carnival would have struggled to identify fleet-wide trends or implement shared best practices, ultimately limiting its ability to scale operational improvements across the fleet.

By adopting the platform approach, Carnival was able to create a centralized, scalable solution that leveraged existing assets and infrastructure. The deployment of IoT sensors across the fleet transformed vessels into data hubs, allowing the platform to operate at quasi-zero marginal cost as additional ships were onboarded. Compared to a startup attempting to build a similar platform from scratch, Carnival had a clear advantage. Its established fleet, coupled with years of operational expertise, provided a foundation that no new entrant could replicate.

Takeaways

The Neptune platform showcases the transformative power of the Platform Thinking Hack "*Data Harvesting*." Looking at the

Platform Transformative Framework, Carnival addressed the problem of a "*Lack of Data for Strategic Insights*" by innovating within a "*primary value-chain activity*"—the operation of its vessels. Rather than creating a new service, the company focused on dramatically improving how data is captured and used to support existing functions such as fuel efficiency, maintenance, and compliance.

This case highlights a critical mindset shift: successful *Data Harvesting* begins by identifying the data needed to solve operational challenges and designing a system that makes it valuable for contributors to provide it. By viewing vessels—and their crews—not just as data sources but also as beneficiaries of real-time insights, Carnival created an ecosystem in which operational teams at sea and on land both gained from data-driven coordination.

By adopting a platform approach, Carnival was able to create a centralized, scalable solution that leveraged critical idle assets—its global fleet, experienced crews, and years of operational know-how. The deployment of IoT sensors across the ships transformed each vessel into a real-time data hub, enabling Neptune to operate at quasi-zero marginal cost as additional vessels were onboarded. A startup attempting to build a similar platform would face steep challenges in acquiring fleet access, domain expertise, and stakeholder buy-in.

AbbVie's Transformation: Leveraging Data to Accelerate R&D

When AbbVie was founded as a spin-off from Abbott Laboratories in 2013, it inherited a legacy of innovation and excellence in pharmaceuticals. Known for its groundbreaking treatments for autoimmune diseases like Humira and its oncology advancements with drugs such as Imbruvica, AbbVie quickly earned a reputation as a leader in transforming lives through medicine. The company is also renowned for its focus on chronic conditions like hepatitis C and its dedication to improving global health. AbbVie's success in addressing some of the most pressing medical challenges has made it a trusted name among healthcare professionals and patients alike.

The Challenge: Bridging the Data Gap in R&D

Drug development is a time-consuming and resource-intensive process, with years spent gathering insights, testing hypotheses, and conducting clinical trials. For AbbVie's researchers, one of the biggest hurdles was accessing comprehensive, real-world health data to inform the early stages of research and development (R&D). They needed a way to collect data, such as genomic information, lifestyle behaviors, and medical histories, that could help them identify trends, refine hypotheses, and accelerate the development of transformative medicines. But how could AbbVie build a system that seamlessly integrated these disparate data streams while also incentivizing individuals to participate?

The Solution: The AbbVie Research Collaborative (ARC)

To tackle this challenge, AbbVie developed the AbbVie Research Collaborative (ARC), a platform designed to connect two critical groups: adults in the United States as data providers and AbbVie's own researchers as data consumers. Through ARC, individuals voluntarily share real-world health data, including medical records, genomic data, and lifestyle information, creating a rich dataset that researchers can analyze in real-time.

This platform exemplifies "*Data Harvesting*" in action: AbbVie designed a value proposition that encourages individuals to contribute data, transforming these stakeholders into customers of the platform. By participating, individuals gain insights into their health and wellness, such as understanding genetic predispositions or identifying potential risks. Individuals who join ARC also gain access to an integrated visual timeline of their health data, which they can share with their physicians to make more informed medical decisions and become active contributors to the advancement of medical science, influencing the direction of AbbVie's research efforts.

From a structural perspective, ARC functions as an orthogonal platform, with individuals on one side and researchers on the other. The main good is the health data provided by individuals, which researchers analyze to accelerate drug discovery and development. The platform leverages uni-directional cross-side network effects:

the more individuals who share their data, the greater the value for researchers. However, the reverse does not hold—researchers' participation does not directly increase the value for data providers.

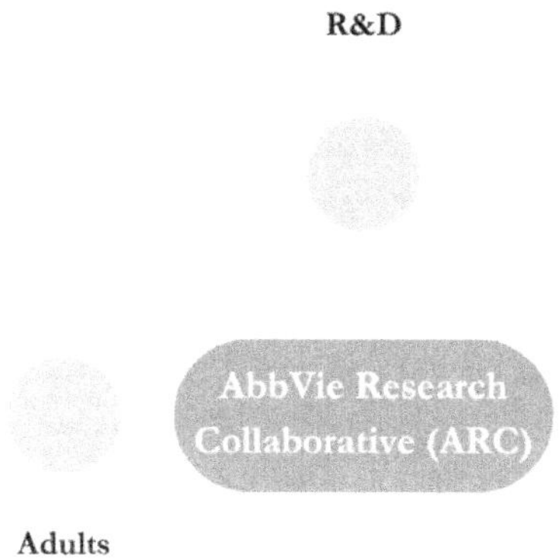

Figure 9.3 – AbbVie's Research Collaborative (ARC)

The ecosystem surrounding ARC is both dynamic and innovative. On the demand side, AbbVie's researchers were already established actors within the ecosystem, seeking solutions to accelerate R&D. On the supply side, the platform transformed adults into new stakeholders, positioning them as key contributors to the innovation process. To engage these individuals, AbbVie employed a combination of trust-building strategies and value-added features. For instance, participants receive access to health insights derived from their data, strengthening their sense of community and shared purpose.

The platform's success lies in its ability to align the incentives of these two groups, fostering a collaborative environment where both sides derive tangible value. By providing researchers with real-time data and empowering individuals to play an active role in shaping medical research, ARC has redefined the traditional boundaries of pharmaceutical innovation.

The Alternative Linear Path

Without the ARC platform, AbbVie would likely have relied on traditional methods to gather the same data, such as commissioning expensive longitudinal studies or purchasing fragmented datasets from third parties. These linear approaches would have required significant upfront investment and yielded incomplete insights, as they lack the depth and real-time feedback enabled by ARC. Moreover, such methods would have perpetuated inefficiencies in R&D, slowing the pace of innovation and increasing costs.

In contrast, the platform approach enabled AbbVie to minimize initial investment by leveraging existing relationships with adults in the United States who trust the company's reputation. AbbVie also drew upon its internal know-how to design a system that identified and integrated the precise data needed for R&D. A startup attempting a similar initiative would have faced significant hurdles, including building trust with data providers and navigating complex regulatory landscapes—challenges AbbVie could address more efficiently due to its established position in the healthcare ecosystem.

Takeaways

In the AbbVie ARC case, the company responded to a growing challenge: a "*Lack of Data for Strategic Insights*" in drug development and medical research. Looking at the Platform Transformative Framework, AbbVie addressed this gap using the Platform Thinking Hack labeled "*Data Harvesting*" to innovate within a "*support value-chain activity*"—R&D. This shift did not alter AbbVie's core business of developing and commercializing pharmaceuticals. Instead, it reflects a profound mindset change: rather than relying solely on internal teams and linear research pipelines, AbbVie built a platform that activates patients—and potential patients—as data providers by offering them valuable services in return, such as personalized health insights, educational resources, and opportunities to contribute to research. This reciprocal design turns participants into engaged contributors, making the platform a powerful support tool for accelerating research while maintaining its alignment with AbbVie's core business.

Participants joined ARC not only for the health insights they received but because they felt part of a mission—helping to shape the future of medicine. AbbVie's ability to activate key idle assets—its scientific expertise, trusted patient relationships, and robust clinical infrastructure—was critical to the platform's success. Unlike a startup, AbbVie didn't need to build trust, recruit researchers, or negotiate data access from scratch. This existing foundation gave the company a significant head start, enabling it to launch a platform with real credibility, depth, and impact—reaffirming its leadership in pharmaceutical R&D.

Looking Across Lack of Data for Strategic Insights Cases

In our exploration of the Platform Thinking Hack "*Data Harvesting,*" we analyzed three distinct cases—News Corp, Carnival, and AbbVie—that illustrate how established organizations can drive innovation by creating services explicitly designed to collect valuable data. Each case highlights the transformative power of Platform Thinking, demonstrating how businesses can build new ecosystems where data collection is not just a byproduct but a core purpose of the service.

Though they belong to diverse sectors, these cases exhibit a common strategy: they identified specific data needs critical to their operations or growth and designed platforms that incentivize stakeholders to provide that data. This proactive approach to *Data Harvesting* contrasts with *Data Exploitation*, as the services were conceived from the outset with data collection as a primary goal.

News Corp launched its **Vertical Video** Platform as a New Service for orthogonal customers to compete in the dynamic digital advertising space. The platform was crafted to attract mobile-first users with engaging, shoppable content, while simultaneously serving as a robust data collection tool. By leveraging its idle asset—deep relationships with advertisers—News Corp aligned the platform's design with advertisers' evolving needs for granular targeting data. Encouraging user interactions transformed casual engagement into a continuous stream of actionable insights. Everybody is winning: advertisers gained precise audience segmentation, users enjoyed personalized content, and News Corp unlocked new value streams beyond its legacy media offerings.

Carnival's Neptune platform addressed operational efficiency within its fleet management, representing an innovation within a primary activity of the value chain. Designed to harvest real-time data from vessels, Neptune provided critical insights to operational departments focused on safety, compliance, and sustainability. By leveraging its idle asset—an extensive, established fleet equipped with operational data systems—Carnival aligned the platform to meet the evolving needs of its operational teams. The platform turned ships into active data providers, enabling Carnival to optimize performance and drive fleet-wide improvements. This created a win-win-win dynamic: operational teams improved decision-making, vessels benefited from optimized performance, and Carnival achieved greater operational excellence.

AbbVie's Research Collaborative (ARC) exemplifies *Data Harvesting* in the realm of pharmaceutical R&D, representing an innovation within a support activity of the value chain—R&D. Recognizing the need for comprehensive, real-world health data, AbbVie created a platform that encouraged individuals to voluntarily share personal health information. By leveraging its idle asset—established trust and relationships with healthcare professionals and patient communities—AbbVie fostered participation and data sharing. This data became a foundational asset for accelerating drug development, while participants benefited from personalized health insights. Everyone is getting value: participants gained personalized health insights, researchers accessed critical data to accelerate innovation, and AbbVie enhanced its R&D capabilities, driving breakthroughs in medical science.

In the initiatives we analyzed from the S&P 500 database, only three concrete cases of *Data Harvesting* emerged. The first employed an open strategy (both sides are outside the company), the second a closed one (both sides are inside the company), and finally, the third a hybrid one. This limited sample underscores the rarity of companies leveraging *Data Harvesting* as a hack—a phenomenon shaped by the low transparency surrounding how organizations gather, aggregate, and anonymize data. As discussed in the previous chapter, companies often hesitate to disclose the details of their data practices, further complicating the ability to identify and evaluate these efforts. Yet, the challenges of uncovering these cases reveal something deeper about the nature of *Data Harvesting*. Similarly to other hacks, *Data Harvesting* requires a fundamental shift in the way organizations perceive and design their processes, which, in this case, is probably even more subtle. It demands reimagining processes as platforms that engage stakeholders in entirely new ways.

The relative scarcity of *Data Harvesting* initiatives can be attributed to the significant paradigm shift this Platform Thinking Hack demands. Managers are asked to address the immediate need to gather data and design value propositions that resonate with data creators, who must be seen as customers and not providers. This dual focus makes *Data Harvesting* uniquely complex. It challenges traditional ways of thinking, which often separate operational needs from customer-centric strategies.

Moreover, *Data Harvesting* blurs the line between internal and external ecosystems. For example, an organization might leverage its relationships with external partners to gather data that benefits internal teams, or vice versa. This interconnectedness reinforces the need for managers to think beyond linear processes and embrace a platform mindset that prioritizes mutual value creation.

Despite its complexity, *Data Harvesting* holds immense promise. When organizations reimagine their processes as platforms, they unlock opportunities to engage stakeholders in ways that traditional approaches cannot. By treating data providers as customers, companies foster trust, collaboration, and innovation. The two cases we examined—though limited in number—demonstrate how *Data Harvesting* can drive transformation across both internal and external ecosystems.

As we synthesize these insights, it becomes clear that *Data Harvesting* is not yet a widely adopted strategy, but its potential to redefine value creation is undeniable. For organizations willing to embrace the paradigm shift it requires, *Data Harvesting* offers a powerful tool to engage stakeholders, create new data points, and unlock untapped opportunities. By reinterpreting processes as platforms, companies can transcend traditional boundaries and position themselves at the forefront of innovation in the platform economy.

Best Practices from Orthogonal Platform Design

Data Harvesting lies at the heart of orthogonal platforms. Traditionally, these platforms are designed to extract insights from existing datasets, transforming them into actionable knowledge. However, the mechanisms of orthogonal platforms work equally well when reversed: instead of merely exploiting available data, they can create tailored services to actively gather the data they need. This switch in perspective underscores the transformative power of the "*Data Harvesting*" hack and aligns with W. Edwards Deming's principle, "*Without data, you're just another person with an opinion.*"

Niantic's Pokémon Go is a compelling example of *Data Harvesting* through an orthogonal platform, illustrating how a seemingly entertainment-focused application is, at its core, a sophisticated data collection tool. While millions of players engage with the game to catch virtual creatures and explore augmented reality (AR) environments, the game's true strategic value lies in the vast amounts of geospatial data it harvests from user interactions.

Far from being an incidental byproduct, data collection was the central objective behind Pokémon Go's design. The engaging gameplay serves as a powerful incentive to encourage users to move through real-world environments, contributing to Niantic's primary goal: gathering rich geospatial data. Every player's movement, location, and interaction with physical spaces feed into Niantic's data ecosystem, providing real-time, global insights that are invaluable for refining navigation, mapping, and AR technologies.

This data fuels Niantic's Large Geospatial Model (LGM), an advanced AI system designed to improve geospatial intelligence. The diversity and scale of the data collected—ranging from GPS coordinates to environmental scans—enable Niantic to enhance its mapping accuracy, develop location-based services, and support innovations far beyond the gaming industry. In fact, Pokémon Go's gameplay mechanics are carefully crafted to maximize data collection, with features like PokéStops, gyms, and AR scanning tasks strategically positioned to drive user movement and engagement in specific geographic areas.

Crucially, players are not mere data providers; they are active participants in a mutually beneficial ecosystem. The game offers an immersive experience that motivates continuous interaction, while Niantic gains the critical data needed to advance its technological capabilities. This creates a everybody wins dynamic: players enjoy a highly engaging AR experience, Niantic strengthens its AI-driven mapping and geospatial technologies, and third-party developers benefit from access to enriched geospatial data for applications in fields like urban planning, autonomous navigation, and location-based marketing.

Although much of the research on orthogonal platforms has been done on cases developed by startups, the insights gained are universally applicable. As discussed in the previous chapter, three foundational principles stand out, but applied to *Data Harvesting*, these principles take on nuanced interpretations:

1. **Leverage Design Thinking to Identify Possible Data Providers**

The central question in *Data Harvesting* shifts slightly: "Who has or can create the data I need?" In some cases, the answer is generic. For example, in the Niantic case, young generations have time to invest and are willing to play. In other cases, the answer must be more precise and targeted. Consider mPower, an app developed by Sage Bionetworks in collaboration with the University of Rochester

Medical Center, designed to collect data from individuals with Parkinson's disease. Launched in 2015 as part of Apple's ResearchKit framework, mPower faced the critical challenge of gathering reliable, real-time health data to advance Parkinson's research. Their solution? Transform smartphones into portable research tools that not only collect data but also empower patients to monitor their condition.

Through tasks like voice recordings, finger-tapping exercises, and walking assessments, combined with self-reported surveys, mPower gathers comprehensive data on motor function, symptom variability, and medication adherence. Participants, motivated by the app's health insights and self-monitoring features, actively engage with the platform, often without viewing themselves primarily as data contributors. This dual-purpose design illustrates how platforms can align user benefits with data collection goals, driving meaningful contributions to medical research.

2. **Design Engaging Services to Meet the Needs of Data Providers**

Once potential data providers are identified, the next challenge is creating a service that both engages them and aligns with your data needs. Pokémon Go serves as a perfect example here as well. The game's high level of engagement was driven by its entertainment value and the strength of the Pokémon brand. While players were deeply immersed in gameplay, Niantic's data-gathering objectives were seamlessly integrated into the experience.

The success of this approach hinges on transparency and ethics. While data gathering doesn't need to be the central focus from the user's perspective, it must be conducted openly[20]. Users should understand how their participation contributes to broader goals without feeling exploited. In this way, engagement is not only sustained but also fosters trust and collaboration.

---

20 See Trabucchi et al., 2023.

Key Questions to Evaluate the Hack's Fit

As organizations consider adopting the *Data Harvesting* hack, three critical questions emerge:

1. Do you require strategic insights to fuel your decision making?
2. Do you have a clear idea of what data do you need to extract those strategic insights?
3. Can you identify who can provide the data you need?

If the answers are all yes, you can reimagine your role as an orchestrator of interacting needs rather than a linear customer in search of insights. *Data Harvesting* is not about purchasing data or coercing stakeholders into participation. Instead, it requires rethinking the organization's role as a platform orchestrator that serves both data providers and consumers. The goal is to create a mutually beneficial ecosystem where all participants derive value.

For forward-thinking companies, *Data Harvesting* represents not just a hack but a paradigm shift—a way to redefine relationships, processes, and value creation in the platform economy. The question is no longer whether *Data Harvesting* is possible, but how effectively organizations can implement it to serve both their stakeholders and their strategic goals.

PART 3
Building Your Platform

9

Where Research Meets Practice: Platform Thinking Journey

A Process Grounded in the Real World

When we embarked on our journey into Platform Thinking, we were driven by curiosity and a desire to decode the transformative power of platforms. Over more than a decade of rigorous research, we have explored countless case studies, engaged with visionary platform thinkers, and collaborated with entrepreneurs and managers who believed in the potential of platform models. We've seen firsthand how companies like AXA, Siemens, and Eni have harnessed this potential to redefine their industries. These stories, introduced earlier in the book, were intended to inspire and ignite the transformative potential that Platform Thinking holds.

Now, it's time to spotlight another critical dimension of our work—our academic roots and the environment that nurtured our research: **Politecnico di Milano**. As Italy's leading university with over 150 years of history, Politecnico di Milano stands at the intersection of three bodies of technical knowledge: Engineering, Architecture, and Design. Founded in 1863 through the joint efforts of industrialists and academics committed to supporting the industrial development of the region, Politecnico has evolved alongside Milan, Italy's industrial and economic capital, and a global hub of innovation.

This strong connection between research and practice remains the heartbeat of our methodology. Our engineering roots instilled in us a pragmatic approach, emphasizing empirical validation and real-world application. Over the years, our research group has grown increasingly intertwined with the Design School at Politecnico di Milano, one of the world's most prestigious institutions in this field.

Here, we learned not just what design is but how design can catalyze business transformation and inspire different types of research activities.

On one hand, the process we present in this chapter draws heavily from design thinking. It leverages tools and methodologies that design has introduced to the business world over the past few decades—emphasizing empathy, ideation, prototyping, and iterative development. On the other hand, our proximity to the design school inspired us to adopt a more active role in research itself. Rather than merely observing and analyzing what others have done (as we did with AXA, Siemens, and Eni), we engaged directly with the subject of our study, proposing solutions and iteratively refining them in collaboration with industrial partners.

This approach aligns with the principles of **Design Science Research (DSR)**[21], an academic paradigm that has its roots in information systems and is increasingly influential in management and innovation studies. DSR emphasizes the creation of innovative artifacts, such as models or methods, that address relevant business problems. These artifacts are designed starting from existing academic literature to solve specific problems and then tested in real-world environments to ensure their utility, quality, and efficacy. Finally, they are fine-tuned for reuse, allowing them to be adapted and applied across different contexts. This approach allows us to build on established theories and frameworks, ensuring that our research not only enriches the broader academic discourse but also contributes to practical advancements in companies and organizations. The DSR process involves iterative cycles of design, implementation, and evaluation, blending theoretical rigor with practical relevance. By focusing on solving real-world problems, DSR contributes to both the advancement of theory and the improvement of practice.

---

[21] See Hevner et al., 2004 and Trabucchi et al., 2024.

Insights from the Platform Thinking HUB: Learning from Real-World Projects

Merging the strong industrial connections that are the foundation of Politecnico di Milano with the profound influence from the design school, we initiated a multi-year **Design Science Research project** supported by a consortium of forward-thinking companies. In 2023, this effort culminated in the launch of the first edition of the **Platform Thinking HUB**[22], part of the **Observatories Digital Innovation** of the School of Management at Politecnico di Milano.

Founded in 1999, the Digital Innovation Observatories were created to enhance awareness in all areas of digital innovation. Today, they serve as authoritative reference points for digital transformation, conducting research, facilitating dialogue, and continuously updating the business community through more than 50 active observatories. Among them, there is the Platform Thinking HUB.

The **Platform Thinking HUB** is more than just a research initiative; it is an active **community of innovation leaders** dedicated to envisioning revolutionary digital business transformations grounded in platform-based mechanisms. Its mission is to foster a collaborative environment where professionals can critically examine platform-based projects, exchange ideas, and apply the methodologies we have developed to drive impactful changes within their organizations.

One manager in the community reflected on this collaborative environment, noting, "*The continuous exchanges with the other partners gave us the opportunity to focus our work on concrete problems with precise outcomes to create new solutions and innovative business models.*"

Another one added: "*This experience has reinforced our belief that innovation and the strategic use of data can not only transform a company, but also redefine the rules of an entire industry.*"

---

[22] More that 20 companies actively funded and participated into the Platform Thinking HUB in the first 3 editions: Angelini Industries, Alpitour, Edenred, Eni, EY, Epta, Fondazione Mondino IRCCS, GPS Bilance, Gruber Logistics, GS1 Italy, Iveco, Leonardo, Open-es, Poste Italiane, Prysmian, Relatech, Retail Reply, SDF, Sintetica, Sisal, Trentino Sviluppo.

Our methodology, the **Platform Thinking Journey**, is deeply rooted in years of academic literature, both from our research and contributions from global scholars. This approach was designed to address real challenges faced by established organizations exploring platform-based solutions. Each year, we guide over 50 managers who apply our methodology to their specific contexts. Through this process, we collect feedback, observe interactions, and continuously refine our approach.

In the first edition of 2023, we introduced a suite of strategic tools, including the Idle Asset Canvas, the Data Board, and the Platform Thinking Matrix. While these tools ignited innovative ideas, it became clear that managing the complexity of platform strategies required more than just isolated tools. Managers from traditional linear firms needed a comprehensive framework to fully realize the potential of Platform Thinking.

Recognizing this, we radically transformed our approach in the second edition in 2024 when each company was asked to identify specific problems or opportunities within their organizations to develop comprehensive platform-based business cases. We introduced the first version of the Platform Thinking Journey, a seven-step process supported by 39 cards. Through a series of workshops and seminars, each organization crafted detailed business cases. Some of these projects have already reached the market, showcasing tangible business impact and the transformative potential of Platform Thinking, while others are in advanced stages of internal discussion, poised to drive significant organizational change.

This iteration revealed valuable insights. Although the seven-step process provided structure, it was often perceived as cumbersome. Some cards were dense, and there was confusion about their optimal use. These constructive critiques led to the third edition in 2025, featuring a refined, cyclical four-phase model and an updated set of cards. This time, the cards were not just tools, but part of interactive workshops crafted like a serious game, complete with guiding questions cards, decision points with alternatives, and checkpoints to facilitate dynamic strategic thinking.

Furthermore, working on constructive feedback on the complexity of managing a card set and all the platform-related concepts, we integrated comprehensive feedback loops that not only validated the four-phase model but also optimized the design cards to be more user-friendly and intuitive. These enhancements, combined with the inclusion of **Platform Thinking Journey GPT**, an AI-powered agent offering real-time support and strategic insights, have significantly elevated the practical utility and impact of our methodology. This virtual advisor encapsulates the breadth of our Platform Thinking knowledge, offering real-time insights and recommendations.

Through these evolving iterations, we have validated our methodology, refined our tools, and, most importantly, fostered a vibrant community of platform thinkers. This section of the book reflects the lessons learned from these collaborative endeavors, offering a roadmap for companies seeking to embrace the transformative power of Platform Thinking.

The 4 Steps of The Platform Thinking Journey

In the rapidly evolving business landscape, where traditional models often fall short in the face of digital disruption, Platform Thinking emerges as a transformative approach. After years of rigorous research, analysis, and collaboration with industry leaders, we've crystallized this approach into a recursive, four-step design process: **Framing, Design, Ignition, and Growth**. This journey is not linear but cyclical, allowing continuous adaptation and evolution—a key trait in the dynamic platform economy.

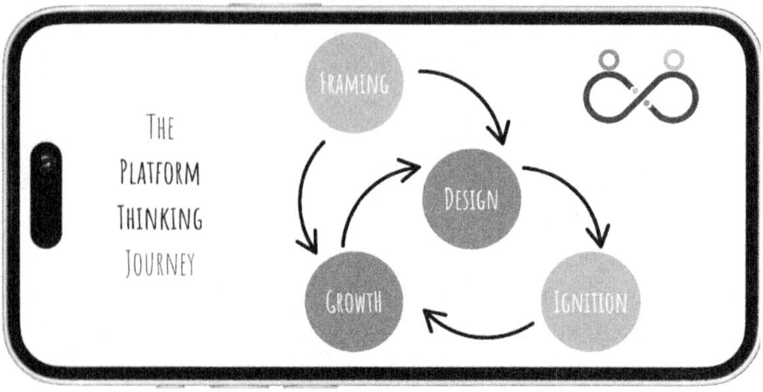

Figure 10.1 – The Platform Thinking Journey

Framing: Defining the Arena

The journey begins with Framing, the phase where clarity is sought amidst complexity. The goal here is to identify the precise area where Platform Thinking can be applied effectively. This involves answering two pivotal questions:

- Where are you fostering Platform Thinking?
- Why are you applying Platform Thinking?

Is the focus on creating new services, enhancing the primary value chain, or optimizing the support value chain? Is it to solve specific business problems (aligned with the five core problems discussed in Part Two of this book) or to exploit opportunities by leveraging idle assets?

These two questions conceptually mirror the central framework of this book, defining the area of application of Platform Thinking.

Through structured reflection and strategic analysis, the framing phase culminates in a clear understanding of the problem to be addressed or the opportunity to be seized. It sets the stage, ensuring that efforts are targeted and impactful.

Design: Crafting the Blueprint

Once the problem or opportunity is framed, the Design phase takes center stage. Here, the objective is to shape the platform's architecture and operational model. Drawing from the typologies of platforms outlined earlier in the book, this phase dives deep into:

- Adopting a user-centric perspective, leveraging design thinking principles to ensure the platform meets the needs of all stakeholders, not just the provider.
- Identifying the core functionalities for each user side.
- Bridging the gap between idea conception and business model design, encompassing potential revenue streams, cost structures, key metrics, and scalability considerations.

This phase is where the abstract becomes tangible, and strategic visions are translated into actionable plans.

Ignition: Sparking the Launch

The third phase, Ignition, focuses on transitioning from design to deployment. This critical juncture involves:

- Defining the go-to-market strategy.
- Selecting key strategic alternatives for platform launch and sides' onboarding, informed by extensive platform literature and case studies.
- Crafting a roadmap that outlines the steps needed to bring the platform to life, from initial pilot projects to full-scale rollout.

Ignition is about momentum—creating the conditions necessary for the platform to attract its first users, generate network effects, and achieve market traction.

Growth: Scaling and Evolving

Growth is not merely the final phase; it is both an end and a new beginning. For nascent platforms, it represents future evolution. For established ones, it can be the entry point into the Platform Thinking Journey. This phase is anchored in the Platform Thinking Matrix, which highlights four strategic alternatives to support platform growth, both onboarding new sides or exploiting the ones already on board. Successful platforms tend to apply Platform Thinking over and over again, becoming 'idle asset hunters', and that's the heart of this phase.

Growth strategies are dynamic, requiring platforms to revisit the design phase continually. This recursive process fosters resilience, adaptability, and sustained value creation, maintaining relevance in the competitive positioning of the platform initiative.

The Platform Thinking Journey is designed to be iterative. As platforms grow and markets evolve, the journey cycles back to Framing, allowing for reassessment and realignment. This continuous loop of Framing, Design, Ignition, and Growth equips managers and professionals with a robust framework to navigate the complexities of platform-based business models, driving transformation and unlocking new sources of value in an ever-changing world. In the next section we dive into the details of the process and the support cards, almost as the instructions for using the Platform Thinking Card Set.

The Platform Thinking Journey Card Set

The transition from concept to execution in platform design is rarely linear. To navigate this complexity and build on our Design School mindset and consultancy experience, we've developed the Platform Thinking Card Set, a strategic toolkit designed to support professionals and innovators through every step of the Platform Thinking Journey. This card set serves three primary goals:

- **Guiding Complex Design Processes:** It provides structure in navigating multifaceted platform initiatives.
- **Supporting Strategic Decisions:** It offers clear alternatives during critical decision-making moments, reducing ambiguity.
- **Providing Conceptual Depth:** Each card links to definitions, real-world examples, and further readings, ensuring decisions are grounded in comprehensive knowledge.

The card set is composed of four interrelated card types, each serving a distinct role in the design process:

- **Triggering Questions:** Strategic questions that frame the Platform Thinking activities within each phase.

- **Design Alternatives:** Multiple strategic options for addressing each triggering question, complete with explanations and supporting examples.
- **Design Tools:** Instruments to foster divergent thinking and support creative ideation, ensuring broad exploration of possibilities.
- **Milestones:** Key checkpoints that verify the coherence and integrity of the design before progressing to the next phase.

In the next chapters, we provide a phase-by-phase explanation of the process and an introduction of all the cards. Then, we provide an extensive how-to guide to manage this type of workshop, introducing a GenAI support tool.

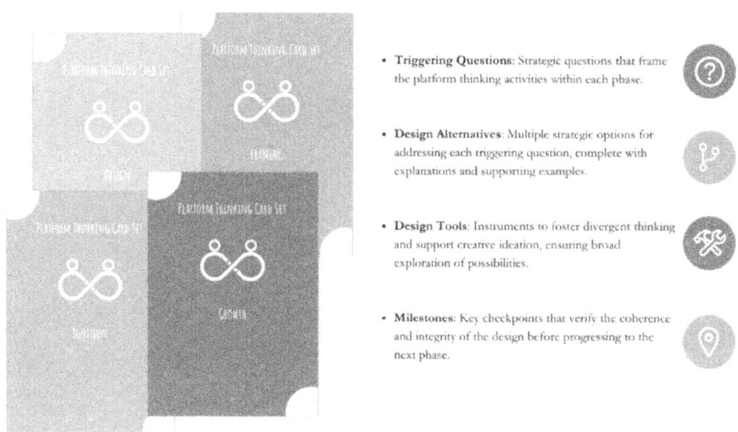

Figure 10.2 – The Card Set

You can by your Platform Thinking Card Set using this QR code. - https://bit.ly/PTJCards

---

10

The Framing Phase

The Process

The Framing Phase establishes the foundation for platform initiatives. Its goal is to clarify where and why Platform Thinking should be applied. This phase is driven by two fundamental triggering questions: Where Are You Fostering Platform Thinking? Why Are You Applying Platform Thinking — to Solve Problems or to Exploit Opportunities?

Let's go through both of them

First triggering question for the Framing Phase

The first triggering question is: Where Are You Fostering Platform Thinking?

Figure 11.1 – Framing: Triggering Question 1

This question helps define the scope and focus of the platform initiative. The card set offers three strategic alternatives:

- **Platform as a New Service:** Developing entirely new value propositions through platform mechanisms.
- **Platform to Innovate a Primary Activity:** Applying platform principles to transform core business activities within the primary value chain.
- **Platform to Innovate a Support Activity:** Leveraging platform models to enhance support functions like HR, IT, or procurement.

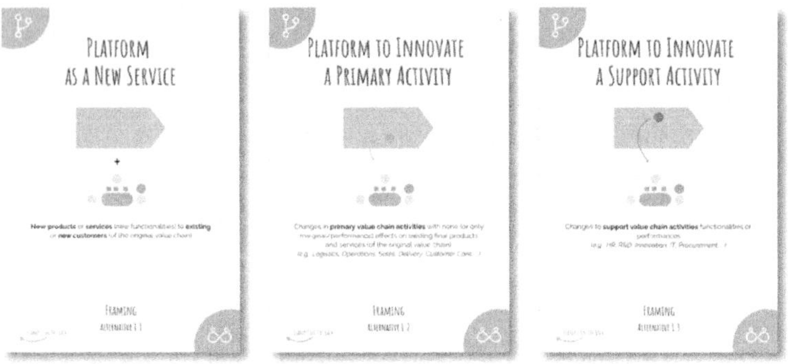

Figure 11.2 – Framing: Alternatives 1

The first triggering question for the Framing Phase concludes with a critical **Milestone**: the **Platform Stakeholders' Map**. This tool spots the main stakeholders to be involved and convinced to approve at the end of the process and crystalizes the answer to the question: Where are you fostering Platform Thinking?

Figure 11.3 – Framing: Milestone 1

Second triggering question for the Framing Phase

The second triggering question is: Why Are You Applying Platform Thinking—to Solve Problems or to Exploit Opportunities?

Figure 11.4 – Framing: Triggering Question 2

This question opens two strategic pathways:

- **Solving Problems:** For organizations addressing specific challenges, Platform Thinking can be applied through five alternatives, corresponding to the key Platform Thinking Hacks discussed in Part Two of this book:

- Enhance or Enable Transactions among Existing Stakeholders
- Solving Customers' Needs by Onboarding New Stakeholders
- Complementing My Product Through Others' Capabilities
- Data Exploitation
- Data Harvesting

Figure 11.5 – Framing: Problem Alternatives 2

- **Exploiting Opportunities:** Beyond problem-solving, Platform Thinking can support in identifying untapped innovation opportunities within existing organizations. This approach focuses on leveraging **idle assets**, categorized into four types:

- Data
- Relationships
- Physical Assets
- Know-how

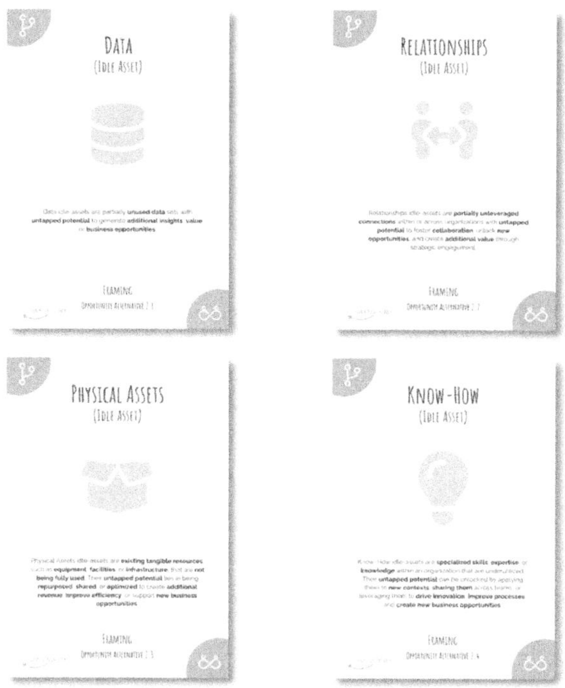

Figure 11.6 Framing: Opportunity Alternatives 2

To support this exploration, two specialized tools are provided:

- The **Idle Asset Canvas:** A Platform Thinking tool that helps identify an organization's available assets and potential platform-based initiatives.
- The **Data Board:** A design thinking toolkit for uncovering data-driven opportunities by identifying potential users of aggregated data.

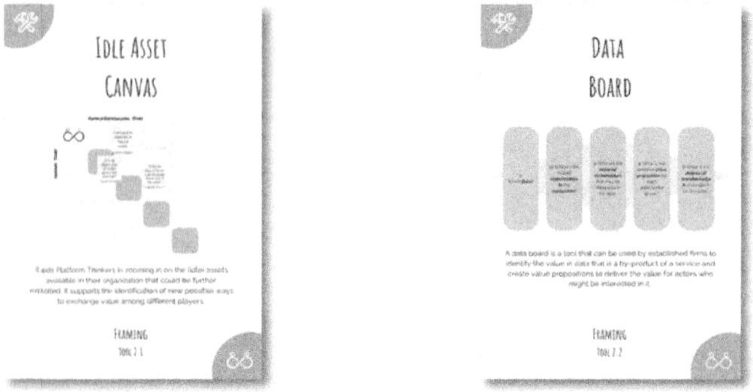

Figure 11.7 – Framing: Tools 2

The Second triggering question for the Framing Phase concludes with a critical **Milestone**: the **Problem Framing Canvas**. This tool crystallizes the insights gained during framing and evaluates the suitability of Platform Thinking through three control questions:

- Where and Why? This question summarizes whether the platform innovates a new service or a primary/support value-chain activity and whether it aims to solve a business problem or exploit an idle asset.
- Who Are the Customers Involved? This focuses on identifying the two sides of the platform, ensuring the presence of distinct user groups.
- Where Do You See Value in the Network Externalities? This assesses the potential for cross-side network effects, validating the platform model's value creation mechanism.

A consistent response to all the questions establishes a solid foundation for the next phases of the Platform Thinking Journey. If the initiative involves creating a new platform, the journey proceeds to the **Design Phase**. If it applies to an existing platform, the next phase is **Growth**.

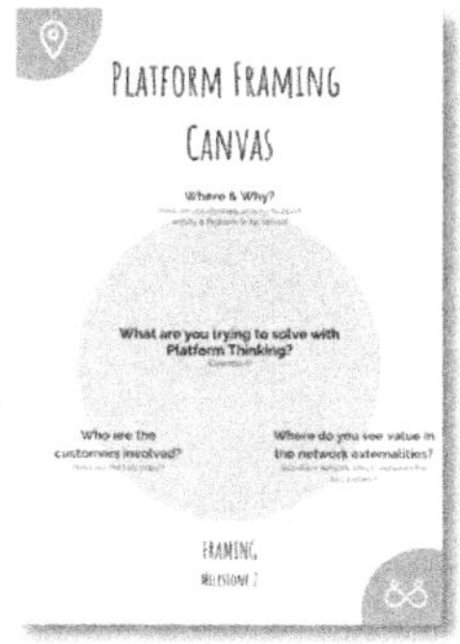

Figure 11.8 – Framing: Milestone 2

11

The Design Phase

The Process

With the framing phase providing a solid foundation, the Design Phase focuses on shaping the platform's architecture and operational model. This phase transforms strategic insights into actionable structures, ensuring the platform is not only conceptually sound but also practically viable. The design process revolves around three triggering questions, each supported by strategic alternatives and checkpoints.

First triggering question for the Design Phase

The first question is: Which is the Best Type of Platform to Sustain Your Project?

Figure 12.1 – Design: Triggering Question 1

Choosing the right platform type is fundamental, as it influences the platform's design, critical success factors, and potential challenges. The three platform typologies introduced in Chapter 2 guide this decision:

- **Transactional Platforms:** Facilitate direct exchanges between users, such as Uber or Airbnb.
- **Innovation Platforms:** Provide a foundation for third-party development, like Apple's App Store.
- **Orthogonal Platforms:** Support complementary interactions between distinct user groups, such as Google's advertising model.

Each typology carries specific benefits and challenges, shaping the platform's dynamics and strategic approach.

Figure 12.2 – Design: Alternatives 1

Before progressing, it's crucial to **validate** the platform structure with a **Platform Type Check** milestone through key questions:

- Are there two sets of customers involved plus a platform provider? This ensures the presence of distinct roles.
- Do the three players (two sides and the provider) play clearly different roles in the system? This verifies role clarity.
- Are there cross-side network externalities? Depending on the platform type:
    - **Transactional Platforms:** Are network effects bidirectional?
    - **Orthogonal Platforms:** Are network effects unidirectional?

- **Innovation Platforms:** Are network effects bidirectional, and can complementors build on the platform?

Figure 12.3 – Design: Milestone 1

Positive responses confirm readiness to advance to the next **triggering question**.

Second triggering question for the Design Phase

We now move from high-level platform design to the side level, with the second triggering question: What are the Main Functionalities Needed from Each Side?

This question explores the platform's operational design, focusing on the specific functionalities required by each user. Unlike the first question, there are no predefined alternatives; instead, the **User Stories** tool supports this process.

Figure 12.4 – Design: Triggering Question 2

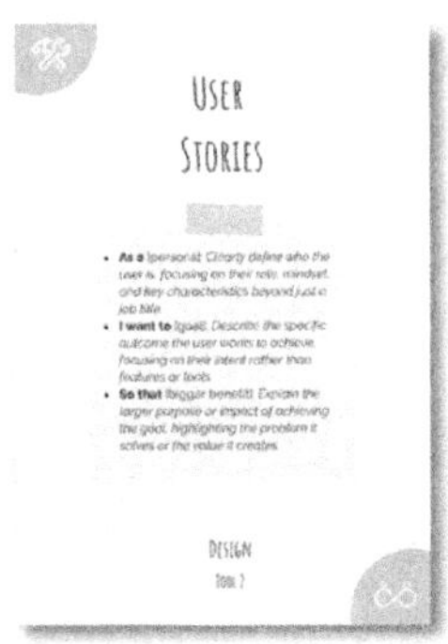

Figure 12.5 – Design: Tool 2

Borrowed from the SCRUM methodology, user stories bridge abstract design with practical implementation. Each story follows a simple syntax:

"As a [user], I need [functionality] so that [desired outcome]."

This structure ensures user-centric thinking, clarifying functionalities and their value. It's essential to develop user stories for all platform sides, capturing diverse perspectives.

The milestone here supports the proper design of the value proposition for **each side**. Indeed, each user side requires validation through the **Value Proposition Canvas**, ensuring coherence among:

- The problem faced by the user.
- The functionalities addressing the problem.
- The value proposition offered to the user.

Alignment across these elements confirms the platform's design relevance and completeness.

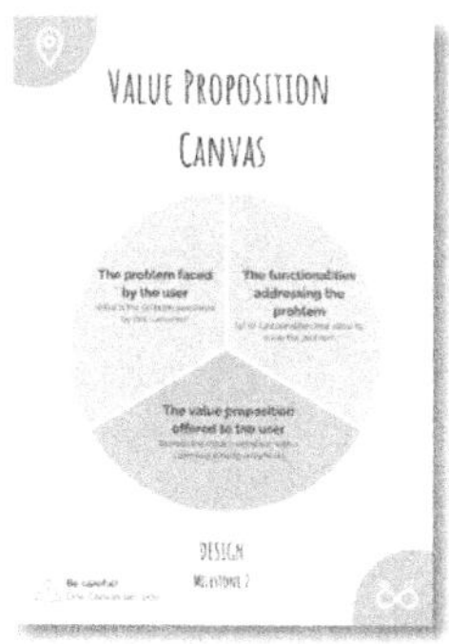

Figure 12.6 – Design: Milestone 2

Third triggering question for the Design Phase

The third and final triggering question for this phase is: How does the Platform Business Model Work?

The final design question addresses the platform's business model, focusing on sustainability and scalability. The **Platform Thinking Business Model Canvas** supports this analysis, building on established frameworks like Osterwalder's Business Model Canvas and Ash Maurya's Lean Canvas, while tailoring them for platform-specific nuances.

Beside the platform representation that sits at the center, the Key Components of the Platform Thinking Business Model Canvas are:

- **Channels:** How the platform reaches and engages its user sides.
- **Key Metrics:** KPIs to monitor platform growth and user activity.

- **Unfair Advantage:** The unique strengths (often linked to idle assets) that provide a competitive edge.
- **Costs and Revenues:** Focused on operational aspects, assessing financial viability.
- **Platform Value Proposition:** The overarching value promise that aligns all stakeholders.

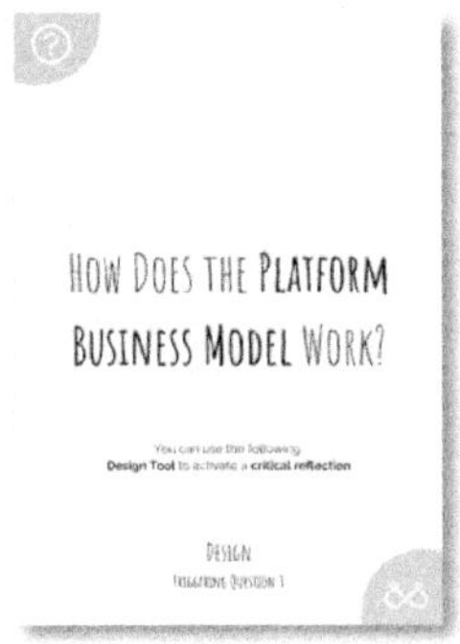

Figure 12.7 – Design: Triggering Question 3

Practical suggestion: Visualizing key flows—money, data, and data-driven value-added services—enhances understanding of the platform's dynamics.

The design phase concludes with a comprehensive **milestone**:

- Sustainability and Feasibility Assessment:
    - Are costs and revenues balanced?
    - Is the design technically feasible?
- Defining the Minimum Viable Platform (MVP):
    - What are the minimum functionalities required to enable platform-based mechanisms? Identifying the MVP guides implementation priorities, informs project planning, and sets the stage for iterative development cycles.

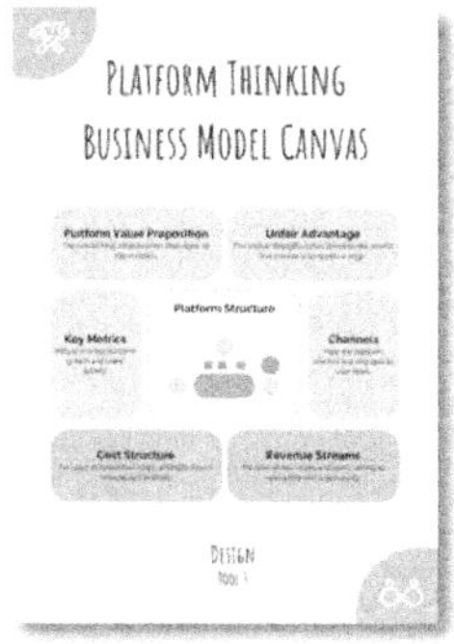

Figure 12.8 – Design: Tool 3

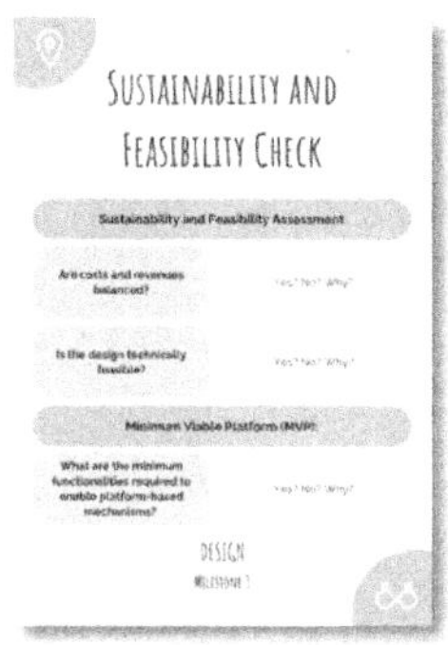

Figure 12.9 – Design: Milestone 3

With the design phase complete, the platform is ready to move into the next stage: **Ignition**.

12

The Ignition Phase

The Process

With a well-structured platform design in place, the Ignition Phase focuses on transitioning from strategic planning to actual deployment. The core challenge here is overcoming the notorious chicken-and-egg paradox—a dilemma that has puzzled platform innovators for years.

The chicken-and-egg paradox refers to the difficulty of attracting users to a platform that lacks active participants on the opposite side. Orthogonal and innovation platforms may not experience this paradox as acutely. Nevertheless, for transactional platforms, this issue is particularly significant, as both user groups (buyers and sellers, drivers and riders, etc.) must be engaged simultaneously to create value. Still, the sequence and strategy of onboarding different sides remain critical decisions that can determine the platform's success.

Therefore, the triggering question here is: How are you Igniting the launch of the platform?

This guiding question focuses on defining the strategies to overcome the chicken-and-egg paradox and successfully ignite platform growth. The goal is to identify the order in which the various sides will be onboarded and the tactics to engage them effectively.

Several strategic alternatives can guide this process:

- **Leveraging an Existing Network:** Utilize pre-existing relationships to promote and scale the platform.
- **Door-to-Door:** Engage potential users directly through in-person interactions.

- **Direct Marketing:** Employ targeted communications via email, phone, or mail to attract users.
- **Bandwagon Effect from the Other Side:** Showcase growing adoption from one user group to attract the other.
- **Involving Key Players:** Engage influential stakeholders to drive broader platform adoption.
- **Simulating One Side:** Generate artificial activity to create the illusion of platform vitality and attract real users.
- **Contract Side:** Secure agreements with key participants to ensure an initial base of activity.

Figure 13.1 – Ignition: Triggering Question 1

Before progressing, it's crucial to **validate** the ignition strategy with a **Roadmap** milestone, answering critical questions:

- Which side will be onboarded first? With which ignition strategy? Why?
- Which sides will follow? With which ignition strategy? Why?

Figure 13.2 – Ignition: Alternatives 1

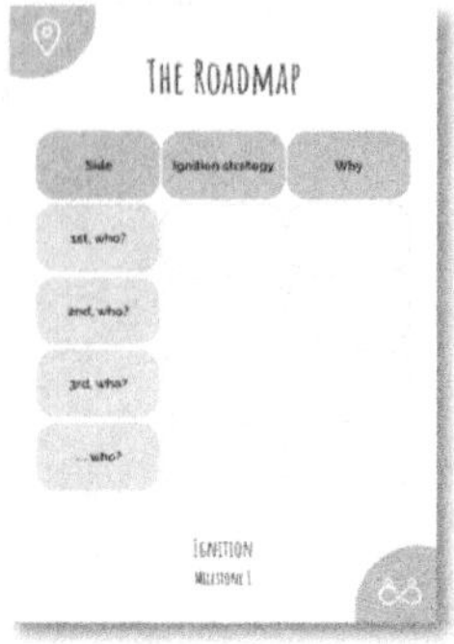

Figure 13.3 – Ignition: Milestone 1

For simple platforms, this roadmap might be straightforward. However, complex platform initiatives may involve multiple sides, some of which were not part of the Minimum Viable Platform identified earlier. The roadmap ensures a clear, step-by-step approach to scaling the platform effectively.

13

The Growth Phase

The Process

The Growth Phase focuses on scaling an existing platform to unlock new opportunities and maximize value. Growth can be achieved through two primary strategies:

- Extension: Onboarding new user sides to the platform.
- Exploitation: Generating new services and functionalities for existing sides.

These evolutions can occur through both transactional and orthogonal logics. The intersection of these perspectives forms the **Platform Thinking Matrix**, which highlights four strategic alternatives that guide the triggering question: How will the Platform evolve?

Figure 14.1 – Growth: Triggering Question 1

To guide the growth process, we identify ten strategic alternatives:

- **Service Enlargement:** Expand the range of services offered to existing platform users, enabling new transactions.
- **Platform Gemini:** Launch a new platform leveraging relationships with existing sides, featuring distinct branding and access.
- **Supply-Side Addition:** Onboard new supply-side customers to serve existing demand, aligning with the platform's value proposition.
- **Demand-Side Addition:** Attract new demand-side customers to benefit from the current supply offerings.
- **Supply-Side Advertising:** Monetize matchmaking services by offering sponsored positions to supply-side users.
- **Side-Oriented e-Ethnography:** Provide data-driven insights as value-added services to one platform side, based on interactions with other sides.
- **Firm-Oriented e-Ethnography:** Leverage platform-generated data to gain insights into customer behavior, informing product development.
- **Enhanced Advertising:** Combine targeted advertising with data-driven insights to increase effectiveness.
- **Data Trading:** Monetize collected data by offering it to third parties, creating new revenue streams.

The Growth Phase concludes with the **Growth Map**, a checkpoint that prioritizes selected growth strategies and integrates them into the platform's ongoing development cycle. This map guides teams back to the **Design Phase** to refine and implement new platform evolutions effectively.

Figure 14.2 Growth: Alternatives 1

Figure 14.3 – Growth: Milestone 1

14

How-to guide: From Workshops to a GenAI Co-Thinker

The Collaborative Origins of the Platform Thinking Journey

As we mentioned, the Platform Thinking Journey is not just a methodology; it's the culmination of a rigorous design science research project developed within the Platform Thinking HUB initiative. Its roots lie in a context defined by collaboration and the integration of diverse perspectives. This foundation is not incidental but intentional, reflecting the very essence of Platform Thinking: the power of ecosystems, interconnectedness, and co-creation.

Over the past three years, we've engaged with more than 100 professionals across various editions of our programs. Their experiences, insights, and challenges have been instrumental in shaping this methodology. Through iterative refinement, real-world applications, and continuous feedback, we've crafted a robust two-step how-to guide designed to support professionals in applying the Platform Thinking Journey effectively within their organizations.

How We Do It: The Workshop Framework

Our approach is both structured and adaptive, built around a series of four workshops conducted over a four-month timespan. Each workshop is strategically linked to one of the phases of the Platform Thinking Journey, creating a cohesive and progressive learning experience. These workshops are not standalone events; they are interconnected, with each session building upon the insights and decisions of the previous ones.

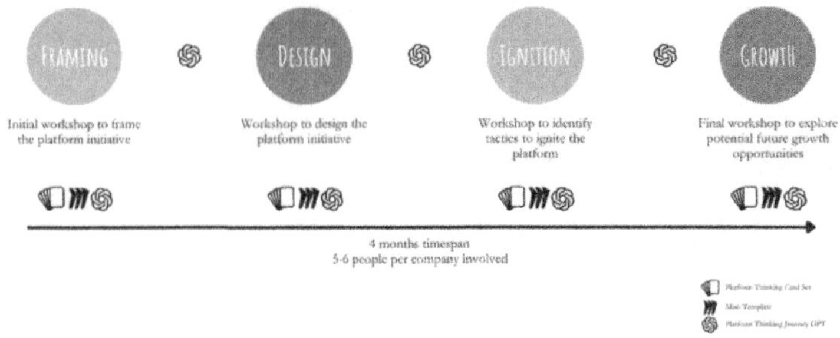

Figure 15.1 – The Workshop Framework

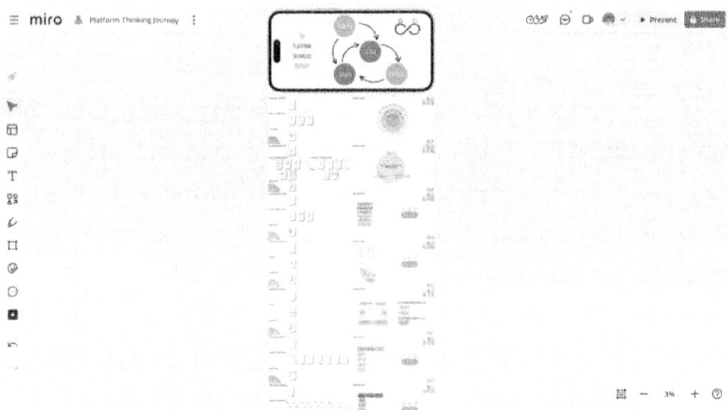

Figure 15.2 – The Platform Thinking Journey Miro Template

To ensure depth and continuity, we involve multiple representatives from each organization. This diversity of voices fosters richer discussions, challenges assumptions, and promotes holistic thinking. But what truly differentiates our workshops is the integration of three pivotal tools:

- **The Platform Thinking Card Set:** Serving as the backbone of our workshops, the card set guides the logical flow of discussions. It helps participants navigate complex concepts with clarity, ensuring that critical elements of Platform Thinking are not overlooked. - https://bit.ly/PTJCards

- **Miro Template[23]:** In an era where digital collaboration is paramount, Miro provides a dynamic, interactive space where participants can co-create, visualize ideas, and track the evolution of their thinking. Its continuity feature allows teams to revisit and build upon their previous work seamlessly across all workshops. - https://bit.ly/PTJMiro
- **Platform Thinking Journey GPT:** Recognizing the inherent complexity of Platform Thinking, we've introduced a dedicated AI assistant—a chatbot trained specifically to support this process. Platform Thinking involves a myriad of decisions, each rooted in nuanced definitions, principles, and strategic considerations. The AI assistant acts as both a guide and a critical thinking partner, offering real-time support, clarifying concepts and sparking reflective dialogue. This ensures that participants can maintain a high level of cognitive engagement without getting lost in the intricacies of the methodology. - https://bit.ly/PTJ_GPT

This how-to guide is structured into two complementary parts:

Part One: Designing and Managing Co-Creation Workshops.

Here, we share **best practices**, **tips**, and **insights** on how to design and facilitate workshops that drive meaningful outcomes. From setting the stage for collaboration to managing group dynamics and ensuring productive discussions, this section equips facilitators with the tools needed to create impactful learning environments.

Part Two: The GenAI Co-Thinker.

This section dives into the role of the GenAI Co-Thinker—the AI assistant we've developed to enhance the Platform Thinking Journey. We explore its capabilities, how it supports decision-making processes, and the ways it fosters deeper critical reflection

---

[23] In our workshops, we use Miro (www.miro.com) and developed templates that can be downloaded for free from the Miroverse collaborative space. There are several other tools available on the market, so feel free to choose the one you prefer.

among participants. Importantly, this AI co-thinker is available to readers of this book, providing a hands-on tool to support their Platform Thinking endeavors beyond the workshop setting.

Together, these two parts offer a comprehensive roadmap for professionals seeking to harness the transformative power of Platform Thinking in their organizations. By blending human creativity with AI-driven insights, we aim to not just teach Platform Thinking but to embed it as a dynamic, evolving practice within the fabric of organizational strategy.

Part One: Designing and Managing Co-Creation Workshops

In this section, we outline the best practices we've gleaned from our extensive experience in designing and managing co-creation workshops.

1. Start with Why

Setting the stage for participants is fundamental. Workshops can serve different purposes: they might aim to open participants' minds to fresh ideas, target specific strategic goals, engage them for the following implementation phase, or be directly linked to project execution. Clarity on purpose ensures the right expectations are set. Whether the goal is exploration, alignment, or actionable outcomes, articulating the "why" helps anchor the process and motivates participants.

2. Engage the Right People

Innovation rarely happens in isolation. The best ideas emerge from co-creation, fueled by radical critique and collaborative evolution. We recommend forming:

A Core Team: Ideally around five people (but ranging from two to ten), this team provides continuity across workshops. Members should be highly motivated, play critical roles in relevant processes, be designated end-users, or possess deep expertise in key areas.

An Extended Team: Up to 20 additional stakeholders are involved through alignment sessions and feedback loops. Their engagement is crucial for projects destined for real-world execution, ensuring both buy-in and valuable perspectives to anticipate constraints. Key moments, even outside formal workshops, should be identified for their involvement.

Special Guests: Inviting user representatives or technical experts during specific sessions can offer fresh perspectives and validate assumptions, enriching the process with real-world insights.

3. Manage the Space

The COVID-19 pandemic reshaped how we conduct workshops. While digital sessions are effective, our best practice recommendation is a **phygital** approach:

Physical Presence: In-person workshops foster direct communication, spontaneous interactions, and deeper engagement. The tactile experience of using the Platform Thinking card set enhances alignment and decision-making.

Digital Integration: Miro serves as a central repository, ensuring continuity across sessions and avoiding the pitfalls of lost sticky notes or illegible handwriting. The GenAI Co-Thinker complements this by providing real-time support, which we'll explore in detail later.

4. Manage the Time

Innovation requires both time and reflection. Our typical framework spans four months, with guidelines as follows:

Workshop Duration: Each session should last a full working day (6-8 hours). Smaller, highly aligned teams might compress some sessions to 4 hours, but longer durations enable deeper discussions.

Spacing Workshops: Ideally, schedule workshops 1-2 weeks apart to allow ideas to mature. Intensive bootcamps (4-5 consecutive days) are feasible for inspiration-driven sprints but less suitable for projects aiming at real-world implementation due to limited time for reflection and validation.

5. Manage the Process

While the journey and card set suggest a phase-by-phase approach, effective workshop management requires additional best practices:

Facilitation: A neutral facilitator is essential. We often act as facilitators in these workshops, playing a dual role: delivering seminars that provide participants with the necessary knowledge to navigate the phases, and guiding group work to foster productive discussions. While our seminars can be substituted by this book, the "*Platform Thinking. Read the past. Write the future*" book, or our MOOCs on Coursera—encouraging participants to engage in preliminary study—the facilitation role should ideally be assigned to someone not directly involved in the design activities. This helps avoid conflicts of interest, ensures time management, and promotes objective moderation. A skilled facilitator will maintain focus, encourage diverse viewpoints, and ensure that the workshop dynamics remain constructive and aligned with the intended goals.

Iterative Reflection: Each key question within the workshop should follow a two-step process to maximize participant engagement and depth of thought:

1. **Individual Reflection:** Allocate dedicated time for participants to reflect and formulate their thoughts independently. This step allows diverse perspectives to emerge, as individuals bring their unique insights without the immediate influence of group dynamics.
2. **Collective Discussion:** Once individual reflections are complete, bring participants together to share their ideas. This collective discussion fosters rich dialogue, encourages critical thinking, and enables the group to build on each other's insights.

This alternation between individual and collective reflection enhances cognitive engagement and leads to more robust outcomes. Contrary to popular belief, effective brainstorming isn't about thinking collectively from the start. True innovation often arises when individuals first process ideas independently, followed by collaborative reasoning and refinement. By integrating these practices, workshops evolve beyond traditional meetings, becoming dynamic environments that drive meaningful innovation and strategic alignment.

By embedding these best practices, workshops become more than just meetings; they transform into powerful catalysts for innovation and strategic alignment.

Part Two: A GenAI Co-Thinker: Introducing Platform Thinking Journey GPT

The creation of the Platform Thinking Journey GPT sits at the intersection of three converging flows.

The first one is **the GenAI Revolution**, when OpenAI launched ChatGPT in the fall of 2022, like the rest of the world, we were fascinated by the power of this technological tool. As innovation scholars, we sought to understand not just its impact on our activities but also its broader implications for the models and theories we study. The introduction of "MyGPTs" in January 2024 transformed OpenAI into an innovation platform, opening new avenues for exploration. We began to view ChatGPT not merely as a tool but as a platform in its own right, capable of supporting transformative thinking.

The second one deals with **Lessons Learnt from Our Platform Thinking Workshops.** In our role as professors and facilitators of Platform Thinking workshops, we've consistently integrated training sessions to equip participants with the foundational knowledge needed to engage meaningfully in workshop activities. Despite the depth and breadth of these sessions, we often found participants grappling with the complexities of platform dynamics, especially those transitioning from linear business models. We frequently had to correct misunderstandings and clarify the proper use of Platform Thinking tools. This recurring challenge highlighted the need for an accessible, reliable source of support that could reinforce key concepts outside of formal training sessions.

The third one are Insights from Thinkers50 Colleagues. Elisa Farri and Gabriele Rosani, provided a critical spark. They introduced the idea of positioning GenAI not just as a co-pilot for efficiency but as a **co-thinker**—a sparring partner within the team[24]. While many use GenAI to enhance productivity in repetitive tasks, their research suggests a more profound potential. When leveraged as a reflective partner, GenAI can guide users through critical thinking processes, pose challenging questions, and validate reasoning. This approach has shown to yield significantly greater returns than mere productivity gains.

These three streams converged in the creation of the **Platform Thinking Journey GPT**. Much like the iterative design process that shaped the Platform Thinking Journey itself, this AI tool evolved through multiple prototypes, tested across diverse settings until we refined it into its current form.

Platform Thinking Journey GPT is a personalized AI agent built on OpenAI's large language model framework as a MyGPT. Its knowledge base is rooted in:

- A decade of our research on Platform Thinking, all the knowledge base that built this book and the previous "*Platform Thinking. Read the past. Write the future.*"[25]
- A comprehensive database of case studies from both pure platform companies and traditional firms applying Platform Thinking
- The Platform Thinking Journey methodology and its accompanying card set

Beyond its extensive knowledge base, the GPT has been fine-tuned from an interaction perspective to serve three key functions:

---

[24] See Farri and Rosani, 2025a, 2025b

[25] See Trabucchi and Buganza, 2023

1. **Clarifying Concepts and Ensuring Accuracy**

It answers questions like "What is a transactional platform?", "What are the defining characteristics of innovation platforms?", or "Can you list examples of orthogonal platforms?"

It validates statements, such as "Is it correct to classify Uber as a transactional platform?"

This role offers participants content support during and between workshops, deepening their understanding of Platform Thinking.

2. **Identifying Relevant Cases from our Platform Thinking Dataset**

The GPT draws on a classified dataset of 140 platform initiatives across the S&P 500. Users get inspiration by exploring and filtering these cases using multiple dimensions, including industry, business problem, idle asset leveraged, platform typology, and type of hack applied.

For example, a user might search for healthcare companies that involved new stakeholders to respond to evolving customer demand and discover cases like Walgreens, Biogen, or Eli Lilly, not included in the book for the sake of space and clarity.

3. **Sparking Reflective Dialogue in the Platform Thinking Journey:**

The GPT responds to queries about the meaning and role of specific questions within the Platform Thinking process.

Rather than providing direct answers, it poses thoughtful, guiding questions to stimulate team discussions.

In essence, Platform Thinking Journey GPT isn't designed to solve your innovation challenges. Instead, it acts as a sparring partner—a thought-provoking team member that asks the right questions to keep the process flowing. You know your company, and you hold the answers. Sometimes, all you need are the right questions to unlock them.

Figure 15.3 – QR Code for Platform Thinking Journey GPT
https://bit.ly/PTJ_GPT

The Dynamic Synergy of Human Collaboration and AI Reflection

The journey from co-creation workshops to the integration of a GenAI Co-Thinker represents more than just a methodological evolution—it embodies a transformative shift in how organizations can harness the power of collective intelligence and technology.

Our workshops remain the heartbeat of the Platform Thinking Journey. They are dynamic environments where diverse minds converge, ideas are challenged, and innovative solutions are co-created. The physical and intellectual spaces crafted during these sessions ignite *The Digital Phoenix Effect* necessary for meaningful change. Here, teams confront real challenges, leverage diverse perspectives, and craft strategies grounded in both creativity and critical thinking.

However, the complexities of Platform Thinking often extend beyond what traditional workshops alone can address. This is where the GenAI Co-Thinker steps in—not as a replacement for human knowledge, but as an enhancer of it. Acting as a perpetual sparring partner, the Platform Thinking Journey GPT complements human efforts by posing thought-provoking questions, clarifying complex concepts, and maintaining a continuous thread of critical reflection throughout and beyond the workshop sessions.

This synergy between human-driven workshops and AI-supported reflection creates a powerful dual engine for innovation. Workshops provide the fertile ground for ideation and collaboration, while the GenAI Co-Thinker ensures that the momentum doesn't fade once the session ends. It keeps the dialogue alive, helps teams revisit and refine their ideas, and supports sustained learning and development.

The true strength of this guide lies not in prescribing a rigid process but in offering a flexible framework adaptable to various organizational contexts. By embracing both the structured, interactive nature of workshops and the adaptive, reflective capabilities of GenAI, organizations can unlock new dimensions of Platform Thinking. This integrated approach fosters continuous evolution, enabling businesses to not only respond to change but to anticipate and shape it. The future of Platform Thinking is not just to be learned—it's to be lived, and co-created, looking at future evolutions.

APPENDIXES

The Platform Thinking Ecosystem

The Digital Phoenix Effect sits at the heart of the **Platform Thinking Ecosystem**, an extensive network and community that Daniel and Tommaso have cultivated over the last decade. This ecosystem, developed through academic research, industry collaborations, and teaching initiatives, is a powerful promotional platform for the book.

QR Code for The Platform Thinking Ecosystem - https://bit.ly/PT_PlatformThinking

---

1. **Platform Thinking HUB**

Platform Thinking HUB, co-founded by Daniel and Tommaso as part of Politecnico di Milano's Digital Innovation Observatorics, is a thriving community of innovation leaders, researchers, and corporate partners dedicated to exploring and advancing platform strategies. With partners such as Eni, Leonardo, Prysmian, GS1, Angelini and Sisal (over 20 partners in the first three editions, sponsored by established firms trying to implement Platform Thinking), the HUB provides a dynamic platform for promoting *The Digital Phoenix Effect.* Each year, the HUB hosts two major events: an Italian conference attended by 1,000+ participants and an international LinkedIn Live event, organized with TheNTWK, that reaches over 2,000 viewers.

QR Code for The Platform Thinking HUB - https://bit.ly/PlatformThinkingHUB

2. **Symplatform**

Daniel and Tommaso also co-founded Symplatform (with Laurent Muzellec from Trinity College Dublin and Sébastien Ronteau from Audencia Business School), an annual international conference dedicated to digital platforms. This unique event, held in Lake Como, gathers more than 100 global participants, from academics to industry leaders, to discuss the latest platform trends and research.

QR Code for Symplatform - https://bit.ly/PT_Symplatform

3. **MOOCs and Online Resources**

Daniel & Tommaso have developed several MOOCs available through Coursera, with over 25,000 students enrolled to date. Additionally, this and the previous books' concepts and tools have been introduced on Miroverse, where the authors' templates have seen 25,000+ downloads, with new card sets and templates from the book made available to help professionals apply platform strategies effectively.

QR Code for courses on Coursera - https://bit.ly/PTCourseraSpecialization

QR Code for Miro Templates - https://bit.ly/PTmiroverse

4. Podcast

The authors' podcast (led by Philip Meier), *Talking About Platforms*, features leading platform researchers and practitioners and has gained traction on Spotify and Apple Podcasts and in the research community.

QR Code for Talking About Platforms - https://bit.ly/PT_TAP

5. **Platform Thinking Journey: Card Set, Miro and GPT**.

This book is supported by three resources for the direct application of the methodology presented, the Platform Thinking Journey. The Card Set to facilitate physical workshops, a Miro template for digital support and the Platform Thinking Journey GPT as a co-thinker.

QR Code to buy the Platform Thinking Journey Card Set - https://bit.ly/PTJCards

QR Code to use the Platform Thinking Journey template on Miro - https://bit.ly/PTJMiro

QR Code to use the Platform Thinking Journey GPT - https://bit.ly/PTJ_GPT

References

Caillaud, B., & Jullien, B. (2003). Chicken & egg: Competition among intermediation service providers. *The RAND Journal of Economics*, 34(2), 309–328.

Cusumano, M. A., Gawer, A., & Yoffie, D. B. (2019). *The Business of Platforms: Strategy in the Age of Digital Competition, Innovation, and Power.* Harper Business.

Dell'Era, C., Trabucchi, D., & Magistretti, S. (2021). Exploiting incumbents' potentialities: From linear value chains to multisided platforms. *Creativity and Innovation Management*, *30*(1), 31-46.

Evans, D. S., & Schmalensee, R. (2016). *Matchmakers: The new economics of multisided platforms.* Harvard Business Review Press.

Farri, E., & Rosani, G. (2025a). *HBR Guide to Generative AI for Managers.* Harvard Business Review Press.

Farri, E., & Rosani, G. (2025b). How AI can help managers think through problems. *Harvard Business Review*, February 2025.

Filistrucchi, L., Geradin, D., Van Damme, E., & Affeldt, P. (2014). Market definition in two-sided markets: Theory and practice. *Journal of Competition Law & Economics*, 10(2), 293–339.

Gawer, A., & Cusumano, M. A. (2014). Industry platforms and ecosystem innovation. *Journal of Product Innovation Management*, 31(3), 417–433.

Hagiu, A., & Altman, E. J. (2017). Finding the platform in your product. *Harvard Business Review*, 95(4), 94-100.

Hevner, A.R., March, S.T., Park, J. & Ram, S. (2004). "Design science in information systems research", *MIS Quarterly*, 28 (1); 75-105.

Jacobides, M. G., Cennamo, C., & Gawer, A. (2018). Towards a theory of ecosystems. *Strategic management journal*, *39*(8), 2255-2276.

Jacobides, M., Cennamo, C., & Gawer, A. (2015). Industries, ecosystems, platforms, and architectures: Rethinking our strategy constructs at the aggregate level. *Unpublished manuscript.*

Jovanovic, M., Sjödin, D., & Parida, V. (2022). Co-evolution of platform architecture, platform services, and platform governance: Expanding the platform value of industrial digital platforms. *Technovation, 118*, 102218.

Karhu, K., Heiskala, M., Ritala, P., & Thomas, L. D. (2024). Positive, negative, and amplified network externalities in platform markets. *Academy of Management Perspectives, 38*(3), 349-367.

Katz, M. L., & Shapiro, C. (1985). Network externalities, competition, and compatibility. *The American Economic Review*, 75(3), 424–440.

Kenney, M., Bearson, D., & Zysman, J. (2021). The platform economy matures: Measuring pervasiveness and exploring power. *Socio-economic Review*, 19(4), 1451-1483.

Magistretti, S., & Trabucchi, D. (2025). Agile-as-a-tool and agile-as-a-culture: a comprehensive review of agile approaches adopting contingency and configuration theories. *Review of Managerial Science, 19*(1), 223-253.

Meier, P., Friederici, N., Krell-Sun, T., & Trabucchi, D. (2024). Strategies for Designing and Growing Business-to-Business Platforms. *Research-Technology Management, 67*(2), 44-56.

Parker, G. G., & Van Alstyne, M. W. (2005). Platform strategy. *Communications of the ACM*, 48(10), 149.

Parker, G. G., Van Alstyne, M. W., & Choudary, S. P. (2016). *Platform Revolution: How Networked Markets Are Transforming the Economy—and How to Make Them Work for You.* W. W. Norton & Company.

Patrucco, A. S., Trabucchi, D., Buganza, T., Muzellec, L., & Ronteau, S. (2024). Technology-enabled multi-sided platforms in B2B relationships: A critical analysis and directions for future research. *Industrial Marketing Management.*

Porter, M. E. (1985). *Competitive Advantage: Creating and Sustaining Superior Performance.* Free Press.

Rochet, J.-C., & Tirole, J. (2003). Platform competition in two-sided markets. *Journal of the European Economic Association*, 1(4), 990–1029.

Springer, V., Randhawa, K., Jovanović, M., Ritala, P., & Piller, F. T. (2025). Platform design and governance in industrial markets: Charting the meta-organizational logic. *Research Policy*, *54*(6), 105236.

Täuscher, K., & Laudien, S. M. (2018). Understanding platform business models: A mixed methods study of marketplaces. *European Management Journal*, 36(3), 319–329.

Trabucchi, D. (2020). Let's get a two-sided platform started: Tactics to solve the chicken and egg paradox. *Journal of Business Ecosystems*, 1(1), 63–77.

Trabucchi, D., & Buganza, T. (2022). Landlords with no lands: A systematic literature review on hybrid multi-sided platforms and Platform Thinking. *European Journal of Innovation Management*, 25(6), 64–96.

Trabucchi, D., Bellis, P., Buganza, T., Canterino, F., Shani, A. B. R., Verganti, R., & Press, J. (2024). Leading impactful research: applying platform thinking to drive collaborative inquiry in the innovation field. *European Journal of Innovation Management*, 27(9), 408-436.

Trabucchi, D., & Buganza, T. (2023). *Platform Thinking: Read the Past. Write the Future.* Business Expert Press.

Trabucchi, D., Buganza, T., & Pellizzoni, E. (2017). Give away your digital services: Leveraging big data to capture value. *Research-Technology Management*, 60(2), 43–52.

Trabucchi, D., Patrucco, A. S., Buganza, T., & Marzi, G. (2023). Is transparency the new green? How business model transparency influences digital service adoption. *Technovation*, *126*, 102803.

Zhu, F., & Cao, B. Y. (2024). *Smart Rivals: How Innovative Companies Play Games That Tech Giants Can't Win.* Harvard Business Review Press.

List of sources for the cases

3 inspiring stories from Part 1

AXA Digital Commercial Platform

- *Aurora launches new policy in partnership with AXA*, Insurance Business UK, 10/05/2024. https://www.insurancebusinessmag.com/uk/news/breaking-news/aurora-launches-new-policy-in-partnership-with-axa-488696.aspx
- *AWS and AXA to Develop Global B2B Risk Management Platform*, PYMNTS, 04/04/2024. https://www.pymnts.com/insurance/2024/aws-and-axa-to-develop-global-b2b-risk-management-platform/
- *AXA and AWS Developing the First Global B2B Risk Management and Prevention Platform*, AXA, 04/04/2024. https://www.axa.com/en/news/axa-and-aws-developping-first-global-b2b-risk-management-and-prevention-platform
- *AXA and AWS Developing the First Global B2B Risk Management and Prevention Platform*, Amazon Press Center, 04/04/2024. https://press.aboutamazon.com/aws/2024/4/axa-and-aws-developing-the-first-global-b2b-risk-management-and-prevention-platform
- *AXA and AWS partner to revolutionise B2B risk management with new digital platform*, FinTech Global, 08/04/2024. https://fintech.global/2024/04/08/axa-and-aws-partner-to-revolutionise-b2b-risk-management-with-new-digital-platform/
- *AXA announces the launch of a strategic program to develop a Digital Commercial Platform*, AXA, 15/06/2022. https://www.axa.com/en/press/press-releases/axa-announces-the-launch-of a-strategic-program-to-develop-a-digital-commercial-platform
- *AXA declares plan for new digital platform*, Insurance Business America, 16/06/2022. https://www.insurancebusinessmag.com/us/news/technology/axa-declares-plan-for-new-digital-platform-409767.aspx

- *AXA launches digital hub for commercial clients' changing risks*, Commercial Risk, 15/06/2022. https://www.commercialriskonline.com/axa-launches-digital-hub-for-commercial-clients-changing-risks/
- *AXA launches programme to build Digital Commercial Platform*, InsurTech Digital, 17/06/2022. https://insurtechdigital.com/digital-strategy/axa-launches-programme-to-build-digital-commercial-platform
- *AXA to build new digital platform for commercial customers*, Life Insurance International, 16/06/2022. https://www.lifeinsuranceinternational.com/news/axa-to-build-digital-platform/
- *AXA XL SVP Rose Hall Introduces the AXA Digital Commercial Platform*, Insurance Innovation Reporter, 23/08/2024. https://iireporter.com/axa-xl-svp-rose-hall-introduces-the-axa-digital-commercial-platform
- *Amazon partners with AXA to develop global risk management platform*, Captive Insurance Times, 05/04/2024. https://www.captiveinsurancetimes.com/captiveinsurancenews/industryarticle.php?article_id=8942
- *Our Risk Management Department plays a key role in the Group's strategy*, AXA, 09/11/2023. https://www.axa.com/en/news/leaders-voice-the-group-risk-management-plays-a-key-role-in-the-group-s-strategy
- *Digitalization of the Insurance Industry: Trends and Innovations*, AXA, 16/06/2022. https://www.axa.com/en/insights/digitalization-of-the-insurance-industry-trends-and-innovations
- *Digitalization of the Insurance Industry: Trends and Innovations*, AXA XL – Fast Fast Forward, 16/06/2022. https://axaxl.com/fast-fast-forward/articles/digitalization-of-the-insurance-industry-trends-and-innovations
- *The climate crisis is getting worse: here's how insurance is helping*, The Insurer, 27/09/2024. https://www.theinsurer.com/viewpoint/the-climate-crisis-is-getting-worse-heres-how-insurance-is-helping/
- *Speech at the Platforms Renaissance event*, Thierry Faining, 20/11/2023. https://www.linkedin.com/events/platformsrenaissance7122895321784840193/theater/

- *Keynote speech at "La Galassia delle Piattaforme"*, Pierre du Rostu, 15/10/2024.
- *Interviews with* **Pierre du Rostu**, 2023–2024.

Open-es

- *Amundi SGR fa il suo ingresso nella piattaforma Open-es*, La Stampa, 22/05/2024. https://finanza.lastampa.it/News/2024/05/22/amundi-sgr-fa-il-suo-ingresso-nella-piattaforma-open-es/NzVfMjAyNC0wNS0yMl9UTEI
- *Come aderire ad Open-es: la piattaforma per la sostenibilità di filiera*, EconomyUp, 03/05/2021. https://www.economyup.it/energia/come-aderire-ad-open-es-la-piattaforma-per-la-sostenibilita-di-filiera/
- *Confindustria Energia entra in Open-es per promuovere sostenibilità settore energetico*, ESG News, 23/04/2024. https://esgnews.it/governance/confindustria-energia-entra-in-open-es-per-promuovere-sostenibilita-settore-energetico/
- *Fasani (Eni): "Alleanza di sistema e inclusione le chiavi del successo di Open-es"*, ESG News, 30/01/2023. https://esgnews.it/focus/interviste/fasani-eni-alleanza-di-sistema-e-inclusione-le-chiavi-del-successo-di-open-es/
- *Fasani (Open-es): oltre 20.000 realtà nella community per la sostenibilità delle imprese*, ESG News, 04/06/2024. https://esgnews.it/focus/interviste/fasani-open-es-oltre-20-000-realta-nella-community-per-la-sostenibilita-delle-imprese/
- *TIM aderisce a Open-es*, Gruppo TIM, 29/09/2022. https://www.gruppotim.it/it/sostenibilita/news/TIM-Open-es.html
- *KPMG, a Milano l'evento conclusivo della I edizione di Open-es Camp*, Affaritaliani.it, 23/02/2024. https://www.affaritaliani.it/economia/notizie-aziende/kpmg-a-milano-l-evento-conclusivo-della-i-edizione-di-open-es-camp-902772.html
- *KPMG, conclusa la I edizione di Open-es Camp*, Affaritaliani.it, 03/03/2024. https://www.affaritaliani.it/economia/notizie-aziende/scatti-d-affari/kpmg-conclusa-la-i-edizione-di-open-es-camp-904421.html

- *Le aziende fanno rete grazie ad Open-es*, StartupItalia, 18/06/2024. https://startupitalia.eu/economy/economia-digitale/open-es-stefano-fasani/
- *Obiettivi ESG, Gruppo Iren aderisce a Open-Es*, La Stampa, 18/04/2024. https://finanza.lastampa.it/News/2024/04/18/obiettivi-esg-gruppo-iren-aderisce-a-open-es/NjlfMjAyNC0wNC0xOF9UTEI
- *Open Fiber si unisce all'alleanza Open-es per sostenibilità supply chain*, Teleborsa, 03/04/2024. https://www.teleborsa.it/News/2024/04/03/open-fiber-si-unisce-all-alleanza-open-es-per-sostenibilita-supply-chain-89.html
- *Open-es – Un'Alleanza Aperta per lo Sviluppo Sostenibile delle Filiere*, TopLegal, 11/01/2024. https://www.toplegal.it/art/open-es-unalleanza-aperta-per-lo-sviluppo-sostenibile-delle-filiere/
- *Open-es camp, l'iniziativa di formazione concreta per aumentare la sostenibilità delle PMI*, ESG News, 29/02/2024. https://esgnews.it/social/open-es-camp-liniziativa-di-formazione-concreta-per-aumentare-la-sostenibilita-delle-pmi/
- *Open-es, la piattaforma aperta a tutte le imprese per un ecosistema sostenibile*, Il Sole 24 ORE, 03/12/2021. https://www.ilsole24ore.com/art/open-es-piattaforma-aperta-tutte-imprese-un-ecosistema-sostenibile-AEEJuI0
- *Open-es, la piattaforma che unisce imprese, procurement e banche per la sostenibilità dell'intero ecosistema*, Innovation Post, 24/01/2022. https://www.innovationpost.it/sponsored-content/open-es-la-piattaforma-che-unisce-imprese-procurement-e-banche-per-la-sostenibilita-dellintero-ecosistema/
- *Open-es, la piattaforma digitale per lo sviluppo sostenibile delle imprese*, Euractiv Italia, 31/03/2021. https://euractiv.it/section/energia/news/open-es-eni-piattaforma-sviluppo-sostenibile/
- *Presentazione OpenESCamp – trascrizione video da Youtube con interviste a Fasani e a partner KPMG*, Open-es, 02/2024.
- *Keynote at the event "La Galassia delle Piattaforme"*, Stefano Fasani, 15/10/2024.
- *Interviews with* ***Lorenzo de Filippi***, 2024.

Siemens Xcelerator

- *Siemens launches Siemens Xcelerator – an open digital business platform to accelerate digital transformation*, Siemens Press Release, 29/06/2022. https://press.siemens.com/global/en/pressrelease/siemens-launches-siemens-xcelerator-open-digital-business-platform-accelerate-digital
- *Siemens Xcelerator – The Open Business Platform That Accelerates Digital Transformation – Part 1*, Siemens Blog, Dr. Ralph-Christian Ohr, 05/07/2023. https://blog.siemens.com/2023/07/siemens-xcelerator-the-open-business-platform-that-accelerates-digital-transformation-part-1/
- *About the Ecosystem*, Siemens Xcelerator Global, 01/10/2024. https://xcelerator.siemens.com/global/en/partners/ecosystem.html
- *API World*, Siemens Xcelerator Global, 01/10/2024. https://xcelerator.siemens.com/global/en/api-world.html
- *How to become a partner*, Siemens Xcelerator Global, 01/10/2024. https://xcelerator.siemens.com/global/en/partners/how-to-become-a-partner.html
- *Siemens Xcelerator*, Siemens Xcelerator Global, 01/10/2024. https://xcelerator.siemens.com/global/en.html
- *Keynote at the event "La Galassia delle Piattaforme", – Bettina Rotermund, 15/102024*
- *Bettina Rotermunds's keynote – TheNTWK speech*, Bettina Rotermund, 27/05/2024.
- *Interviews with* ***Bettina Rotermund***, 2024.
- *Siemens CEO – Launch of Siemens Xcelerator*, YouTube video transcript, 29/06/2022. https://www.youtube.com/watch?v=KM2QWMM5T9Y

15 cases used in Part 2

AbbVie

- https://www.abbvie.com/who-we-are/our-stories/abbvie-research-collaborative.html
- https://www.abbvie.com/science/areas-of-innovation/patient-focused-drug-development.html

- https://www.abbvie.com/science/areas-of-innovation/ai-and-data-convergence.html
- https://www.voluntis.com/abbvie-and-voluntis-to-develop-companion-digital-therapeutics/

Catterpillar

- https://digital.cat.com/node/2966
- https://www.youtube.com/watch?v=KyHwQzjF6Qc
- https://www.caterpillar.com/en/careers/career-areas/digital.html
- https://www.digitalcommerce360.com/2023/06/21/caterpillar-advancing-digital-acceleration-campaign/
- https://ohiocat.com/digital-toolbox-and-resources/
- https://www.caterpillar.com/en/legal-notices/cds-privacy-notice.html

Carnival

- https://www.microsoft.com/en/customers/story/1624878639257824742-carnival-corporation-travel-transportation-azure-stack-hci
- https://news.microsoft.com/source/features/digital-transformation/carnival-corporation-sails-edge-tracking-oceans-data/
- https://www.keytech.it/carnival-corporation.html
- https://akcruise.org/carnival-opens-fleet-operations-center-seattle/
- https://www.datacenterdynamics.com/en/news/carnival-corporation-deploys-azure-edge-solution-on-its-cruise-ships/
- https://www.carnival-news.com/2018/05/10/carnival-cruise-line-unveils-largest-most-technologically-advanced-operations-center-in-cruise-industry
- https://www.dayone.network/works/dive-in-with-neptune-technology/
- https://www.seatrade-cruise.com/safety-security/carnival-corp-hikes-safety-with-new-fleet-operations-center-in-seattle
- https://www.carnival-maritime.com/press/news-7.34273.html
- https://www.rivieramm.com/news-content-hub/news-content-hub/carnival-installs-stm-on-entire-fleet-55488

Chipotle

- https://www.businessinsider.com/chipotle-launches-virtual-restaurant-farmesa-through-cloud-kitchens-2023-3
- https://www.qsrmagazine.com/news/chipotle-opens-its-first-digital-kitchen/
- https://www.qsrmagazine.com/news/chipotle-launches-its-virtual-restaurant-brand-farmesa/

Dish

- https://media.dish.com/
- https://media.dish.com/solutions/addressable
- https://about.dish.com/2025-05-12-Dish-Media-Unveils-AdvantEdge-TM-%2C-A-Game-Changer-in-Unified%2C-Data-Driven-TV-Advertising
- https://about.dish.com/2023-05-31-Dish-Media-Brings-Linear-TV-to-the-Digital-Ad-Marketplace-with-Dish-Connected-TM
- https://www.elastic.co/customers/dish-media
- https://www.linkedin.com/company/dishmedia
- https://www.cbinsights.com/company/dish-media-sales
- https://www.radioadvertisinghome.com/dish-advertising/

Domino's

- https://anyware.dominos.com/
- https://thestrategystory.com/2020/07/11/dominos-digital-transformation/
- https://www.wired.com/2016/04/dominos-anyware-pizza/

Intuit

- https://turbotax.intuit.com/personal-taxes/online/live/how-it-works.htm
- https://turbotax.intuit.com/personal-taxes/online/live/full-service/
- https://turbotax.intuit.com/personal-taxes/online/live/premium/
- https://quickbooks.intuit.com/live/
- https://quickbooks.intuit.com/live/full-service-bookkeeping/
- https://quickbooks.intuit.com/accounting/live-tax/

- https://www.intuit.com/expert-careers/tax-preparers/
- https://www.intuit.com/expert-careers/apply-now/

Kraft Heinz

- https://news.kraftheinzcompany.com/press-releases-details/2022/Kraft-Heinz-Partners-with-Google-to-Accelerate-and-Scale-Ambitious-Digital-Transformation-and-Sustainable-Innovation-Agenda/default.aspx
- https://consumergoods.com/kraft-heinz-invests-consumer-insights-kraft-o-matic-data-platform
- https://adage.com/article/marketing-news-strategy/how-kraft-heinz-using-its-kraft-o-matic-software-boost-innovation/2401471/
- https://www.ciodive.com/news/kraft-heinz-google-cloud-transformation/619219/
- https://www.datamation.com/big-data/kraft-heinz-partnering-google-digital-transformation/
- https://brand-innovators.com/kraft-heinz-leverages-google-tools-for-consumer-personalization/
- https://liveramp.com/blog/consumer-insights-rely-on-aligning-internal-and-technical-partners/
- https://www.cloudcomputing-news.net/news/kraft-heinz-partners-with-google-cloud-for-cloud-data-insights/

Kroger

- https://www.grocerydive.com/news/kroger-goes-for-endless-aisles-with-new-marketplace-strategy/583260/
- https://www.kroger.com/d/ship
- https://www.thekrogerco.com/vendors-suppliers/
- https://www.thekrogerco.com/vendors-suppliers/partner-pass/
- https://www.thekrogerco.com/vendors-suppliers/supplier-hub/
- https://www.thekrogerco.com/vendors-suppliers/supplier-hub/supplier-hub-help/

Masco

- https://masco.com/masco-employees-learn-from-human-library/

- https://masco.com/masco-becomes-founding-partner-for-new-human-library-app/
- https://humanlibrary.org/masco-announced-as-founding-partner-for-human-library-app/
- https://humanlibrary.org/new-human-library-online-reader-service/
- https://humanlibrary.org/the-human-library-500/

Merck's and Co.

- https://www.merck.com/research/
- https://www.merck.com/news/merck-announces-the-launch-of-the-merck-digital-sciences-studio-to-help-healthcare-startups-quickly-bring-their-innovations-to-market/
- https://www.mds.studio/
- https://www.genedata.com/company/news/details/press-release/genedata-and-merck-co-develop-digital-platform
- https://www.genedata.com/platform/profiler
- https://www.nature.com/articles/d42473-024-00195-z
- https://medcitynews.com/2025/02/merck-is-embracing-ai-but-we-always-have-a-human-in-the-loop-exec-says/
- https://arxiv.org/abs/1506.07116
- https://www.prnewswire.com/news-releases/merck--co-digital-transformation-strategy-analysis-report-2023-accelerators-incubators-and-other-innovation-programs-302051944.html

New Corp

- https://www.newscorpaustralia.com/news-corp-australia-announces-vertical-video-platform/?utm_source
- https://www.newscorpaustralia.com/news-corp-australia-launches-groundbreaking-shoppable-in-video-campaign/?utm_source
- https://www.newscorpaustralia.com/digital-media-assets/social-stories/?utm_source
- https://www.newscorpaustralia.com/sydneys-new-home-of-news-the-daily-telegraph-launches-dttv/?utm_source
- https://www.newscorpaustralia.com/the-total-video-suite/?utm_source

- https://www.newscorpaustralia.com/video-reach-and-targeting-expanded-with-in-article-news-shorts-and-liveramp-safe-haven/?utm_source
- https://www.newscorpaustralia.com/news-com-au-is-australias-number-one-in-news/?utm_source
- https://www.newscorpaustralia.com/whats-on/news-corp-australia-steals-the-show-at-imaa-whos-who-in-the-media-zoo-event/?utm_source

PACCAR

- https://www.paccar.com/news/current-news/2023/paccar-and-platform-science-announce-strategic-equity-investment/
- https://www.peterbilt.com/news-and-events/press-releases/peterbilt-and-platform-science-build-a-new-ecosystem-of-connected-products
- https://www.kenworth.com/about-us/news/kenworth-and-platform-science-announce-partnership-to-integrate-innovative-virtual-vehicle-solution-in-kenworth-trucks-1/
- https://www.truckinginfo.com/10190785/paccar-platform-science-integrate-virtual-vehicle-solution
- https://www.fleetowner.com/technology/article/21264168/paccar-makes-minority-equity-investment-in-platform-science
- https://www.worktruckonline.com/10190754/paccar-to-add-virtual-vehicle-platform-to-trucks
- https://www.ccjdigital.com/technology/telematics/article/15306073/paccar-to-deploy-platform-science-virtual-vehicle
- https://www.platformscience.com/trimble-on-virtual-vehicle
- https://www.prnewswire.com/news-releases/paccar-and-platform-science-announce-new-collaboration-to-integrate-innovative-virtual-vehicle-solution-in-kenworth-and-peterbilt-trucks-301725837.html
- https://www.ttnews.com/articles/paccar-plans-platform-science-integration
- https://www.constructionequipment.com/trucking/news/21546072/paccar-brands-partner-on-fleet-platform
- https://www.fleetowner.com/technology/article/21258376/paccar-platform-science-partner-on-integrated-telematics-for-kenworth-peterbilt-trucks

Royal Carribean

- https://www.royalcaribbean.com/faq/questions/what-the-benefits-of-booking-hotel-packages
- https://www.royalcaribbeanpresscenter.com/press-release/1594/royal-caribbean-introduces-hotel-booking-engine-royal-caribbean-hotels/

Target

- https://roundel.target.com/
- https://corporate.target.com/press/releases/2019/05/target-s-roundel-puts-a-new-spin-on-retail-media-net
- https://www.adweek.com/brand-marketing/target-rebrands-its-in-house-media-company-as-roundel/
- https://www.marketingdive.com/news/target-rebrands-in-house-media-company-as-roundel/554293/
- https://www.businessinsider.com/target-rebrands-media-company-roundel-retail-media-2019-5

List of Figures

Index

About the Authors

Daniel Trabucchi and ***Tommaso Buganza*** are Professors both based at the School of Management, Politecnico di Milano, where they are part of the LEADIN'Lab, a research laboratory dedicated to leadership, design, and innovation. Together, they have published over 100 articles in top academic journals, such as the *Journal of Product Innovation Management*, *Technovation*, and *Information System Journals*, as well as in many leading conferences, working on Platform Thinking. Recognized for their contributions to management and innovation, both were included in the 2024 **Thinkers50 Radar list**.

Daniel is Associate Professor of Platform Thinking, while Tommaso, is Full Professor of Leadership & Innovation and chairs the International Product Development Management Conference.

They are co-founder of **Platform Thinking HUB**, a research community within Politecnico's Digital Innovation Observatories, focused on advancing platform strategies for traditional industries, working with numerous established firms both working at the national and international level. They co-founded and lead **Symplatform**, an international conference connecting platform scholars and practitioners. They both teach within MBAs and Executive MBAs programs at Politecnico di Milano and in other international universities like Trinity College Dublin, and Tsinghua University in Beijing (China).

Both are co-authors of *Platform Thinking: Read the Past. Write the Future*, a book that has been translated into Italian and Chinese and shortlisted for the Business Book Award 2024.

Together, they aim to offer a unique blend of rigorous research, practical industry insights, and educational impact.

QR Code for Daniel Trabucchi's LinkedIn Profile
https://bit.ly/PT_Trabucchi

QR Code for Tommaso Buganza's LinkedIn Profile
https://bit.ly/PT_Buganza

Acknowledgements

When *Platform Thinking – Read the Past. Write the Future* came out in May 2023, we were following a vision. It felt like giving shape to a dream: sharing a decade of research, projects, ideas, and intuitions in one place. We had never published a book before and didn't quite know what to expect. What we found was a new world — of discovery, connection, and exploration. And here we are, just two years later, writing the acknowledgments for a second book. A book born directly from that experience, rooted in that research, enriched by the people we met and the opportunities we lived — all thanks to that first book we hold so dear.

The Digital Phoenix Effect is not just a continuation — it's a different book. It stands on the shoulders of ten years of research that brought *Platform Thinking* to life, but it also captures two intense, fast-moving, unpredictable years shaped by deep conversations, global shifts, and new technologies. In these pages, we built upon our foundation, but we also explored new directions, thanks to the managers, thinkers, and fellow authors who let us into their worlds and helped us refine our own approach to platform-based innovation.

We owe a huge thank you to all those *Platform Thinking* introduced us to — people who opened new doors, gave us their trust, and shared their time and stories.

Thank you to **Kaihan Krippendorff**, for welcoming us into his Outthinker network and into a broader conversation with the world's Chief Strategy Officers. And thank you for opening the path to the **Thinkers50** community — where we've found energy, stimulation, and generosity. A warm thanks to **Des Dearlove** and **Stuart Crainer** for making us feel at home in this vibrant community, which not only inspired our research on the human side of platforms but also brought us in touch with fellow thinkers and collaborators.

A heartfelt thank you to **Elisa Farri** and **Gabriele Rosani** — their work on GenAI and Co-Thinking, and their generous lunches, deeply influenced the third part of this book and the development of our Platform Thinking Journey GPT. We can't wait to see where our shared research takes us next.

Thanks to **Giuseppe Stigliano**, who challenged our storytelling style and helped us better frame the business problems platform thinking can solve. And to **Elizabeth Altman**, who continues to guide us in finding that sweet spot between rigorous research and managerial impact.

And of course, our deepest gratitude to **Annabelle Gawer**, **Marshall Van Alstyne**, and **Geoffrey Parker** — pioneers of platform thinking who not only shaped our early academic journey but have since become trusted interlocutors in our ongoing exploration of this field. We will always be grateful for the paths you opened.

Alongside these international thought leaders, we also want to thank the **doers** — those who helped us develop and apply our methodology. When *Platform Thinking* was published, we had just launched the **Platform Thinking HUB**, our applied research initiative within the **Osservatori Digital Innovation at Politecnico di Milano**. Three years later, we're proud of what this initiative has become, and we owe that to many.

Thanks to **Alessandro Perego** for believing in our vision and making it real. To **Valeria Portale**, **Alessandra Luksch**, **Damiano Frosi**, **Valentina Pontiggia** and **Marta Valsecchi** for their help in launching the project. To **Silvia Gadola** and **Elisabetta Puglielli** for turning the HUB into a vibrant space for dialogue and action. And to all the companies that partnered with us along this journey: *Angelini Industries, Alpitour, Edenred, Eni, Ernst&Young, Epta, Fondazione Mondino IRCCS, GPS Bilance, Gruber Logistics, GS1 Italy, Iveco, Leonardo, Open-es, Poste Italiane, Prysmian, Relatech, Retail Reply, SDF, Sintetica, Sisal, Trentino Sviluppo.*

We also want to recognize the over 100 managers who contributed their experience and insights. A special thank you to **Stefano Brandinali**, **Carlotta Dainese**, and **Camilla Folladori** —

for the reflections, the meals, the honesty. And to **Francesco Caio**, the brain trust behind much of our thinking — thank you for always being there.

Our gratitude extends to the three platform thinkers whose stories open this book. Thank you, Pierre du Rostu, Bettina Rotermund, and Stefano Fasani, — for sharing your journeys and for the boldness of your work. We're eager to see where your platforms will go next.

And of course, thank you to those who were already part of the first book and are still here today. To the researchers who've walked alongside us, and to our academic home: **LEADIN' Lab**, **MOSAIC**, and the whole **School of Management of Politecnico di Milano**. To our academic communities — **IPDMC**, **CINet**, and our very own **Symplatform** — thank you for always pushing us to go further.

A special nod to **Philip Meier** and *Talking About Platforms*, which continues to connect us with incredible academics worldwide. And to **TheNTWK**, **Marina Planas**, and **Anna Noakes Schulze** — thank you for the support, the collaboration, and even the first read of this book.

Above all, thank you to the people who give meaning to everything we do: our wonderful and patient wives, **Ludovica** and **Aline**; the not-so-little **Clara**; and the very little **Calliope**.

And thank **you** — yes, you — for reading this book. We hope you'll find something in here that helps you, inspires you, or simply makes you think.

And finally… thank you to our **3.5 writing weeks**. They were intense, funny, and becoming our way of writing books. Beauty generates beauty — at least, we like to think so.

Daniel & Tommaso

Milano, June 2025

Printed in Dunstable, United Kingdom

63920399R00178